P9-BJA-397

OUR ELUSIVE CONSTITUTION

SUNY Series in American Constitutionalism
Robert J. Spitzer, editor

OUR ELUSIVE CONSTITUTION

Silences, Paradoxes, Priorities

Daniel N. Hoffman

STATE UNIVERSITY OF NEW YORK PRESS

Published by
State University of New York Press, Albany

© 1997 State University of New York

All rights reserved

Printed in the United States of America

No part of this book may be used or reproduced in any manner
whatsoever without written permission. No part of this book may be
stored in a retrieval system or transmitted in any form or by any means
including electronic, electrostatic, magnetic tape, mechanical,
photocopying, recording, or otherwise without the prior permission in
writing of the publisher.

For information, address State University of New York Press,
State University Plaza, Albany, N.Y., 12246

Production by Marilyn P. Semerad
Marketing by Dana E. Yanulavich

Library of Congress Cataloging-in-Publication Data

Hoffman, Daniel N., 1942–
    Our elusive Constitution : silences, paradoxes, priorities /
Daniel N. Hoffman.
        p.   cm. — (SUNY series in American constitutionalism)
    Includes bibliographical references and index.
    ISBN 0-7914-3501-6 (hc : alk. paper). — ISBN 0-7914-3502-4 (pbk.
: alk. paper)
    1. Constitutional law—United States. 2. United States-
-Constitutional law—Philosophy. 3. Law and politics. I. Title.
II. Series.
KF4550.H63 1997
342.73′02—dc21   96-48971
                                                                         CIP

10 9 8 7 6 5 4 3 2 1

*To the memory of James Roland Law,
my former dean and friend,
the best candidate I have known
for a legitimate title of nobility.*

AUGUSTANA UNIVERSITY COLLEGE
LIBRARY

CONTENTS

PREFACE

*T*his project's primary stimulus was Walter Murphy's NEH seminar at Princeton in the summer of 1985. The fires lit there were slow burning, but relentless. Of course, I brought to the seminar what I had learned from many superb teachers and from eager and persistent students.

I also brought discomforts that come with the benefits of being trained both in law and in political science. The gap between the (typical) lawyer's "internal" perspective and the (typical) political scientist's "external" one is difficult to bridge, but sitting astride it provides frequent reminders of how much nonsense is talked on both sides. Lawyers pass off partisan politics as "craftsmanship," while political scientists pass off earnest strivings for justice as "ideology" or "self-interest." My resolve, of course, has been to make both mistakes in equal measure.

I have profited greatly from the advice and encouragement of perspicacious readers, among them Sanford Levinson, Frank Michelman, George Anastaplo, John Mack, René Lebeau, Dorothea Martin, and the extremely helpful anonymous reviewers of the State University of New York Press.

A sabbatical granted by Johnson C. Smith University was crucial to the project's completion. The manuscript also benefited greatly from my family's stylistic advice and moral support; charges of anti-semicolonialism are hereby dismissed. Thanks are also due to Clay Morgan and Marilyn Semerad of the State University of New York Press for their sagacious, patient, and courteous assistance.

An earlier version of chapter 4 was published in Morton Halperin and Daniel Hoffman, editors, *Freedom vs. National Secu-*

rity (New York: Chelsea House, 1977). Earlier versions of chapter 6 were published in 19 *Polity* 74 (1986) and in David Freeman, editor, *Political Concepts* (Dubuque: Kendall/Hunt, 1994). An earlier version of chapter 7 was published in 49 *Review of Politics* 515 (1987). Thanks are due to all of the above for granting permission to print the revised versions.

I cannot resist suggesting that the People of the United States, and especially the Framers of the Constitution, are partly responsible for the remaining flaws of this book.

INTRODUCTION

$\mathcal{M}$ any readers of this book will be teachers—teachers of public law or political science at various levels. That is as it should be, for the book largely deals with questions that have arisen in my classroom experiences, as I sought to explain what constitutionalism is and why it is important. Indeed, several of its chapters are my own responses to essay questions originally presented to students in constitutional law, law and politics, or political theory courses. Yet constitutionalism cannot be grasped as a merely academic subject, and this work is not intended for an exclusively academic audience.

Sometimes it appears that constitutionalism as we know it today is not really constitutive for our political culture. One might almost say that constutionalism is a sort of cult. A few insiders take its occult practices seriously; following Weber's threefold typology of authority, one might wonder whether the sway of this cult is traditional, charismatic, or rational in its basis. Meanwhile, most people, though recognizing some of constitutionalism's symbols and slogans, organize their actual experience in quite different ways— power resides not in the law but in men.

When threatened with moral and fiscal bankruptcy, the typical behavior of adherents of different sects/cults is remarkably similar. We *try to go on*. We deny that the Holy of Holies is empty; or we proclaim its emptiness as a triumph over idolatry.[1] Either way—any way—we go on. So . . . .

The stimulus for this book is a sense that much of American constitutional theory, as currently practiced, is irrelevant. Irrelevant, that is, to the ongoing political life of our society. While there are a

1

great many schools of thought, it is useful at the outset to identify two broad groupings.

Constitutional theory of the traditional sort (first-order theory) is concerned with expounding the Constitution. By interpreting the text, and/or the principles and practices associated with the text, first-order theory seeks to provide an account of the basic substantive and procedural norms by which Americans, and especially our public officials, have lived, do live, and/or ought to live. First-order theory may be broad or narrow in scope, descriptive or prescriptive in method, and more or less tightly focused on the constitutional text, as opposed to implicit principles, conventional practices, judicial interpretations, and so forth. All of these variants pretty much take it for granted that the Constitution in some meaningful sense actually constitutes the polity: that it plays (or, at the very least, offers to play) a central unifying, disciplining, energizing role in political life. Like China's Great Wall, it maintains harmony and wards off the barbarians. However, contemporary first-order theory, in its heroic efforts to bridge the often formidable gaps between our constitutional text and the real world of modern politics, often fails to make adequate contact with either.

Nowadays, many of our most brilliant minds are concentrating on second-order theory, which is concerned primarily not with the Constitution itself but with interpretive methods and foundational questions. Second-order theory ostensibly aims at making it possible to do first-order theory more successfully. However, its paths often seem to lead us ever farther away from the Constitution and from first-order theory. Can it be that the barbarians have already smashed the wall, but its guardians, for want of an alternative, go on performing ever more esoteric rituals with its fragments?[2]

"Barbarian" may be a bit strong, but it is clear enough that the average citizen today is no avid constitutionalist. It would seem that even most college students have little interest in or aptitude for constitutional theory. Moreover, opinion surveys indicate that insofar as Americans come to understand the axioms of our classical constitutionalism, they are likely to have significant disagreements with said theory.[3] A *fortiori*, most of us are not enthusiastic participants, or even spectators, of the abstract, metaconstitutional games that second-order theorists play.

In short, second-order theory is academic, obscure, and seldom directly speaks to the questions that inspire what general interest first-order theory can command. Moreover, there is reason to doubt whether its driving impulse—the search for a solid theoretical foundation—is worth pursuing.

People are not computers. It is doubtful whether a comprehensive, consistent theory could fully describe and regulate a human society; if it could, the resulting system might constitute (literally) the most horrible tyranny imaginable. In any event, the Constitution of the United States is not such a system, and no such theory is available to us. Moreover, it seems plausible that the very looseness of our constitutional system is a significant part of the reason that the United States, for all its problems, is so far from being that most horrible tyranny.

It remains, then, spurning the allures of what I like to call "ismism," to explore significant lacunae, inconsistencies, and practical weaknesses in our constitutional thought. Still, to do first-order theory often seems to require more suspension of disbelief than one can easily manage. Some of the problems are more widely recognized than others.

One obvious point will be mentioned only in passing: it would seem that *no one* proposes to read the entire Constitution literally (including those who sometimes pretend that they do). To establish this, we need not embroil ourselves with those provisions, universally regarded as vague or ambiguous, that can scarcely be said to *have* a literal reading. Instead, consider the apparently straightforward provision that "Congress shall make no law . . . abridging the freedom of speech." With regard to this provision, at least, Justice Hugo Black was one who notoriously insisted upon a strict, literal reading.

Yet, where the First Amendment says "Congress," Justice Black (with help from the doctrine of "incorporation") applied this prohibition to all officials of the federal, state and local governments, plus others acting under some cloak of governmental authority. On the other hand, where the amendment says "no law," even Black was willing to uphold certain restrictions on or punishments of speech—sometimes by openly recognizing a compelling countervailing interest that supported the restriction, and sometimes by simply adopting narrow, artificial, and in my judgment implausible readings of the terms *abridgment* or *speech*.[4]

This example is by no means unique nor particular to one thinker. Article I, section 5 declares that "Each House [of Congress] shall be *the judge* of the elections, returns, and qualifications of its own members"; yet the Supreme Court has held that a House's refusal to seat an apparently duly elected member may be subject to judicial review.[5] Article I, section 8, authorizes Congress "to establish *an uniform rule* of naturalization"; yet the constitutionality of "private bills" that admit a single person to citizenship seems accepted by all.

Congress is also empowered "to establish an army and a navy"; did anyone insist on the need for amendments in order to establish a separate air force and marine corps? Article II, section 2 requires senatorial consent to treaties; but the Supreme Court has developed a concept of "executive agreements" requiring no such consent.

Each of these departures from literality can be justified in various ways. Indeed, no doubt it can be argued that each is consistent with a literal reading of the *document as a whole*. The larger point, however, is that any stranger (or naive law student!) carefully reading the Constitution with only a lexicon to guide her would certainly be shocked over and over in learning what our jurisprudence has made of it—whether the lexicon was published in 1789, 1889, 1989, or any combination of the above.

This is not a criticism of lawyers and judges, but a consequence of the nearly universally recognized necessity for interpretation. Madison argued in *The Federalist* that the ambiguity inherent in language and the defects in our intelligence make interpretation necessary.[6] Whether such interpretation is performed well or poorly, openly or deviously, *ad hoc* or according to an elaborate second-order theory, it will gradually lead the Constitution's meaning further and further away from any common-sense understanding. As the Constitution becomes less accessible, the layman is apt to retreat either into outright apathy or into a partisan, media-manipulated preoccupation with the latest sensational decisions of the official interpreters.[7]

Beyond the ambiguity inherent in language, the passage of time changes both the ordinary meaning of words and the context in which they must be used. The consequences are magnified by the extremely cumbersome provisions of Article V for amending the Constitution. Because the changes in our society and politics have far outpaced the changes in our written Constitution, the document has become, in several important respects, downright obsolete. There are major institutions, such as the political party, the giant multinational business corporation, and the international organization, whose existence is not constitutionally acknowledged. There are others, such as the national executive bureaucracy and the electronic media of mass communication, whose current size, functions, and impact are vastly different from those of their historic counterparts. Crucial modern governmental functions, such as education, health, welfare, and environmental protection, are provided for only by implication.

At the same time, large parts of the Constitution have all the relevance of provisions on "letters of marque and reprisal." It is no wonder that the weight of constitutional controversy has come to focus on the most open and sweeping of its clauses—those involving the central concepts of 'liberty,' 'equality,' 'due process,' 'necessary and proper,' 'executive power,' and so forth. For much of today's needed constitutional work, only these are available. Yet the heavy reliance on these provisions requires complex interpretive techniques that make it ever harder to maintain the vital distinction between law and politics—whence the ostensibly obligatory digression into second-order theory.[8]

In short, for a constitution to *work*, it must express meaningful principles understood and supported, on the whole, by a consensus both of elites and of masses. What sort of principles? Ulrich Preuss puts it this way: "A society is constituted when it is confronted with itself in suitable institutional forms and normatively guided processes of adjustment, resistance, and self-correction."[9]

This is quite a stringent test to propose for a society which seems increasingly fragmented and alienated. On the one hand, *politics* has become a dirty word, so that candidates for our highest offices constantly denounce each other for engaging in it. Meanwhile, academic controversy aside, knowledge of the law, respect for law, and the impact of official interpretations of law are apparently very shallow.[10]

Some years ago I attended a conference of the Critical Legal Studies movement, at which a leader of that movement solemnly announced that "constitutional theory is dead." This announcement did not prevent him and many of his colleagues from continuing to engage in what looked very much like constitutional theorizing, even sometimes of the first-order variety. The reason, I think, is the absence of an appealing alternative.

The logically possible alternatives would include framing a new constitution or adopting a nonconstitutional form of politics. The idea of a fresh constitutional start can be tempting in the abstract. Yet when we observe the actual workings of Congress and of interest-group politics, or review the substance and fate of recent proposals for constitutional amendment, it is easy to understand why few Americans, liberal or conservative, are eager for a new convention.[11] At the same time, a glance at news from around the world reminds us that, for all its defects, our constitutional discourse still seems to play an invaluable role in "combining the requisite stability and energy in government with the inviolable attention due to liberty and to the republican form."[12]

Studies of public opinion and knowledge leave room for doubt as to how far the lack of demand for thoroughgoing constitutional reform comes from satisfaction with the Constitution, and how far it comes from apathy. Either way, thoughtful observers have reason to fear what effect radical reform attempts might have on a polity whose coherence and stability seem to depend more on continued adherence to its Constitution than on the mutual trust that comes from strong social and cultural bonds. As Bernstein puts it:

> If constitutional revision is to succeed, the American people must be prepared to engage in a profound and far-reaching discussion of fundamental principles, driven by an equally powerful conviction of the need for constitutional change and neither condition has been met.[13]

If we do not want to dispense with constitutions and cannot have a new one, we must make the best of the one we have. That project, surely, must be a collective one, to which different people contribute in different ways. Many brilliant scholars are currently so engaged.[14] Some argue the need for, and demonstrate the possibility of, keeping the discourse going. Some focus on the important question of *whose* discourse it is, and especially on the proper bounds of the judicial role. Some continue the search for a viable, comprehensive constitutional theory. Some modestly and perhaps wisely confine themselves to addressing narrower doctrinal or empirical issues.

This book is an effort to contribute to first-order theory, while avoiding the dogmas and unexamined assumptions to which such theory so often falls prey. It pursues a twofold strategy: criticizing certain important theories and specific doctrinal interpretations that I find problematic or unsatisfying; and pointing out issues which have not yet been sufficiently addressed, whose elaboration promises to clarify, rectify, or reconcile existing interpretations. Because of the Constitution's many silences and ambiguities, this effort will require a good deal of attention to extratextual materials.

Some disclaimers may help to avoid misunderstanding. This study is selective in its scope, eclectic in its method, and tentative in its conclusions. There are no special pretensions either to philosophical or to empirical rigor; indeed, my purpose is largely to raise questions and to place them in relationship to each other, rather than to provide definitive answers.

Nevertheless, at some junctures I shall take very definite stands. Here the reader may notice assertions that seem to lack adequate support. Some are not carefully argued because they seem to me too obviously correct to require it. In other cases available evidence is cited but not discussed in detail, due to limitations of space. And in some cases I frankly rely upon intuition or common sense, recognizing that skeptics demanding hard proof will be unpersuaded. Yet if the reader is moved to articulate more clearly and to share with others her own beliefs and the bases therefor, I will have achieved a large part of my objective—to provoke a broader, more meaningful constitutional discourse.

The plan of this book expresses my understanding of the structure of American constitutionalism. Its core concerns are the rule of law—procedural regularity, functional specialization, and other restraints on the use of power—and the relationship between the individual and the state, where the individual is primarily a holder of reserved rights and the state a holder of powers delegated to it collectively by the people. The paradigmatic constitutional controversy, in our day at least, involves a conflict between a governmental authority purporting to exercise such a power, and an individual protesting that the act in question violates a personal right. In part I, I explore the distinction between "law" and "politics," with all that implies for the appropriate role of the courts. In part II, I explore our conceptions of the people, the state and its powers. In part III, I explore our conceptions of the person and the kinds of rights she possesses.

My thesis is that these three inquiries are essential to the maintenance—some would say restoration or genesis—of a *constitutional* polity in the United States. Given our history, customary ways of thinking, and authoritative texts, a viable constitutional polity depends upon (among other things) the extent of agreement among us on those three issues: the meaning and value of the rule of law, of the public interest, and of the flourishing of the person. What is called for is not a rigid orthodoxy, but an ongoing constitutional dialogue that participants can find meaningful, principled, and fruitful.

Today, the shared vision of "unity, justice, tranquility, security, welfare and liberty" (to paraphrase the Preamble) that such dialogue promises to produce for the people of the United States is difficult to discern. How far our polity can today provide these goods and, in particular, how far the Constitution is part of our solution are therefore questionable. What guidance we are able to find in the Constitution of course depends on what the Constitution actually says and how it has historically been interpreted. Even more decisively, it depends on what we now choose to make of the Constitution, with all its silences, paradoxes, and (largely implicit) priorities.

Law and Politics—
What, Where, and How?

*T*he major theme of this part is the relationship between law and politics and the way that relationship bears upon the respective authority and competence of courts, of legislatures, and of the citizenry. A secondary theme is the distinction between ordinary and constitutional politics and the corresponding distinction between ordinary and constitutional law. It is widely believed—in the academy, at least—that the legitimacy of our political system, and especially of judicial review, depends on the theoretical coherence and the proper application of these distinctions that are necessary to confine each decision-making agency to its proper role.

In the orthodox account, ordinary politics is the province of the elected, "political" branches of government, which, spurred by communication and pressure from the citizenry, formulate public policy by enacting ordinary law. Constitutional politics is special in that supermajorities are required to bring a proposal to fruition, so that the resulting declaration becomes entrenched as "the will of the People"—a higher form of law. The judicial role is to interpret and enforce both ordinary law and constitutional law, while abstaining from "political" involvement. Whereas their applications of ordinary law can be modified through the modalities of ordinary politics, the courts' constitutional decisions are, orthodoxy holds, corrigible only through constitutional amendment.

It is curious how little attention the literature has paid to the significance of Article V for the whole debate on judicial review. Yet a necessary, if seldom stated, assumption behind defenses of judicial activism seems to be that the Constitution is too difficult to amend, making judicial interpretation a far superior method of adaptation when changing circumstances bring to light defects of omission or commission in the text. Bernstein,[1] for example, sets forth the advantages of reliance on interpretation, custom, and usage over frequent resort to Article V. The latter is not only cumbersome, he argues, but often politically costly. It is not guaranteed to resolve neatly the problems an amendment's framers sought to address, and may even bring new, unforeseen problems in its wake.

How then would the argument go if the Constitution were easier to amend? Would the case for judicial restraint then be an easy winner—or is there, for example, a distinction between matters of high principle that require wide public involvement, and technical improvements that can easily and safely be made without such involvement? Either way, are there good arguments in principle against making it easier to amend and for continuing to use judicial review instead? Madison, for example, makes a case in *The Federalist* against frequent appeals to the people on constitutional questions, arguing that regular amendment would soon diminish reverence for the Constitution itself.[2]

As a practical matter, there seems no prospect that amending Article V will become a live issue—assuming at least that we do not advertently or inadvertently call a new constitutional convention with a wide-open agenda. (It is highly doubtful that Congress or the states could confine a convention to considering only a single issue. The 1787 convention itself ignored the guidelines under which it was convened.) Although one activist has recently proposed amending Article V to provide for ratification by national referendum rather than by the states,[3] the idea has attracted very little attention. A lower threshold for constitutional amendment thus is not in the cards. Nor, for that matter, is Ackerman's proposal[4] that some fundamental rights (etc.) should be made immune to future amendment.

Little is known about the empirical consequences of making a constitution easier or harder to amend, even though comparison of the fifty states, and of historical changes within many of them, appears to offer abundant research opportunity. One might hypothesize that states where constitutional amendment is easier have less judicial activism, since they do not *need* it as much. Of course, the largest obstacle to testing this hypothesis is the operationalization of "judicial activism," a contentious and elusive concept that some find downright incoherent, useful only for bashing one's political opponents. The only remotely relevant study I am aware of did not engage the issue of judicial behavior; it made the unsurprising finding that in states where amendment is easier, more amendments occur.[5]

One operational hypothesis might be that invalidating acts of the political branches is the essence of judicial activism; restraint means taking seriously the presumption of constitutionality. A very different one would hold that, on the contrary, invalidation is, typically at least, not an activist exercise, but rather an upholding of traditional constitutional norms in the face of attempted innovation. Thus, for Ackerman,[6] the *activist* move is to reinterpret the Constitution so as to *legitimize* the reform—a step courts would not find so tempting if formal amendment were easier. It seems impossible to decide between these opposing operational hypotheses without getting into the substance of specific rulings and their rationales, as well as additional variables, such as partisanship.

Before we get more deeply into questions about the appropriate role of courts, it is worth pausing to consider why we have courts in the first place. In particular, what is the rationale for entrusting lawmaking and law interpretation to separate and independent institutions?[7]

Today we take this arrangement so much for granted that we seldom look closely at its origins. At the time of the framing, the separation of powers was far from a clear and settled axiom. The Massachusetts legislature was called (as indeed it still is) the "General Court"; bills of attainder had recently been used in Virginia and elsewhere. The Constitution sought to establish a different system. Madison, in *The Federalist*, cites Montesquieu as authority for the proposition that to let the legislature be the judge is to invite tyranny.[8] Neither he nor Montesquieu elaborates very fully the reasoning behind this claim.

The argument appears to rest on the premises that laws ought to be, first, general in their coverage—in particular, their burdens must fall on the legislators themselves just as they do on others—and, second, impartial in their application—with equal protection for all individuals and groups, without regard for the favor or disfavor in which they are held by those in power. Since the prejudices of lawmakers may naturally tempt them to violate these norms, an independent judiciary will serve as a salutary check against such abuses.[9]

To assess this argument, we need to consider how it applies to at least two different cases: a law that is impartial on its face, but sub-

ject to possible bias in its application; and a law that is overtly designed to further some interests at the expense of others. In the former case, Madison's claim is apparently that judges are more likely
than legislators to carry out impartially the law's true policy, because judges cannot be corrupted by the desire for reelection or for
quick profit before their term expires. Legislators, in contrast, cannot be trusted to act impartially if allowed, as the old saying goes,
to "be judges in their own cause."

In the case of an overtly biased law, the separation of powers can
avail us only if judges have the power and the duty to prevent such
a corrupt law from being carried out. In short, for Madison's argument to make sense, courts must be in some effective sense "above
politics," and they must use the power of judicial review to ensure
that the legislature does, properly speaking, legislate. Yet, as we
shall see, there is much room for doubt about the reality of both
these claims.

There are other possible arguments for a separation of powers,
based not on fear of tyranny but on the efficiency of a division of
labor between bodies favored with different competencies. Thus, we
have come to view legislatures as specialists in policymaking, in
representation of constituents' desires and interests, whereas
courts are specialists in the realm of principle, precedent, and textual interpretation. Members of each body ostensibly come to have
distinctive skills, informational resources, and career incentives appropriate to the respective tasks assigned them.

It is interesting that, while debate about how capably legislators
represent (and how capably judges judge) is immediately and
nakedly partisan, the incompetence of judges as policy makers is
sometimes taken as a scientific fact.[10] How can this be so, if we cannot agree what good policymaking consists of? Moreover, if it is so
clear that legislators have the structural advantages commonly attributed to them, how and why has the predominant role in policymaking in fact devolved upon the unelected bureaucrats of the
executive branch?

As difficult as they may be to answer, these questions seem crucial for our understanding not just of the proper role of the judiciary, but of the reality, depth, and thrust of the Constitution's
impact on our political life. In chapter 1, I focus on the claim that
courts can and must avoid deciding "political questions." In chapter
2, I explore more broadly the relationship between the citizen and
the state, the concept of representation, and what it can mean to
engage in a specifically "constitutional" form of politics.

⊰§ Chapter 1 §⊱

The Myth of the
Political Question

Ours is a government of laws, not of men.

—John Adams

*T*he "political questions" phenomenon can be studied as a *doc-trine*, by exploring the ramifications of the law/politics di-chotomy which underlies and necessitates the doctrine; or it can be approached as a question of institutional *behavior*, by asking under what circumstances courts have in fact sought to avoid deciding cases "on the merits." This chapter will pursue each approach in turn.

The "political questions" doctrine states that courts must and do avoid deciding questions that are not legal but political in nature. This is upheld by judges and many academicians, even though we routinely find courts deciding about controversial matters such as abortion, election districting, affirmative action, prayer in schools, and police misconduct. What then is the doctrine, and what does it achieve?

There is a threshold question that must be addressed if this in-quiry is to have any point: Is all law, in fact, "nothing but" politics carried out in a certain style? If this reductionist critique is valid, then the "rule of law" turns out to be a mere ideological disguise for, say, the hegemony of a ruling class. In that case, it would not really matter much which government institution—legislative, executive, or judicial—the ruling class used to effect its will and repress the ruled in a particular case.

E. P. Thompson responds powerfully to this critique in a well-known essay where he argues that law, to perform its acknowledged ideological functions, must be seen as upholding "standards of universality and equity": "If the law is evidently partial and unjust, then it will mask nothing, legitimize nothing, contribute nothing to any class's hegemony."[1]

Thus, the rhetoric and the rules of law normally have a dual, potentially contradictory function: "They may disguise the true realities of power, but, at the same time, they may curb that power and check its intrusions. And it is often from that very rhetoric that a radical critique of the practice of the society is developed . . . ."[2]

Thompson concludes with a suitably dialectical prescription: "We ought to expose the shams and inequities which may be concealed beneath this law. But the rule of law itself, the imposing of effective inhibitions upon power and the defence of the citizen from power's all-intrusive claims, seems to me to be an unqualified human good."[3]

This argument indicates that the law/politics dichotomy is by no means inconsequential, since law can impose significant constraints upon politics. If so, the "political questions" doctrine is worth taking seriously. First, it might make a significant difference whether the courts become involved in a given controversy or whether they abstain from involvement; second, we cannot say *a priori* that it is impossible to give a principled account of the sorts of cases in which judicial involvement is inappropriate.

While Thompson seems convincing on the point that the law/politics dichotomy is consequential,[4] his argument is by no means sufficient to prove that its consequences are necessarily entirely benign. As Jennifer Nedelsky has powerfully argued, a major use of this dichotomy in the American context has been to establish a domain of higher "law" in which the judicial power was supreme and the "political" process forbidden to intrude.

Nedelsky's study focuses on the constitutional visions of three of the Framers: James Madison, Gouverneur Morris, and James Wilson. Her primary concern is the consequences for democratic politics of the Framers' emphasis on the protection of private property. Her thesis is that our constitutional tradition has tended to limit democratic participation more than to foster it. Nedelsky does not discuss the modern "political questions" doctrine, but she does give a penetrating account of the Federalist theory of judicial review elaborated by John Marshall. Insofar as the modern doctrine comports with and follows from the classical theory (as it surely claims to do), Nedelsky's analysis suggests that, while the "political questions" doctrine purports to *limit* the judicial power, its primary purpose may be indirectly to *defend* that power against those who criticize judicial review as profoundly undemocratic. As Nedelsky puts it: "The establishment of judicial review added the law-politics distinction to the conceptual foundation of American constitutionalism. This distinction was the justification for the courts' authority to define the limits to government."[5]

The objective was not a neutral one of defending personal rights. Rather, it had a decidedly partisan character: "The Federalist strategy was to try to remove the most fundamental and most threatened issues from the contested political realm by designating them 'law.'"[6]

In cases such as *Marbury v. Madison*, the Court pursued its strategy precisely by *avoiding* overt partisan confrontation: it claimed authority to adjudicate legal *rights*, not political *interests*.[7] In *Marbury* the power of judicial review was established, but the interests of Federalist would-be officeholders were sacrificed.

This approach of course depended upon a general consensus on certain basic principles that could be stipulated as fundamental rights: "Everyone agreed that property was a fundamental right, although there were serious differences over what constituted violations of property rights. Property was thus a perfect issue around which to build judicial review . . . ."[8]

The next step in Chief Justice Marshall's strategy in *Marbury* was the equation of the courts' role in enforcing the Constitution— the "supreme *law* of the land"—to its role in enforcing the common law. Thus the separation of powers itself fell under their jurisdiction—even though that separation had been supported from its birth[9] by the old maxim that "no man shall be judge in his own cause!" "This subtle confusion of categories of law sustained the claim that the political structure itself . . . should be thought of as law. The structure was the Federalists' solution to the problem of democratic excess."[10]

The political consequences, according to Nedelsky, have been quite faithful to the Federalist vision, despite all the democratizing changes in the political and legal systems: "[T]he protection of property *required* disproportionate power for the few with property since they needed to be able to defend themselves against the many without."[11]

Nedelsky's critique of Marshall's project focuses on the courts' necessary reliance on consensual, *seemingly* "self-evident rules of justice to define the bounds of legitimacy": "Once we acknowledge the mutability of basic values, the problem of protecting them from democratic abuse is transformed."[12]

Here, Nedelsky briefly takes issue with Ackerman's "dualist" formulation of democratic theory (see below):

> First of all, what counts as mere private interest or higher public values is itself part of the terms of constitutional discourse. And these terms are constantly shifting, not static until moments of focused attention on constitutional debate. . . . Judicial review has, in fact, provided a means of insulation from ordinary politics which has proven capable of ongoing change.[13]

Where Ackerman's Founders were dualist democrats who cherished property along with other rights, Nedelsky's were essentially distrustful of democracy and virtually obsessed with property. Where Ackerman's Court has essentially preservationist functions, hers has been a bastion of conservative activism. Accordingly, where he focuses on preserving what is best in the liberal-constitutionalist-democratic tradition, her critique culminates in a proposal for a more radical rethinking:

> The autonomy the Madisonian system sought to protect could be achieved by erecting a wall of rights between the individual and those around him. Property was the ideal symbol for this vision of autonomy . . . . A proper conception of autonomy must begin with the recognition that relationship, not separation makes autonomy possible. . . . Political liberty is a dimension of autonomy as well as a potential threat to it. . . . And once the setting of boundaries is rejected as the ruling metaphor, we will need a new understanding of the nature of law. Not only will the task of law cease to be drawing boundaries of rights between the individual and the collective, but the boundary between law and politics will blur. . . . And those transformations are, in any case, underway.[14]

Unfortunately, Nedelsky has little to say about the specific role that law and courts would play in her more participatory democratic system. Like Roberto Unger,[15] she has some difficulty explaining why *any* sort of law is appropriate—much less essential—in a fluid political system committed to ongoing, open-textured discourse, in which the axiom of self-government requires that all questions remain perpetually open to (re)consideration. I shall refrain from considering further the details of her argument, noting only its implications about the likely historic functions of the "political questions" doctrine: to safeguard the legitimacy of judicial review by avoiding "political" controversy and, at the same time, to further the courts' own specific political agenda by securing urgently desired outcomes. The hallowed *Marbury* precedent suggests that, where these two aims conflict, the courts may well give priority to their long-run institutional potency, even if abstention entails substantial short-run political costs.

While the Marshall Court's legacy and doctrines can be criticized on numerous grounds, we cannot criticize them simply for having acted politically until we offer a clear account of how law and politics could, in principle, be completely separated. If this cannot be done, then the Court can be charged, at worst, with failure to offer an adequate and candid account of the distinction between the sort of politics in which courts may properly engage, and the sort in which they may not—and with practicing *sub rosa* a politics of the latter sort.

In Nedelsky's view, the Court's primary error stemmed from its hostility to inclusive, participatory democracy. Historians will continue to debate the extent to which such hostility was in fact deliberately built into the constitutional design. The crucial point, however, is that—purposely or not—the Framers did leave open ample space for ongoing debate between very different conceptions of our polity. Such debate has always been the stuff of American constitutional politics, conducted inside and outside the courts.

The labeling and classification of the different conceptions and their advocates is a tricky business—a matter, moreover, pertaining more to rhetoric than to science, whether one is labeling oneself or others. Yet it seems useful to observe that, from the outset, constitutional politics has focused on competing views of the relative values of:

1. energetic government vs. individual liberty;
2. national unity vs. local control;
3. elite leadership vs. popular participation;
4. virtue and normalcy vs. inclusiveness and tolerance;
5. stability vs. expansion (economic and territorial).

These issues were already visible in the constitutional ratification debates, but have since undergone many transformations. The complex, overlapping interaction of these issues in different periods and the changing perspectives induced by changing circumstances will confound any effort to reduce our history to, for instance, a bipolar contrast between two enduring paradigms. Nevertheless, it may be useful to employ certain familiar (if much-abused) terms as a rough shorthand for concerns with which they have often been associated. I take liberalism to refer to a focus on the liberty and flourishing of the individual; republicanism to refer to a focus on the self-government and flourishing of the united community; and democracy to focus on the norms of inclusiveness, equality, and expansion.

Each of these ideas can be shown to be, when pushed to extremes, in sharp conflict with each of the others—and, moreover, already to contain within itself the seeds of contradiction. The clash between individual liberty and effective government is a central preoccupation of *The Federalist*; expansion can easily make both harder to achieve. In general, personal flourishing is not ensured for all by a merely negative conception of liberty. The goal of unity places in question the boundaries of the "self" that is to govern; and, the larger the community, the more problematic equality and tolerance become. To these obvious points, at this stage I need add only a few others.

First, the term *conservativism* is largely absent from my schema. The reason is that I understand the conservative impulse not as a political theory or idea but as a situational opposition to change— which cannot be grasped or evaluated until it is specified *which* changes the speaker opposes and why. (Needless to say, the advocacy of "change," as such, is equally meaningless.)

Second, these terms as I use them do not map at all neatly onto the platforms of our political parties. Today there is no truly liberal major party, and the Democratic party is only vaguely democratic. The Republican party, in contrast, seems highly republican, *if* one understands republicanism to be an essentially authoritarian, intolerant doctrine.

Thinkers such as Michelman[16] and Sunstein[17] have attempted recently to reinterpret the republican tradition, emphasizing the possibility and attractiveness of accommodating it to the facts of diversity and the norms of tolerance. Their aim is to overcome the fragmentation and decay that beset the public realm, without reverting to the homogeneous exclusiveness of the Puritan colony or the small rural town. While their different suggestions are intriguing and often tempting in principle, they seem quite inconsistent with the ways in which republicans have generally historically spoken and behaved.

Michelman is keenly aware of the exclusionary impulses to which "solidaristic" versions of republicanism have succumbed. He attempts to show that "pluralistic" republicanism is equally inter-

nally coherent, and more consistent with our tradition and situation as a whole. The difficulty lies in specifying a range of shared "understandings about the ordering and direction of social life" that is, on the one hand, sufficient to make dialogic politics possible and inviting, yet, on the other hand, still tolerant of the variety of existing "perspectives on human interests and needs."[18] This challenging task remains to be accomplished.[19]

From experience, I doubt that Michelman's appeal to shared contexts of "language, culture, worldview, and political memory,"[20] admittedly essential to motivate a dialogue about the common interests of the whole community, would resonate effectively with citizens such as, for example, my African-American students, whose political discourse seems not just distorted but *constituted* by the opposition between "us" and "them." Yet today's conservative judges, to whom Michelman charitably imputes a sincere if inchoate republican theory, often have no difficulty determining that *those* citizens' interests, issues, and perspectives are special, deviant, and not legally valid.

Sunstein argues persuasively that, even in the aftermath of the New Deal reforms, our jurisprudence continues to incorporate a significant measure of "status-quo neutrality," meaning that actions altering the existing distributions of wealth and power tend to be more vulnerable to constitutional challenge than measures reinforcing the status quo. While he denies that such a bias is genuinely neutral and offers new readings of *some* constitutional rights that are less biased toward the status quo, he also concedes (perhaps too quickly) that status-quo neutrality is clearly ensconced in provisions such as the contracts clause of Article I, section 10 and the takings clause of the Fifth Amendment.[21]

It may be that cultural diversity, nihilistic egalitarianism, and the unabashed "liberal" pursuit of private interests are part of our problem, but it seems unlikely that a resuscitated and updated classical republicanism will prove to be our solution. In order to heal, unite, and reinvigorate this polity, it will be necessary to identify concrete projects and symbols that are not, in our present context, inherently divisive. The abstract philosophical underpinnings of republicanism may not be an insuperable obstacle, but its history, symbols, and current agenda are another matter.

Returning to our central theme, the different strands of constitutional thought place different values on the public and private domains of life, and thus suggest different assessments of the rule of law and the law/politics distinction. At one extreme, law is a regrettable but necessary invasion of private freedoms and an essential safeguard against governmental tyranny. The law/politics distinction urges courts to safeguard personal rights against political usurpation. At the other extreme, politics is an essential instrument of collective self-determination and safeguard against private vice. The law/politics distinction safeguards the public interest against selfish "special" interests and cautions courts to be wary of interfering with the will of the People.

An unusually interesting effort to reconcile and synthesize these different views is Bruce Ackerman's theory of "dualist democracy." Ackerman's ambitious, ongoing project is to specify historically and theoretically sound criteria for the constitutional integrity of American politics. Such criteria will test the validity of various governmental (particularly judicial) and popular actions. Ackerman hopes to persuade us that neither the accumulated amendments to the constitutional text nor the sometimes dramatic departures in judicial interpretation (especially those associated with the New Deal) have made the constitutional regime incoherent and illegitimate. To this end he combines a periodization of the constitutional regime with a distinctive theory of judicial review.

"We, the People,"[22] in his view, have constitutionally established a unique, "dualist" system of shared responsibilities, which uses different political and legal mechanisms at different times to accomplish different purposes. For ordinary public decisions, normally we employ representative institutions, influenced through elections and interest-group politics. Such "ordinary politics" is not sufficiently egalitarian or broadly participatory to reflect true popular sovereignty. Indeed, in this context "the People," strictly speaking, does not exist as a political agent. Only on special occasions does the People intervene by, after due deliberation, *constitutionally* transforming government's responsibilities.[23] This claim promises to resolve the tension between the "liberal" and "republican" strands in our tradition.

Various questions can be raised about Ackerman's theory and the way he applies it to specific historical cases. For present purposes, the key point pertains to his concept of 'dualism' itself: the thesis that our polity operates in two temporally discrete modes—ordinary politics (the self-centered, liberal-individualistic world of private citizens) and constitutional politics (the public-spirited, republican world in which alone "the People" deliberates and acts).

The device of temporal separation succeeds only if clear-cut definitions of the two modes can be developed, generating a workable "either-or" rule of recognition. Otherwise, we would be unable to distinguish between ordinary law (the product of ordinary politics) and higher law (the will of "the People"), which takes precedence over ordinary law. Ackerman's insistence that the Constitution can be and has been basically transformed *without* resort to the Article V amendment process makes this problem especially severe. How are citizens, and judges in particular, to know when such a transformation has occurred?

The first American constitutional regime (leaving the revolutionary transition and the Articles of Confederation aside) of course began with the convention of 1787. Ackerman's claim that the post–Civil War amendments signaled a constitutional regime change is relatively easy to accept (although even here, Ackerman finds it necessary to distinguish between "transformative amendments" such as the Fourteenth and mere "superstatutes" like the Twenty-sixth). But the claim that the 1936 elections signaled a regime change of equal stature is another matter entirely. While it makes little sense to question the constitutionality of the Fourteenth Amendment (assuming proper ratification) and of statutes clearly enabled thereby, it makes perfectly coherent sense to question the constitutionality of statutes "enabled" by the 1936 elections. For a court to reject a constitutional challenge simply by citing a decisive electoral mandate would be to replace a constitutional form of democracy with a plebiscitarian form.

Recognizing the inadequacy of voting, taken alone, as a method for conducting constitutional politics or a test for recognizing it, Ackerman offers a fairly elaborate framework for recognizing moments of "higher lawmaking" and thus legitimizing their products. The overall process consists of four stages: signaling, proposing, deliberating, and codifying. Signaling refers to placing an issue on the agenda, by demonstrating that the issue has, in the country at large, "extraordinary support" in terms of "depth, breadth, and decisiveness." Depth refers to the *quality* of public involvement: the citizen has "deliberated as much about her commitment to a national ideal as she thinks appropriate in making a considered judgment on an important decision in her private life." Breadth refers to the *numbers* of citizens in support. As a rule of thumb, Ackerman proposes that a signaling movement should have the *deep* support (in the above sense) of 20 percent of the citizens, and the simple support of an additional 31 percent, to place its initiative on the agenda. The third criterion, decisiveness, responds to the paradoxes inherent in majority voting rules when more than two options are offered; it requires that the initiative enjoy enough support to "decisively defeat *all* the plausible alternatives in a series of pairwise comparisons."[24]

These criteria are subject to various objections. The definition of depth seems far too vague to use in a rule of recognition. The breadth criterion is even more troublesome. My problem is not with the specific numbers offered, but with the appropriateness of understanding breadth of support in gross numerical terms. The rationale for requiring broad support in the first place, as I understand it, is to filter out initiatives whose motivation is essentially *factional*—whose support is based on self-interest rather than a conception of the public good. Since factions come in all sizes, a gross numerical threshold has no relevance for this purpose. Rather, a case-specific analysis of *who* supports the initiative is needed. The ERA movement might need different levels of support from males and females, for example. For Reconstruction, we would separately measure Northern and Southern support.

Ackerman would probably answer that such painstaking care is not needed at the signaling stage. After all, the proposal must still pass several major hurdles; at this stage, taking a proposal more seriously than it deserves is far more acceptable than is the opposite mistake.

At any rate, Ackerman does not directly employ the aforesaid criteria in his study of historical cases. Instead, he reverts to rigorous, institutionalized procedural devices which he takes as embodying those criteria. Ostensibly, these devices are functionally adequate to accept for further consideration proposals having the requisite depth, breadth, and decisiveness, while rejecting at the outset proposals that lack them. The devices include, first, the amendment proposal procedures of Article V, and second, a modern, alternative system:

> [I]f a President can convince Congress to support the enactment of transformative statutes that challenge the constitutional premises of the preexisting regime, the American public treats his success as a higher lawmaking signal similar to the proposal of a formal constitutional amendment under the classical system.[25]

The classical system of course continues with the formal ratification procedure. In the modern system, the continuation is quite different.

> Precisely because of their revolutionary character, many of these statutes will be invalidated by the Supreme Court. This will return the burden of initiative back to the political

branches: Does the constitutional movement have sufficient strength in the country to challenge the Court with a second round of statutes that refine and deepen the legal meanings adumbrated the first time around?. . . .

[T]he modern system relies very heavily on the good judgment of courts. After making their "switch in time," they must reflect upon the deeper meanings of transformative statutes and seek to codify them in transformative opinions that will guide constitutional development in the regime ahead.[26]

This treatment, referring abstractly to the three branches without regard to the working of party systems, organized interests, and the special features of periods of divided government, seems excessively austere and unhistorical. Nor does Ackerman go deeply into studies of political sociology. For all his recognition that the typical citizen is *ordinarily* moved by private and not by public-spirited concerns, the required widespread capability for transcending this attitude on special occasions of constitutional politics is not convincingly demonstrated. Ackerman's model may thus fail to deal realistically with some fairly typical cases—let alone with unique examples of constitutional politics such as Dorr's rebellion or the post–Civil War amendments.

Even sticking to the formal level, Ackerman fails to provide clear criteria for courts to use in deciding whether to "switch," thus acknowledging that a legitimate constitutional transformation has occurred, or whether to adhere to precedent until the formal amendment procedure has been used. Once again, is "sufficient strength in the country" to be measured simply by some number or magnitude of victories in presidential elections and/or congressional votes? Does not the coherence of the ordinary law/higher law dichotomy depend on our ability to distinguish between cases where the Court interprets the Constitution *incorrectly*—errors we could in good faith set right by "transformative" Court appointments and other techniques proper to "ordinary politics"—and cases where the Court's *correct* decision persuades us that the Constitution itself is in some respect no longer right for us—a problem properly corrigible only through very distinct procedures reserved for "constitutional politics"?

The ongoing debate in political science over the identification of "critical" or "realigning" elections provides a useful caution.[27] This is a far simpler issue, in two senses. First, a realignment can be established by analyzing changes in demographic voting patterns, without undue regard to the issues advanced in the campaign or direct evidence about the motives of individual voters. Second, the concept is used as a heuristic device for periodizing political history. To label a given election as "critical" is not really right or wrong; it is more or less explanatorily useful. The debate has produced very little closure; yet the task confronting a court faced with "transformative" legislation is far more demanding.

But perhaps the problem is more than one of measurement. Why isn't there a deep contradiction between the idea that in normal times the People does not exist, and the idea that even normal politics can and should pursue *the public good?* How can a nonexistent entity *have* an interest, and how could we know it if it did? Note: we cannot answer this just by referring back to the vision of the public good last announced (or cumulatively announced) at moments of constitutional politics. The People do not then address what specific actions should be taken to meet specific problems; they speak at a very abstract level. Indeed, if they tried to legislate in the ordinary sense, they would not be acting *constitutionally* at all. In moments of constitutional politics perhaps the public good, like "the People" itself, comes to exist by the very process of self-recognition. But how can we, mere private citizens, recognize it? This "People" is reminiscent of Wittgenstein's lion! "If a lion could talk, we could not understand him."[28] How can a republican politics confined to special constitutional moments "constitute" an ordinary politics whose participants and aims are so different?

One possible source of comfort, which Ackerman's theory obliges him to forego, is the *textuality* of the Constitution. Ackerman sees constitutional politics as especially serious, deliberative, and participatory, as well as fundamental in its concerns. Well and good; but these attributes are hard to measure and largely matters of degree. The "higher law" that emerges from such politics has also been distinguished—in the American tradition, at least—by its textual nature and its elaboration through specialized procedures, which support workable rules of recognition. It is this tradition that so often lures us into quasimetaphysical and, in my opinion, ultimately futile debate over whether or not a specific principle can "actually" be found "within the four corners" of the Constitution.

Now, Ackerman needs to break decisively with this tradition in order to validate his third, New Deal regime and its new approach to constitutional transformation. (Indeed, this outcome imperative seems to be a major impulse behind his theoretical innovations.) If the Constitution is a text, then it did not change in 1937. On the other hand, if it is not a text, then the distinction between constitutional politics and constitutional law threatens to disappear. If the constitution can be radically overhauled without amending the text, what exactly is there left for courts to "interpret" during times of ordinary politics?

Ackerman recognizes the need for a concept of (preservationist) constitutional interpretation, as opposed to (transformative) constitutional politics; thus, he insists that *Brown*[29] and *Griswold*[30] are exercises in the former mode, not in the latter. In the end, it appears that dualist democracy must consist of more than the two stipulated forms of *politics*; it also needs both ordinary and constitutional *law*. Ackerman's temporal dualism and preservationist view of the judicial role imply a view of the law/politics dichotomy: law for him is essentially (in Unger's term) frozen politics.[31]

Note that by expanding the scope of constitutional politics beyond the framework of Article V amendment procedures, and also by labeling certain less transformative constitutional amendments as mere "superstatutes," Ackerman blurs *in both directions* our understanding of which rules are currently entrenched in the Constitution. On the one hand, matters not mentioned in the Constitution can come to have "constitutional" status. (This is, after all, already a consequence of traditional judicial review.) On the other hand, can we not now imagine a court saying (for entirely new reasons[32]) that a purported constitutional amendment is itself unconstitutional? That, although we *thought* we were doing constitutional politics, on close inspection it turns out we were only doing ordinary politics, because our deliberations did not have the depth, breadth, and so on that constitutional politics requires? After all, if the People did not follow the procedures laid down, courts cannot sanction that and still *be* courts.

One bloc on the court might view the distinction between ordinary and constitutional politics as itself purely procedural. Thus, courts are not themselves doing politics when they enforce the (procedural) distinction between substance and procedure. This bloc might still split, however, on whether the procedures laid down are simply those of Article V or whether the courts should look (perhaps in both directions) beyond mere formalistic compliance with those procedures.

Another bloc would predictably view the distinction between ordinary and constitutional politics—not to mention that between substantive and procedural distinctions—as ineluctably substantive. This bloc might still split, however, on whether it is proper for *courts* to make such substantive judgments.

A third bloc, on or off the court, might point out that such technical discourse as this is profoundly alienating, inaccessible, and irrelevant to the people at large. What we care about most is, in the short run: are we to have our way on this issue, or not? And in the long run: whose country, and what kind of country, is this?

To an extent, whether judicial review continues as a legitimate institution may well depend on the popularity, especially with elite opinion leaders, of major court decisions.[33] Yet in the long run, more esoteric arguments about the judicial role will continue to influence the fate of proposals for reform. To justify their actions in terms that we can recognize, courts must be able to discern the difference between ordinary and constitutional rules and to protect the boundary between ordinary and constitutional politics. To allow a confusion between the two would allow "ordinary majorities" to accomplish the sort of major change, potentially affecting fundamental rights and entrenched against future reform, that is reserved for special "supermajorities."

For Ackerman, this would be the ultimate evil. Indeed, he even professes interest in the idea of insulating rights such as free speech from the Article V amendment process, as the Framers did for the equal representation of states in the Senate. For, while he is far less critical than Nedelsky is of the courts' historic performance in preserving and reconciling constitutional principles, he knows we cannot trust them—nor even the sovereign People!—absolutely.

With these considerations in mind, let us quickly review the Supreme Court's own original assertion of its special constitutional role. In *Marbury v. Madison*,[34] the Supreme Court justified judicial review as a direct consequence of the competence and responsibility of the courts to say what the law is—a duty it could hardly perform without adverting to the Constitution, since that document is "the supreme law of the land." The courts can and must interpret the Constitution, in other words, because the Constitution is law.

To these assertions of Chief Justice Marshall, President Jefferson retorted that *all* public officials were sworn to uphold the Constitution, and therefore needed to interpret it on relevant occasions. Moreover, the people—not the courts—were sovereign; hence the decisive role in constitutional interpretation ought to belong to the branch of government closest to the people, namely the legislature. It is to make the laws, after all, that Congress is chosen.

Defenders of judicial review replied by appealing to the paramount need for a nationally uniform, stable, and nonpartisan understanding of our Constitution. Given the separation of powers, federalism, and the realities of party and faction, the elected, "political" branches would be unable to develop and sustain that understanding. The courts, with their professional skills, devotion to precedent, hierarchical structure, and insulation from political pressures, could hope to do so.

This argument may appear simply to expand upon the claim that the Constitution is law. On closer inspection, however, it becomes clear that a significant distinction is involved—between ordinary law, subject to and produced by the ordinary political process, and higher law, superior to and insulated from that process. Since the Constitution is, in its very essence, a safeguard against abuses of power by elected officials, those officials cannot be entrusted with the last word on its interpretation. The only alternatives are the courts—or the people themselves. If (as Madison argued in *The Federalist*[35]) the people cannot safely be called upon to play such a role, then the courts must do so. But now, the claim that judicial power is no threat to democracy because courts engage only in legal interpretation, not political decision making, loses its *structural* sense. It is no longer true that courts simply carry out the policies of the other branches and can easily be corrected by them if they misinterpret those policies. Mistakes in constitutional interpretation are corrigible only by special constitutional lawmaking procedures which, history shows, very rarely succeed.

If so, the claim that judicial review is rife with gravely undemocratic implications must be refuted primarily by reference to the particular kinds of questions courts decide and/or the kinds of reasoning they employ. (One can also try to argue that the appointment process is indirectly democratic, but, without assuming a special judicial *competence*, the case for an elected judiciary is hard to rebut.)

The claim that courts engage only in a special sort of decision making that does not threaten democratic values brings us back to the law/politics dichotomy, which, once again, seems to raise the possibility that there are *some* constitutional questions that courts must not decide, because they are intrinsically "political"—that is, questions for the law*maker*, not the interpreter. If the courts themselves are to be responsible for identifying such political questions, moreover, it must be possible to do so in a judicial—that is, a principled—manner. Yet, as Nedelsky points out in her critique of Ackerman, even if there is to be a line between law and politics, it does not follow that the drawing of that line is itself a strictly legal exercise. To the extent that the Constitution makes Congress responsible for fixing the courts' jurisdiction, one might expect the opposite to be the case.

Let us now take a brief look at three criteria that might be invoked to define the boundary between law and politics. They are bias, competence, and authority.

In ordinary language, the most common sense of the term *political* refers to the domain of political parties and election campaigns. While there are enforceable laws regulating some aspects of this (formally) largely "private" domain, judicial involvement in general is tricky, since it risks compromising the crucial nonpartisan image of the judiciary.

Now, to hold that this kind of potential bias always makes a question *political* would create serious problems. If we must recuse the entire judiciary from involvement in overtly partisan controversies, why would the same risk of bias not extend beyond electoral matters, to *any* issue (such as abortion, affirmative action, or federal/state relations) on which political parties have taken sharply opposed positions? Moreover, judges have personal affiliations based on region, class, race, ethnicity, gender, religion, and so on as well as those based on party. Why can we trust them with controversies between citizens of different states, religious freedom cases, civil rights cases, and so forth? This ordinary-language sense of the term *political* simply discredits the very possibility of "judicial independence."

Apparently, then, the bias criterion can only prompt a prudential, contextual judgment: given the issues presented by the case, the stakes involved, the alignment of political forces, and the perceived position (balanced or unbalanced, moderate or extreme) of the courts with respect to that alignment and that issue, what are the prospects for a judicial decision being accepted as unbiased—and how great is the need for the courts to make such a decision?

The second possible criterion, competence, bespeaks the notion that judges are trained to apply distinctive materials and methods in their decision making. In the traditional view, judges deal with questions of principle, not policy; are informed by authoritative texts, not public opinion or social theory; determine rights and duties, rather than weigh interests; and seek to do justice, not find acceptable compromise. It follows that they can perform successfully *as* judges only when appropriate principles and texts are available; otherwise, their decision would be based on nonjudicial reasoning—typically, on the sort of weighing of interests that is the stuff of ordinary politics and, not coincidentally, is often encumbered by personal and/or partisan bias.

One difficulty with this competence criterion is that it is not inherently limited (as the "political questions" doctrine is) to *constitutional* questions. More serious, the argument once again appears to prove far too much. Few jurisprudents nowadays believe that all or most cases, and especially the controversial "hard" ones, have right answers that are clearly determined by the "plain meaning" of available legal materials or the "original intent" of their authors. Even the persistent advocacy and practice of a "balancing of interests" approach to judicial review did not prevent Felix Frankfurter from being identified as a prime defender of "judicial restraint" and opponent of "activist policymaking."

In light of the ascendant Legal Realist thesis that interpretation *normally* looks beyond as well as to the text, the argument from competence cannot establish the *nonjusticiability* of all cases posing "political questions." More plausibly it suggests that courts should avoid unduly open-textured *grounds of decision* (such as the Ninth Amendment) and should avoid imposing *remedies* that call for judicial fact finding or open-ended supervision that will unduly tax the courts' administrative capacities. Once again, the ground of decision and the shaping of remedies are prudential choices; the only case requiring abstention from the outset on principle would be one where a majority agreed that the available texts and precedents provided inadequate guidance for any judicial ruling on the merits.

Since "cases of first impression" are inevitable in any domain of textual interpretation, it is hard to theorize abstractly any conditions for abstention on this ground that would not jeopardize the basis for judicial review itself. What makes the cases arising under the Ninth Amendment or the guarantee clause qualitatively more difficult than those arising under the due process or privileges and immunities clauses?

The third criterion, authority, is geared more specifically to *constitutional* politics. It refers us to decisions on constitutional lawmaking (as opposed to interpretation) so momentous that they can legitimately be made only by the sovereign People (or, perhaps, as Jeffersonians would have it, those uniquely qualified to speak for the people). In Ackerman's terms, such decisions are *transformative* rather than *preservative* of existing constitutional doctrine.

This approach would reserve from judicial decision only a small fraction of the questions normally termed "political," whether by ordinary language or by judicial doctrine. While such abstention may sound attractive in principle to believers in democracy, it still requires an ability on our and the courts' part to distinguish lawmaking from interpretation. Yet this distinction is notoriously the grist of incessant partisan political strife! What *we* see as an obligatory, preservationist adjustment of existing rules in light of changed circumstances, *you* see as a willful, transformative departure from well-settled understandings. Rarely would a majority have good reason to agree that this debate is too close to call. Once again, if they did so, the judgment would smack of prudence, not principle.

However problematic the criteria of bias, competence, and authority may be, they appear to exhaust the range of *arguably* principled criteria for judicial abstention from "political questions." Conspicuously absent from the list are *clearly* prudential factors such as possible noncooperation by other officials with a judgment, financial costs of compliance, or the destabilizing implications of a ruling that some longstanding practice is and has been unlawful. These criteria must be excluded because they are purely circumstantial: they in no way depend on the nature of the *questions* presented or on the methods and materials needed to resolve them, and thus involve no issues of principle rooted in the separation of powers and the law/politics dichotomy—unless there is to be a principle that following the law must always be convenient for the authorities or for society in general. But that "principle," to quote Justice Stewart only slightly out of context, would not be "law as the courts know law."[36]

One further try at delineating the scope of "political questions" would reverse the figure/ground perspective: instead of asking what questions courts are *least* suited to decide, we can ask what questions elected politicians are *best* at. When are their competence and their authority most clear? When is their "bias" least disabling? Because this question depends essentially upon a theory of representation, its further exploration will be deferred to chapter 2.

The Judicial "Political Questions" Doctrine

Having laid out some of the background theoretical issues, let us turn now to an overview of judicial pronouncements on the questions at hand. As the courts' practice has historically developed, the term *political* is used primarily in an institutional-positivist sense. It refers to any decision typically made by (or, more technically, ostensibly reserved by the Constitution or laws for) nonjudicial officials—the so-called political branches of government. The theoretical distinction appears to involve elements of all three criteria—to be between matters susceptible to governance by legal *rules* and impartially supervisable by courts, and matters whose successful handling requires official *discretion*, accountable ultimately to voters.

This rules/discretion approach was already used in *dicta* in *Marbury v. Madison*,[37] long before the formulation of the "political questions" doctrine itself. In order to obtain the relief he sought from the Supreme Court, Marbury had to prove that he had been appointed

as a justice of the peace, and that the Jefferson administration had wrongfully withheld his commission. When both the executive branch and Senate declined to provide him with the documents he requested, Marbury subpoenaed several officials to testify. At trial, however, cabinet members protested that, in light of the separation of powers, they could not be compelled to answer any questions regarding confidential policy discussions within the executive branch. Marbury's counsel replied that the existence and disposition of documents of public record, such as Marbury's commission, could not be regarded as a confidential matter; but he reassured the Court that he did not mean to open all executive business to public view: foreign policy discussions between the president and the secretary of state, for example, were not subject to judicial intrusion or compulsory disclosure.

At trial the Court ordered the witnesses to testify to their knowledge about the preparation, signing, and sealing of the commission but declared that, since what was subsequently done with it was legally irrelevant to the merits of Marbury's case, questions on that point need not be answered. Then, in its opinion, the Court addressed the broader question whether Secretary of State Madison, in light of his official position, had immunity from a writ of mandamus: insofar as in this case he was performing record-keeping duties imposed by law, he was subject to the writ; however, had he been acting in his capacity as confidential foreign policy agent of the president, he would not be so subject, for such matters "respect the nation, not individual rights."[38]

On one level we see here an embryonic "state secrets privilege," adumbrating the distinction, further criticized in chapter 4 below, between a judicial realm of law and an executive realm of prerogative, carved out in the interest of national security. A still broader immunity, hinted at in the *Marbury* trial colloquy but squarely claimed and adjudicated only in the twentieth century, would establish an "executive privilege" covering all policy discussions among high executive officials. The idea here appears to be that all policy making involves the exercise of political discretion—a matter inherently immune to legal regulation. In *United States v. Nixon*,[39] the Court held that there is such a privilege regarding presidential communications with subordinates, but that the privilege is not absolute.

Neither in *Marbury* nor in *Nixon* did the Court actually refrain from inquiring into or deciding any matter essential to disposing of the case at hand. The "political questions doctrine," properly so called, pertains to questions that the courts *do* abstain from deciding. Scholars have had difficulty finding a consistent, principled pattern to these cases; some have concluded that it is simply a matter of *ad hoc* judicial avoidance of cases where expected challenges to their neutrality, expertise and/or authority are difficult to rebut—and, in particular, cases where the "political branches" may therefore be tempted to defy judicial orders.[40]

Historically, cases involving the political questions doctrine have generally fallen into the categories of electoral politics (cases arising under the guarantee clause of Article IV), constitutional amendment politics (cases arising under Article V), and foreign policy (cases arising under the divine prerogative of Charles I and, according to Locke, William III). The Article IV and Article V cases revolve around issues of bias and authority, while the foreign policy cases involve the third criterion, competence, as well.

While the foreign policy cases (discussed in chapter 4) focus attention on the relations among branches of the government (not to mention those among nation-states), the others focus more directly on the relationship between our government and the American people. In both contexts, the question goes to the appropriate outer limits of the rule of law—whether as a restraint on the conduct of government officials or on that of the people themselves. If we take the rule of law and personal rights to be concerns central to liberalism, the authority and proper structure of government to be concerns central to republicanism, and equality and the power of the people to be concerns central to democracy, then the evolution of the political questions doctrine can be understood as an aspect of the triangular contest between liberal, republican, and democratic conceptions of our polity which has been a major theme of our constitutional history.

The courts are clearly an elite institution—if indeed that couplet is not redundant. Their expertise and impartiality must be in some sense *above* the level of the ordinary person if their assigned function as impartial arbiter is to be successfully performed. For citizens to tolerate this role is part of the mystery of authority in a republican regime. As Thompson points out, they will not continue to do so unless the "rule of law" provides returns. What consoles the disappointed litigant may of course vary greatly, depending on circumstances and beliefs.

In 1804 the Supreme Court's primary audience, in an important sense, was Federalists who needed a good reason to remain within the polity and accept the authority of Jefferson's odious administration. (Secession continued to be a discussible option for the Hartford Convention of 1814.) Only a constitution above ordinary politics in some meaningful sense could continue to command Federalist allegiance in times like those. And for such a constitution to matter, it had to be enforceable—which, in context, meant enforceable by the Federal[ist] courts. Thus Marshall's opinion in *Marbury* was an essential step in nation building—clearly, though, one dependent on the distinction between law and politics, if the pronouncements of Federalist judges were to be accepted as legitimate by the Jeffersonian political majority.

One part of the bargain, evident as early as *Marbury*, was the judicial undertaking to avoid interfering with *imperialism*, if only their power to intervene on behalf of *republican* values was granted. Territorial imperialism, as the Louisiana Purchase and the War of 1812 showed, enjoyed ample Jeffersonian support. The Federalists' *quid pro quo*, in a sense, was what Hunt terms "legal imperialism."[41]

The *McCulloch v. Maryland* decision[42] went further, establishing—to the dismay of Southern states-rights republicans—a specific *nationalist* conception of republicanism as authoritative: henceforth, subdivisions of the polity should not expect the federal courts to inscribe in the Constitution an unduly crabbed view of the nation's agenda. Rather it would be for the political branches to determine that agenda—unless, of course, individual rights (especially property rights) were at stake. Thus the Marshall Court, while holding the line against "excesses of democracy," sought to legitimize and support liberal and nationalist-republican principles simultaneously.

The few cases of perceived internal contradiction between liberal and republican principles provoked interesting responses. Such contradictions surfaced most sharply when pursuit of the imperatives of national security, as perceived by the political branches (especially the executive), ran afoul of rule-of-law values.

Little v. Barreme,[43] for example, arose out of the Adams administration's "quasi-war" with France. Congress had authorized the seizure of ships bound to French ports, but, under presidential order, certain ships coming *from* French ports also had been seized. In 1804, long after the quasi-war's end, the Marshall Court held emphatically that, insofar as the president's order had exceeded his statutory authority, it was null and void. There was no hint that the question was in any sense inappropriate for judicial resolution. This decision of course risked no embarrassment to any ongoing foreign policy.

The courts again endorsed the rule of law over executive prerogative in 1806. William Smith (John Adams's son-in-law) and

Samuel Ogden were charged with violating the Neutrality Act by participating in a Venezuelan insurrection against Spanish rule. The defendants claimed to have acted with government approval— in modern terms, it was allegedly a covert official operation. The circuit court ruled this defense legally irrelevant: the defendants were culpable even if President Jefferson or his aides had ordered them to break the law. Conveniently, this made it unnecessary to enforce the subpoena sought by defendants to prove their contention; Congress also would block efforts by critics of the expedition to expose governmental involvement. Ultimately, the jury found the defendants not guilty; both the rule of law and imperialism emerged unscathed—the first in form, the second in substance.[44]

The War of 1812 produced little significant judicial activity, because its opponents lacked an appropriate institutional base from which to challenge it. New England Federalists opposed to Jefferson's prewar trade embargoes had some state government support but ran afoul of national supremacy in foreign policy. Wartime dissidents had even less to go on. When President Madison ordered a call-up of New York's militia and the governor acted accordingly, Private Jacob Mott refused to comply, arguing that the power to call out the militia belonged only to Congress. The Court, however, held that Congress had delegated this power to the president—and with it, by implication, the sole authority to determine when the exercise of that power was necessary.[45] The Court decided the case, but accepted the presidential decision as binding.

A rather different set of issues was presented by the national and state governments' treatment of native Americans over the years. Indian policy had a unique mix of institutional components: in ascending importance, state laws, federal laws, and treaties (negotiated primarily by the War rather than the State Department) all played a role. All of the above were frequently violated, and attempts at enforcement could produce major struggles over jurisdiction as well as the substance of policy. Most of the struggles, however, were conducted by military and political rather than legal means.

An unprecedented situation arose when the State of Georgia seized the lands guaranteed by treaty to the Cherokee Nation, and the Cherokees sought redress in the Supreme Court. The Court expressed sympathy for the plaintiff, characterizing Georgia's conduct as in effect an act of war. It also expressed concern about the ability of a court to provide an effective remedy; the "political branches" alone were equipped to make war or respond to it. Yet the Court stopped short of declaring the case a nonjusticiable "political question." Instead, it observed that, under Article III, its jurisdiction was confined to cases brought by the United States, a state of the Union, a foreign state, or an individual. Since Article I, section 8 listed "foreign nations" and "Indian tribes" separately (and also for independent, historical reasons), it was clear that the Cherokee were not a "foreign nation." Hence the Cherokee Nation lacked standing to sue.[46]

A cynical reader might well suspect that the "real reason" for the Court's abstention was either lack of genuine concern for the Cherokees or sheer political cowardice. Yet a year later, when the same issues were brought to Court in a different procedural posture, the Court heard the case and issued a decision favorable to the Cherokees. The petitioner this time was a white missionary who had entered the Cherokee lands in defiance of Georgia's new laws. The Court held those laws and his arrest thereunder invalid and ordered Georgia to release him.[47] The state did not comply, and President Jackson took no action. Indeed, he was reported to have said, "The Court has made its decision; now let *them* enforce it." This would have been a nearly perfect occasion (nearly, because Georgia's defiant attitude was a real threat to the Court's nationalist jurisprudence) to concoct a "political questions" doctrine, but John Marshall's Court did no such thing.

On the whole, Marshall's activist approach seemed highly successful. Indeed, at first the Marshall Court could even suggest that it had an affirmative *duty* to decide any case arising under its jurisdiction.[48] Yet that Court's activism was prudently limited in its political thrust: *Marbury* was the only case in which his Court overturned an act of Congress. While judicial review had greater substantive impact with regard to state legislation, this impact was focused, as Nedelsky argues, on property rights (together with the related issues of the boundaries between state and federal tax and regulatory powers).

While Nedelsky's critique of the undemocratic implications of the Marshall Court's constitutional doctrine is powerful, we must bear in mind the extent to which democratic theory has subsequently evolved, the extent to which the Court's view of property rights enjoyed consensual support, and the limited scope, individually and as a whole, of their constitutional decisions. Nedelsky is quite aware of these facts but seems to underestimate their significance for her claim that the "most fundamental and most threatened" issues were insulated from ordinary politics by judicial review. Conspicuously left to other forums, after all, were the key struggles of the early Jacksonian era over political issues such as expanding suffrage, slavery, tariffs, or a national bank.

This pattern, however, reflected no explicit judicial refusal to decide and stemmed largely from the politicians' apparent lack of interest in turning to the judiciary for fundamental assistance. *Pace* De Tocqueville and Nedelsky, many major issues were not formulated at the constitutional level, and much constitutional politics was carried on outside the courts. Thus, the question of judicial abstention from deciding "political questions" scarcely arose.

No instance of explicit judicial abstention arose until several significant shifts had occurred. Territorial expansion introduced new issues and new political actors. The democratic and the abolitionist movements, variously sheltered and to a degree energized by the constitutional order, produced crises that seemed at times to threaten both the rule of law and the Union itself. The evolution of the party system produced electoral results that weakened the politicians' unity and resolve; and the Supreme Court acquired new personnel, with Roger Taney replacing John Marshall as chief justice. These developments produced new incentives for politicians to seek judicial intervention, and a mix of new temptations and anxieties for the courts themselves.

Taney's Court, when confronted with a tumultuous struggle over constitutional politics at the state level, implemented for the first time the inchoate notion of judicial abstention from "political questions," acting in a manner that enabled the Court to rebuff the destabilizing political movements while professing strict neutrality. Meanwhile, by declining to elaborate its own principled, nationally binding interpretation of the guarantee clause, the Court in effect redefined the rule of law, at the state level, as whatever the political status quo had produced.

In other decisions Taney had already begun to redefine nationalism itself, significantly modifying the Marshall Court's rulings on the boundaries between state and federal powers in ways that generally favored states' rights. Later, he would see no need to abstain in cases where *national* action threatened central rule-of-law values such as *habeas corpus* or the property rights of slave owners. The Court's view of its proper role shifted in tandem with the new meanings attaching to liberal, republican, and democratic values and the tensions among them.

Luther v. Borden[49] resulted from the "Dorr War" episode of the 1840s, further discussed in chapter 3. Luther, a follower of Dorr, sued Borden for trespass, in light of the latter's entry and search of his home. Borden claimed to have acted properly, as an officer of the established Charter government. Luther replied that, because the Charter government was not "republican" in form, it had, under Article IV of the U.S. Constitution, no legal authority. On the contrary, the people of Rhode Island, led by the Dorrites, had exercised *their* inherent authority (as declared by the Declaration of Independence) to "alter and abolish" the Charter government.

It was in this context that the Taney Court declared enforcement of Article IV's guarantee of a "republican form of government" to be a function committed exclusively to the "political branches," not to the courts. Since Congress had accepted the delegates elected under the Charter government and the president had promised it military assistance if needed, the Court had to regard the matter as closed.

For practical purposes, it was just as if the Court had ruled for the defendant on the merits. The plaintiff got no damages, the Charter government's rule was not disturbed, and Dorr (not a party to the case) remained in prison. The only difference was that the Court had avoided the responsibility for defining the term *republican* and dignifying the Charter government with that label. Instead, as commentators such as Rodgers and Dennison have it,[50] the rule laid down was that 'republican' means what those at the apex of official power say it means.

The Dorrites had candidly acted outside the law, in the name of the sovereign People. The Court "saved" the rule of law by passively subordinating it to a "politics" that, for all its procedural regularity, had neither liberal rights consciousness nor democratic responsiveness to recommend it.

As abstract jurisprudence, this was pure "neutral" positivism. As historically situated constitutional politics, the commentators argue, it may have been motivated by an aversion to radical change—especially violent change—and a desire (with an eye toward slavery) to shield state political institutions from federal judicial intervention. The Court resisted the destabilizing potential of popular sovereignty in *Luther*, just as it was to do, using different doctrinal techniques, in *Dred Scott*.[51]

Dred Scott was, in retrospect and in the ordinary-language sense, as "political" a case as might be found. Yet, as is well known, the *Dred Scott* Court not only declined to abstain but shunned available paths to a narrow decision, instead reaching out to entrench slavery against interference by either national or territorial majorities.[52] Acting in what Nedelsky sees as its established mode, the Court tried to constitutionalize the most vexing political issue of the day and remove it from the sphere of ordinary electoral and legislative politics.

Yet, unlike Marshall's Court, it could not appeal to an existing elite consensus on basic national principles. Rather, it had to reinterpret constitutional federalism as an agreement fundamentally to disagree. Its pseudorepublican emphasis on the states' powers, even in fixing the definition of national citizenship itself, and its pseudoliberal reading of the Fifth Amendment as protecting slaveholders' property rights while ignoring the right to liberty of black inhabitants, gave to the Court's notion of the rule of law a blatantly sectional cast.

Chief Justice Taney would later strive, with equal "impartiality," to uphold the rule of law against Lincoln's emergency actions; yet, in practice, the attitude of judicial permissiveness toward status-quo state-level politics signaled in *Luther* and *Dred Scott* could only transfer with the shifting political balance to transformative national politics. Thus the doctrinal way was paved for judicial acquiescence in the vastly expanded national government, augmented by presidential emergency powers and delegated bureaucratic authority, that emerged during and after the Civil War.

At this early stage, the Court's understanding of its new abstention doctrine was apparently bound to questions arising under the guarantee clause. For example, no justice saw the cases arising from Lincoln's emergency actions during the Civil War as presenting "political questions." Taney, indeed, was quite prepared to hold some of those actions unconstitutional; but the Court's majority generally ruled otherwise, deferring, as Taney already had in *Luther*, to the president's conception of the national interest and the measures necessary to secure it.[53] Extraordinary times prompt extraordinary measures; but these, once accepted, have a tendency to become ordinary. As Dennison puts it, "[T]he old republic died giving birth to the republican empire."[54] Given a new political alignment and bolstered by the Reconstruction amendments, the postwar Court reshaped the synthesis of liberal, republican, and democratic ideas.

In some ways the new order and new judicial role harked back to the nationalism, judicial activism, and zeal for bourgeois property of the Marshall Court. The "political questions" doctrine, as Taney had applied it, did not fit well into this agenda. Yet the doctrine could hardly be abandoned outright in the new regime (Ackerman's and Lowi's[55] Second Republic), whose democratic pretensions, sectional-partisan political cleavages, and presidential-congressional struggles kept judicial review as controversial and problematic as ever. Adapted to new conditions and applied to novel sorts of issues, the Court's application of the doctrine was to prove notably inconsistent. For example, in cases involving the guarantee clause, the Court abstained from ruling on Southern challenges to the federal appointment of state government officials under the Reconstruction Acts,[56] and later on whether Oregon's and Ohio's initiative and referendum devices were "republican."[57] However, the Court did interpret the guarantee clause in several other cases; thus, it reached and rejected on the merits an argument that the clause required the states to grant female suffrage.[58]

As in the Taney era, the political questions doctrine counseled deference to nonjudicial political authorities—not to insurgent movements. The *democratic* component of the synthesis continued to require only judicial deference to the results of the electoral process and the officials installed thereby (so long as they respected the rule of law). Yet in so deferring—whether by abstention or by rulings on the merits—the Court modified the earlier, more purely *republican* constitutional synthesis in several respects. On the whole and in the long run, it accommodated the political gains of the Reconstruction and Progressive movements, with the associated expansion of suffrage and shifts of power from the state to the national level, from rural to urban areas, from older to newer, corporate forms of property, and from Congress to the executive branch. Since abstention and upholding on the merits are very similar in practical effect, there was little occasion for rethinking "political questions" until the crisis posed by judicial resistance to the New Deal.

Once again, a democratic movement came into direct conflict with established notions of property rights. As always, the definition of property rights seemed a "legal" issue if anything was; no question of outright nonjusticiability could arise. Instead, as explored below, after protracted struggle the Court determined that the Constitution did not incorporate any specific theory—such as Adam Smith's or Spencer's—of the proper relationship between politics and markets. Hence, the scope of government intervention—so long as it had some "rational basis"—was henceforth to be settled largely through the political process, not through constitutional litigation. The matters insulated from ordinary politics and confided to the special care of the judiciary would involve not property but personal liberties and political rights.

The new controversies did not involve the guarantee clause, but the political questions doctrine was now sometimes applied to certain (*i.e.*, uncertain) cases founded on other provisions. Legal scholars will struggle to find or develop consistent doctrinal principles; political scientists tend to be more content with plausible nondoctrinal explanations of judicial behavior.[59] As is not surprising, none of the efforts has yielded a completely consistent account. Let us look more closely at the Court's recent reasoning and behavior.

The fullest and clearest modern judicial statement of the doctrine came from Justice Brennan in *Baker v. Carr*:

> Prominent on the surface of any case held to involve a political question is found a textually demonstrable constitutional commitment of the issue to a coordinate political department; or a lack of judicially discoverable and manageable standards for resolving it; or the impossibility of deciding without an initial policy determination of a kind clearly for nonjudicial discretion; or the impossibility of a court's undertaking independent resolution without expressing lack of the respect due coordinate branches of government; or an unusual need for unquestioning adherence to a political decision already made; or the potentiality of embarrassment from multifarious pronouncements by various departments on one question.[60]

It is interesting to compare this six-part formulation to the three criteria developed above (bias, lack of competence, and lack of authority). First of all, the bias criterion does not explicitly appear. Indeed, it was Frankfurter in his dissent who warned that the Court, by overruling precedent and intervening for the first time in reapportionment disputes, was abandoning neutrality by "injecting itself into the clash of political forces."[61] As we noted above and Justice Brennan apparently recognized, this argument proves too much: critics of a Court decision can plausibly use it in virtually *any* case—certainly any case that is grist for political controversy.

The competence criterion is reflected in Brennan's second and third items, which appear to be opposite sides of the same coin—judicially manageable standards versus nonjudicial discretion. Once again, the criterion seems sound in principle yet elusive in application. Many of the Court's path-breaking and controversial decisions, such as those on school busing, police behavior, prisoners' rights, and abortion, have been criticized as nonjudicial, "activist," or biased in their reasoning or their remedial orders.

Yet it is important to note that litigants, judges, and critics have seldom argued for judicial abstention in these cases. Rather, critics tend to argue that the Court should reject on the merits novel claims of right that lack foundation in the constitutional text and precedents. Given the richness and diversity of the interpretive methods our tradition now makes available, it is easy for a critic to challenge a judge's method and/or result in a given case. It is far harder to establish that the very question presented was political, and not susceptible to resolution by the process of "judicial interpretation."

Without an established orthodox theory of interpretation, we cannot agree on how to label performances "noninterpretive." Moreover, the difficulty seems more than a passing disorder. Arguably, slogans aside, there has never really been such an orthodoxy. Even in the heyday of "classical legal thought," for instance, there was ample room for judicial disagreement over reasons as well as results.[62] At any rate, the history of recent Supreme Court nominations (that of Bork, in particular) suggests that, currently, commitment to an interpretive orthodoxy may be the most disqualifying of all judicial attributes. In a wonderful dialectical reversal, it has become identified as commitment to a *political* agenda. Thus, one who criticizes the Court for deciding "political questions" *ipso facto* tars herself with the same brush.

Some say that the process of filling Supreme Court vacancies has been newly "politicized" in recent years. In fact, the process has always been and must be political. Yet it does appear that the form of this politics has been fleshed out and transformed, due in large part to the partially successful efforts of academics to make more predictable the consequences of a given nomination. Those efforts have altered our view of the boundary between the realms of law and of politics, creating a paradigm clash that is not easily ignored.

Scholarly research has undermined the traditional, legalist assumption that justices approach each case with an utterly open mind and respond only to the legally controlling aspects of a case. Indeed, the political-scientific study of judicial behavior has often understated the role of legal reasoning in generating judicial votes. Be that as it may, the inquiry has made it more intellectually legitimate to attempt to predict how a new justice will vote—whether the analysis proceeds from social background factors or from a close reading of the nominee's legal writings and answers to senatorial questions. At the same time, it has become more difficult for presidents and senators to confine their attention and comment to the ostensibly neutral judicial "qualifications" of a candidate. Indeed, to do so has come to seem irresponsible or disingenuous.

Once innocence is lost, at any particular time the current analytical models, as well as pending or anticipated issues on the Court's docket, will direct attention to specific lines of inquiry concerning a prospective justice, opening the door for participation by interest groups and/or scholars who wish to speak to the matters in question. Since careful inquiry is obligatory, such participation has become a normal, even an essential, part of every nomination to the highest court.

From the standpoint of traditional judicial ethics, grounded in legalist ideology, to ask a nominee how she would approach specific future cases is to improperly pressure her to prejudge those cases. From a slightly different perspective, these inquiries impel the nominee to abandon the judicial role: she is not asked actually to decide a case, but to assist in a process of scientific observation, by providing data that will allow others to predict her own future behavior. But if the prediction is successful, the question is not so much whether the candidate can still judge impartially, but rather why she should bother to judge at all. To the extent that the scientific program is tenable, it implies that to select the justices is to decide the cases. The results are, as it were, automatic, so that the procedure known as judging becomes more or less superfluous. Shall the justices perhaps cite their Judiciary Committee testimony as adequate authority for their subsequent decisions?

Returning now to Brennan's discussion of the "political question," the criterion of authority figures in his first, third, fourth, and fifth items: textual commitment to a coordinate branch, initial discretionary policy determination, respect for coordinate branches, and unquestioning adherence to a decision already made. Most striking here is the consequence of Brennan's premise that the political questions doctrine is rooted in the separation of powers: if the courts lack authority to decide, it is because that authority is vested in the "political branches"—never, apparently, directly in the sovereign People. Brennan's view of constitutional politics, therefore, is quite distinct from Ackerman's dualism. Just as *Luther v. Borden* put the rule of law before popular sovereignty, the cases where the Court later abstained on issues arising under Article V[63] had been couched in terms of deference to *Congress* and not to the will of the People. Moreover, the vitality and scope of those precedents is highly uncertain in light of subsequent "political questions" decisions.

It appears that, while the three branches are formally "coordinate," the relationship described by Brennan leaves the courts, for practical purposes, in a distinctly subordinate position. Clearly the powers textually committed to them are by far the slightest. Indeed, the textual basis for judicial review itself continues to be disputed. There is also room for debate, though, about the powers committed to other branches. For instance, it is hard to find a clearer "textual commitment" than the rather curious constitutional provision that "Each House shall be *the* Judge of the Elections, Returns and Qualifications of its own Members" (emphasis added).[64] Yet the Court intervened in the House's refusal to seat Adam Clayton Powell, holding that the definition of the term *qualifications* was a justiciable question.[65] And indeed, this was not without a principled justification, for an absolutely literal reading of this "commitment" would make each house potentially the final judge *in its own cause*—exactly what the separation of powers aimed to prevent.

More important, in the normal course of affairs it is the courts who will give "unquestioning adherence" to "initial policy determinations" made by the other branches. Indeed, despite the theoretical primacy of policy *making* over its *execution*, the "vigor, secrecy, and despatch" with which the executive is endowed, together with the modern drift toward delegation of congressional powers, leaves the executive branch in a highly advantaged position whenever the needs for unity and authority are salient. If it counsels abstention from constitutional struggles between Congress and the presidency, then, the "political questions" doctrine can only support (certainly in the long run) the aggrandizement of the latter.

Thus the stress on unity, implicit in Brennan's fourth item, explicit in the fifth, and culminating in the final item's concern for the "potentiality of embarrassment" inherent in the separation of powers, is the Achilles heel of Brennan's analysis. Such fear of separated powers might provide reason for citizens to advocate *amending* the Constitution; it cannot provide grounds for a court to decline enforcing it. As Justice Brennan's examples make clear, the thrust of his concern for unity pertains to foreign affairs; as is argued in chapter 4, the logic of this concern is highly threatening both to the individual rights of citizens and to their ability to hold government accountable for its policies.

Since *Baker*, in fact, the only significant applications of the political questions doctrine have been in foreign affairs, with some intimations regarding certain activities of political parties.[66] Fortunately, as noted above, the Court has not yet succumbed to the temptation to total abdication of its responsibilities in this area. For instance, in *Goldwater v. Carter*,[67] "only" four justices thought the question of the Senate's role in treaty abrogation was "political." This question, we may note, is distinguishable from the repeatedly adjudicated one of presidential removal power *only* in its foreign policy context—not in terms of textual commitment, manageable standards, or potentials for domestic controversy and institutional embarrassment to the courts.

The political questions doctrine, ostensibly a defensive response to the charge that judicial review is undemocratic, proves to be no impediment when courts redraw election districts, designate new "suspect classifications," or identify new "fundamental rights." Yet what began by tentatively subjecting popular sovereignty and nationalism to the rule of law threatens to end by abandoning the rule of law to nationalism and the Imperial Presidency. John Marshall would be astonished, and so should we.

The rule of law is not vitiated by the truisms that law arises from political processes and has political effects, and that the exercise of judicial review is often controversial. It can be depreciated, of course, by rulings that appear arbitrary, unprincipled, and willful— or by the tendency of disappointed parties to so label decisions with which they disagree.

Courts have various means available for reducing their vulnerability to such criticism. Holding sensitive cases nonjusticiable does not appear, in general, to be either essential in principle or particularly effective in maintaining a "neutral" image. Careful opinion writing, consistency across cases, and striving for unanimous or near-unanimous decisions might all be more useful than a doctrine neither coherent in theory, consistent in application, nor effectual in outcome—in a word, mythical.

Of course, no improvements in judicial craftsmanship or strategy will lay to rest the tensions between law and politics. Politics by nature cannot be permanently frozen. Moreover, a structural challenge to the "rule of law" idea seems to arise from the downright unruly character of the process by which our polity responds to judicial decisions. Alexander Bickel[68] once portrayed the judicial role as involving not judicial supremacy (which indeed would be undemocratic), but rather a dialogue with the political branches of government. He neglected, however, to note the peculiarity of a "dialogue" in which participants are free to ignore each others' moves and may find it politically distasteful or not worthwhile to make a timely, direct response. Thus, judicial interpretations or even invalidations of a law are often simply ignored by politicians.

If a process is to be called "the rule of law," would we not expect it to be structured like the judicial branch itself—to feature a prescribed series of hierarchical steps, leading to clear-cut decisions that we can recognize as authoritative and final? Would we not expect it to be very clear where the ultimate authority lies and how we are to know when that authority has spoken?

Historically, the norm of rule of law is not necessarily linked to the separation of powers or any other specific constitutional structure. The idea, as adopted from the British tradition, simply requires some sort of safeguard against arbitrary rule; judicial review was certainly no staple of British thought. Moreover, thoughtful scholars such as Brigham, Burgess, Barber, and Levinson can urge that the rule of law would in fact be more secure without "the cult of the court," because politicians and the public would then have to take more seriously their own responsibilities to interpret and abide by the Constitution.[69] Though empirical evidence is hard to come by, they dismiss the lawyers' reflexive fear of cognitive and functional anarchy.

What we surely do require, though, is some credible account of the law/politics distinction. Without it, we cannot fathom Thompson's approval of the rule of law, but must accept Hunt's assertion that the state is incapable of abiding by that norm.[70] What sense could then be made of *constitutional* government?

Despite the centrality of judicial review to our conventional understanding of the law/politics distinction, we need to pay careful attention to the nonlegal as well as to the legal aspects of the constitutional separation of powers system. This system is structurally open-ended, nonhierarchical, and often ambiguous in its outcomes. That one or more officials, elected or appointed, claim to speak in the name of the People does not self-evidently make it so. If the ultimate authority is the sovereign People, that authority can speak in many voices and through many channels. In this sense, Ackerman's dualism seems to understate the system's complexity.

Moreover, some version of this complexity is implicit in the law/politics dichotomy itself. While law, to do its work, must be seen as fixed and certain, politics by the same token needs to be open and fluid. The Constitution's location at the very crux of the essential but paradoxical law/politics dichotomy requires that the Constitution's meaning be at once clear and unclear, settled and open to revision. Thus its role and value for us must remain endlessly precarious and elusive.

‑§ Chapter 2 §‑

Representation and Constitutional Politics

There's no such thing as democracy, and it's a good thing, too.

—after Stanley Fish

$\mathcal{M}$uch of the debate over judicial review and its place in a democratic political order has been carried on against a set of wildly unrealistic background assumptions. In particular, it is taken for granted that the system whereby legislators and executives are elected renders them, unlike federal judges, effectively accountable and responsive to the will of the People. Ostensibly, then, the "political branches" *represent* the people in a way that judges do not, which makes "judicial policymaking" putatively illegitimate. To the extent that this assumption is unwarranted, the debate needs to be recast.

We begin by elaborating on the concept of representation in political theory. Then we explore the way representational issues are treated in the Constitution and constitutional law. We will find that these are discrete and divergent discourses—and that important questions are neglected in all of them.

Even if we confine ourselves to (largely American) political theory, the diversity of the literature on representation is already striking. There is disagreement over how a representative body should be composed, how it should operate, and what the members' primary responsibilities should be. There is disagreement over what legislatures actually accomplish, their instrumental and/or ideological functions. There is even disagreement over whether representation is inherently good (that is, better than both authoritarianism and direct democracy), a practically unavoidable second-best choice, or a downright bad thing (essentially unworkable and unfair).

Some of this debate is the stuff of ordinary politics, whose presence should neither surprise nor disturb us. Some of it, however, goes to the basic, structural arrangements on which a constitutional polity heavily relies, theory tells us, to sustain its legitimacy in the face of the disappointments that ordinary politics will inflict. Failing a consensus (or something like it) on the fairness of these arrangements, the integrity of the entire enterprise seems compromised.

Of course, it by no means follows that a Constitution must embody a comprehensive and completely consistent theory of representation. To speak of constitutional politics is to acknowledge the fact of ongoing, often bitter disputes over rather fundamental issues. What seems essential, if politics is to remain constitutional, is that disputes be contained within the bounds of norms and procedures to which all major interests on the whole claim allegiance. This may not always be possible, and if possible, it may have unhappy effects for certain excluded interests or issues. Yet, since representation is manifestly a core feature of our political system, the claim that our Constitution provides *no* standards of fairness in representation would uproot the distinction between constitutional and ordinary politics—leaving the very foundations utterly up for grabs.

Normative Theory

Hanna Pitkin[1] traces the concept of a 'representative' back to medieval times. The modern understanding, she says, stems from Hobbes, for whom the representative is an artificial person created by the social compact, and thereby *authorized to act for* and to command all his subjects. Later thinkers added the idea that representatives must be *accountable* to the represented, a result typically accomplished through election and reelection.

A distinct component of our understanding, Pitkin notes, is the idea—espoused by John Adams, among others—that a representative body should faithfully mirror the composition of society at large: *descriptive* representation, in the sense of a "representative sample." A representative, such as a chief executive, may also *symbolize* the values, traditions, and glories of the polity. Judges, she holds, can be deemed representatives in several senses. They are agents (officers) of the state and of the sovereign People; their comportment symbolizes and their decisions embody the values of the society, such as its conception of justice; and their behavior often responds to interest-group pressures or popular demands. It is noteworthy that the several senses of representation imply different and sometimes conflicting views of the judicial role.[2]

Since the same multidimensionality pertains to the representative functions of nonjudicial officers of the state, questions arise as to how representatives must behave if they wish to perform their roles well. For example, should an elected representative act according to constituents' immediate desires or according to their long-run best interests? Should she focus on the interests of her particular district or on those of the whole polity? On those of the majority who elected her, or on those of all the people?

As Pitkin notes, it is one thing to represent an individual, whose will and interests can at least sometimes be easily ascertained and followed. In the case of large, diverse groups, however, their will and interest are for representatives to *construct*—not passively to observe. Representatives are advised to look to the best interests of society at large, while remaining ever mindful of constituents' actual feelings and grievances. When faced with fundamental cleavages, however, consensus may be impossible to construct. In such cases, formalistic or mirroring modes of representation may be all that are attainable. Hopefully, those outvoted will be comforted by having received a respectful hearing.

Pitkin also makes interesting observations about the way our understanding of representation shifts according to the nature of the issue in question. She distinguishes political decisions on matters of taste from those on questions of knowledge—a continuum, not a dichotomy. Since matters of taste are subjective, collective decisions will emerge from bargaining, not from rational persuasion. Questions of knowledge, in contrast, are susceptible to correct solution. Here, representatives either seek to persuade each other or they delegate the issue to administrative experts. The ideal political process will produce representatives who can channel each decision into its proper path.[3]

Charles Beitz[4] focuses on certain questions regarding the design of a fair political structure for a society—in particular, one that satisfies the norm of political equality. A valid theory, he says, must go beyond formal procedural equality. It must take account of the actual social structure (especially the existence of "intense or permanent minorities")[5] and distinctions among types of issues, that is, "the importance or urgency of the interests at stake" for the various groups.[6] In short, it must take account of expected political outcomes.[7]

Beitz begins by rejecting two unsatisfactory approaches to political fairness. First, aggregate welfare maximization fails as a standard because, by allowing the tradeoff of one individual's welfare for that of another, it denies the equal respect owed to each citizen.[8] The second alternative rejected by Beitz is a requirement of equal influence. Even if "fair institutions should express public recognition of the equal worth of persons,"[9] and even if we assume that everyone is the best judge of his own good and entitled to his own view about the good of society, it does not necessarily follow that "everyone has an equal right that these judgments be reflected in public policy."[10] After all, it would be absurd to hold that a norm of "equal respect and concern" precludes us from judging one person's opinion or claim more meritorious than another's.[11]

The inadequacies of these approaches suggest that discrete and potentially inconsistent values are implicated in the choice of decision procedures.

> These include the predictable consequences of the procedures for the content of public policy and the conduct and quality of public political debate, the prospects for political stability and for the coherent administration of policy, the transparency of the procedure itself from the point of view of ordinary citizens, and the ease with which they may enter into it effectively. . . . [I]t also matters that outcomes normally bear some predictable and consistent relationship to the array of individual preferences about outcomes that come to exist in society and that are actually expressed in the political process.[12]

Indeed, the complexity of the task follows fairly directly from the multidimensional complexity of our concepts of power, equality, and democracy. Beitz identifies three specific guiding concerns ("regulative interests") which remind us of Preuss's definition[13] of the term *constitution* itself:

1. recognition—
    public institutions should not establish or reinforce the perception that some people's interests deserve less respect or

concern than those of others simply in virtue of their membership in one rather than another social or ascriptive group;[14]

2. equitable treatment—
   citizens might reasonably refuse to accept institutions under which it was predictable that their actual interests . . . would be unfairly placed in jeopardy;[15] and

3. deliberative responsibility—
   the resolution of political issues on the basis of public deliberation that is adequately informed, open to the expression of a wide range of competing views, and carried out under conditions in which these views can be responsibly assessed.[16]

Beitz then applies his theoretical framework to four key issues of electoral design. The first is the choice between proportional representation (PR) and districting systems. Unlike winner-take-all districts, PR systems can allow virtually all votes to count, creating legislatures in which each member's self-selected constituency solidly supports her.

Beitz acknowledges that PR—or certain forms of it at least—is unique in its ability to produce a legislature that mirrors the population; and he refutes on empirical grounds most of the arguments that attribute to PR a variety of undesirable effects, such as instability. Nevertheless, he is unable to conclude that PR is inherently fairer than districting systems.

Beitz argues that in most cases it is possible to construct a districting system that is, on balance, equally fair. Yet he ignores the point, relative to the recognition interest, that a formally equal vote, to be cast in a district gerrymandered to be noncompetitive, may well be experienced by the would-be voter (or nonvoter) as a futile gesture. He also ignores the key symbolic dimension of recognition associated with the presence or absence in the legislature of a due number of members of the group(s) with which one most closely identifies.

Beitz's second design issue is fairness in districting. He distinguishes first of all between formally equal procedural resources for affecting election outcomes, such as are provided by the one person, one vote rule, and "equal prospects for electoral success," which, unlike equal procedural resources, depend significantly on the actual distribution of political preferences.[17] He goes on to argue that an adequate theory of political equality must concern itself with both kinds of equality in order to address issues of qualitative as well as quantitative unfairness in voting rules.

To point out the limited value of a formally equal vote is to critique the notion of neutrality in districting plans. Beitz argues not only that explicitly nonpolitical criteria for districting may be hard to find, but also that there is little to recommend them in any case: "Whatever criteria are used to construct a district system, some interests will be advantaged and others disadvantaged . . . . [A] general principle of qualitative fairness must specify the kinds of outcomes that fairness forbids."[18]

At this juncture a key question arises: Why should we care so much about equality of prospects for electoral success? After all, electoral success in no way guarantees an equal chance that the voter's policy preferences will be satisfied.[19] Beitz thus takes up the case for a stronger, more substantive standard: equality in the distribution of preference satisfaction, that is, "political decisions should satisfy the preferences of each member of the population an equal proportion of the time."[20]

Beitz does not acknowledge that this standard can be understood in (at least) two radically different ways. Suppose, for example, that a society were divided into two stable factions, one constituting 90 percent of the population and the other 10 percent. On one reading, members of *each* faction are entitled to have their way half the time, so that each citizen has her way half the time. But this would be a very strange account of *democracy*, because it seems to disregard the basic idea of majority rule. On this account, the fact that most people agree with my view on an issue would give me no advantage whatsoever.

The obvious alternative reading would be that each individual gets her way for one day of the hundred-day cycle, so that the larger faction has its way 90 percent of the time. But the minority would be unlikely to accept this as a fair reading of the principle set forth: how can you say that everyone has her way an equal proportion of the time, when *each of them* has her way 90 percent of the time and *each of us* has her way only 10 percent? Beitz's insistence that only individual rights, not group rights, are at stake does not seem to provide a satisfactory response, for each member of our group seems *individually* disadvantaged in comparison to each member of the other.

But there is a deeper problem. Even if we could agree on a way to satisfy each individual's preferences an equal proportion of the time—why would we *want* to? Can we really mean to take the stand that, *a priori*, all preferences are equally valid? Regardless both of their moral attractiveness and of how many people hold them? Bearing in mind Pitkin's distinction between matters of taste, of principle, and of expertise, the suggestion seems adverse both to the republican idea of civic virtue *and* to the democratic idea of majority rule. All that can recommend it is the liberal idea of neutrality between the preferences of different citizens; yet Beitz rejects neutrality as an incoherent and arbitrary standard.

The chief defect of the principle of equal preference satisfaction is that it lacks any satisfactory conception of the political activity of elected representatives. We do not have a right to have our preferences satisfied *per se*. Rather, we have a right to participate and to have our representatives participate, by voting, persuasion, bargaining, and other lawful means, in the complex, multistaged processes of interest articulation (in which particular needs and demands are voiced) and interest aggregation (in which the various concerns are combined, traded off, and compromised by the representatives) that transform private preferences into public policy.

As Beitz recognizes, it is a mistake to treat the existing distribution of preferences as a given. In the process of shaping public policy, voter preferences are themselves shaped and reshaped. Even if they were not, policy would seldom if ever exactly track the preexisting preferences of any identifiable voter. Thus, instead of a right to have those preferences satisfied, it is necessary to return the focus to the fairness of the process: Under what conditions can I fairly be expected to abide by the results of a process, even though I am disappointed with those results? With regard specifically to districting, when and how can we claim that the losers in a winner-take-all election are still meaningfully represented?

The specific reforms Beitz recommends to address current fairness issues include "increasing the proportion of districts in which the normal or expected partisan voting strength is relatively evenly divided,"[21] and, where necessary, creating safe districts to ensure a voice for "geographically concentrated and politically isolated" minorities.[22] Beitz acknowledges that both strategies entail forms of gerrymandering aimed at a rough proportionality of representation—for parties in one case and minority groups in the other. Unfortunately, he fails to consider carefully whether the two strategies are mutually compatible, either in theory or in practice.

The theoretical difficulty is in viewing voters simultaneously as individual choosers whose preferences are fluid and as members of fixed social groupings whose interests are objectively given. The practical difficulty is in trying to increase simultaneously the number of competitive seats and the number of safe ones. Beitz does not discuss such examples as the effect on the Democratic party in the South of recent race-conscious redistricting plans driven by the Voting Rights Act.

Beitz's third issue is agenda formation. The rules of primary concern here are the prevalent limitations on access to the ballot, which tend strongly to favor major-party candidates. Beitz's goal is to "ensure public presentation of positions responsive to the needs and interests of all significant portions of the citizenry."[23] The regulative interests imply a preference for broad and coherent campaigns over those that focus on single issues, and for a number of alternatives limited so as to facilitate informed comparison. Still, "it would be a bad thing for the urgent needs of *any* group to be left out of political account, and all the more so if the group were already disadvantaged . . . ."[24]

Later, he reinforces this point by endorsing rules that would open party governance, including candidate selection and platform formation, to broad participation by party members, and also rules granting ballot access to minor party and independent candidates. Otherwise, important positions might go unrepresented.[25] Thus, Beitz rejects the view that parties, as formally private organizations, are constitutionally exempt from state regulation of their internal decisionmaking procedures: "The framing of issues for public deliberation, the mobilization of excluded groups, and the selection of candidates for office are all vital public functions . . . ."[26]

Beitz's fourth and last design issue is campaign finance. One possible governing principle is that "all interests and points of view [should] receive financial support and expression in proportion to the numbers of their adherents."[27] A competing one is that *candidates* (not voters and not interests or ideas) are entitled to equal treatment. While Beitz holds that voters' interests should take priority over those of candidates or speakers, neither of these principles, he argues, is tailored to the primary public goals of preventing corruption and ensuring fair access. Rather than equality in either of the above senses, these two goals imply, on the one hand, ceilings on maximum expenditure by or on behalf of any candidate and, on the other hand, floors or minimum resources that must be made available to anyone having enough support to be deemed entitled to compete. Because of the different marginal utilities that any precise amount of spending or spending increase will have for different candidates, the norm of equality has no clear-cut bearing on either of these goals.

Beitz's overall conclusion is that

> there is no general reason to treat formally egalitarian procedures as enjoying any special privilege and no reason to think that inegalitarian or countermajoritarian procedures (such as judicial review, supermajority requirements, and the like) must necessarily be unfair.[28]

Yet, if judicial review is to play a constructive role in resolving issues of fair representation, adequate standards must be found in constitutional doctrine—a matter which Beitz treats only in passing.

While Beitz's theory suggests some important reforms (see chapter 8), his ideas are, for the most part, well embedded in American ideas and institutions. However, some approaches to representation even more novel than PR have recently begun to attract attention. One of these, advocated by Robert Grady, is functional representation—a species of corporatism.[29] Corporatist systems identify "functional interests," such as economic, ethnic, or religious groupings, as primary units of representation, alongside or instead of territorial units.

Grady's thesis is that our system of interest-group pluralism has allowed organized functional interests to attain a predominant role in our politics, without requiring that these interests be democratically structured or subject to public norms in their exercise of influence. The functional interests are active makers of public policy, working in conjunction with their chief counterparts: unelected bureaucratic experts to whom virtually unlimited authority has been delegated by law. The result is that the overall role of democratically accountable officials has been severely eroded, undermining the legitimacy of public policy and of government in general.

Grady's solution is not to suppress the functional interests but to incorporate them formally into the process and subject them to publicly formulated standards of conduct. While on the surface this proposal may seem radical, Grady argues that functional representation would actually be more faithful than interest-group pluralism is to the underlying impulses of American democratic theory. He reminds us that Madison, alongside his proposals for institutional balancing and protecting property, stressed the importance of commitments to political equality and to guarding against the evil effects of economic inequality. While decrying factionalism, Madison supported harnessing factional interests to serve the public good by extending the public sphere. He did not advocate efforts to suppress factions or to pretend they do not exist.

Finally, while the circumstances of Madison's time made territorial representation seem natural, Grady argues that for many people today, functional association and occupational status are more central to personal identity and political interests than is geography. With the important caveat that unorganized interests and individuals must also have access to representation, this historical transformation makes a turn to functional representation an asset, even an essential, for "restoring real representation."

Lani Guinier's theory of representation pays less attention than does Grady's to economic organizations, but is equally critical of our territorial districting system. Her ideas received wide publicity when President Clinton nominated her to head the Justice Department's Civil Rights Division. One of her most striking proposals was a system of cumulative voting. Instead of creating territorial districts in which minorities are able to see their preferences prevail, cumulative voting has all members chosen at large, with each voter having a number of votes equal to the total number of seats to be filled. The voter then decides, in a sense, with which group or groups to be counted. She may cast all her votes for a single candidate or distribute them any other way she chooses.

In her recent book,[30] Guinier argues that such a scheme bespeaks a "one vote, one value" principle that is consistent with, but superior to, "one person, one vote." Dispensing with both gerrymanders and quotas, it provides cohesive minorities with real prospects for electoral success. More broadly, it comes closer than current approaches to affording *each* voter an equal opportunity to elect a like-minded representative of her choice. It minimizes wasted votes—both those cast on behalf of losers in single-member district races, and those cast superfluously on behalf of candidates who clearly would win without them. It empowers citizens and encourages coalition building and deliberation in the legislature, instead of entrenched incumbency, group or territorial parochialism, and alienating, winner-take-all politics.

As Peter Schuck also argues,[31] single-member districting harms minority interests far more than partisan gerrymandering does; thus, the heavy reliance of voting rights strategists on single-member districts dominated by minorities has had disappointing, even counterproductive results.

Guinier's critique of the winner-take-all, single-member district system is extremely compelling and has significance well beyond the issues addressed by the Voting Rights Act. She notes the feudal origins of the composition of Parliament on territorial lines, and the eighteenth-century Whig view that "interests," rather than individuals, were to be represented. While the liberal strand in American thought emphasized representation of persons, this principle never entirely replaced its predecessors—as shown by the design of the Senate, the ongoing malapportionment of state legislatures, and, Guinier argues, the continued preference for *territorially* defined (that is, inherently gerrymandered) constituencies.

Guinier denies that the one person, one vote standard has constitutionalized a purely individualist theory of voting rights; she notes that both Congress and the Supreme Court have explicitly recognized a group right of historically disadvantaged minorities to effective political participation. It is unclear what turns on this debate, given the possibility of formulating the issues, inelegantly if need be, in terms of individual rights. Indeed, Guinier is careful to show how her proposals would enhance individual voting rights, including those of nonminorities. A great strength of her approach is its emphasis on the respects in which politics can be a "positive-sum" rather than a "zero-sum" game, in which all sides get something of value.

There are, however, a number of theoretical and practical problems with her analysis. Theoretically, the ambiguous concepts of 'equal opportunity to be part of a winning coalition' and 'right to have one's interests satisfied a fair proportion of the time' are not elaborated with sufficient clarity. For example, it is one thing to claim an immunity from arbitrary or malicious dilution of one's vote—but quite another to claim that one's chances of winning must be equal, without regard to how many other voters share one's preferences. The latter claim could be satisfied only if representatives were chosen at random—clearly not what Guinier intends. The suggested right to satisfaction of one's interests is still more perplexing—first, because Guinier repeatedly insists that her concern is for *procedural* fairness, not a substantive theory of distributive justice; and second, because the notion of a "fair proportion of the time" provides no measurable standard, especially in light of Guinier's recognition that issues differ in importance and preferences differ in intensity. Given her commitment to a genuinely deliberative politics and her professed distaste for quotas, it is difficult to see how this notion can be applied, beyond the easy but rather empty claim that for some groups to *never* win is unfair. (Insofar as some "public goods" are provided from which *everyone* benefits, even victims of blatant discrimination could not pass the rigid test of proving they never win.) On these matters, Beitz's thinking seems significantly clearer.

Another conceptual difficulty pertains to Guinier's unsteady use of the term majority. Early on, the very possibility of majority rule is earnestly questioned and conceded only for purposes of argument, yet "the tyranny of the majority" is still taken seriously enough to serve as the book's title. In the epilog, the same phrase is offered as a "metaphor" for the quasi-monarchist theories of Reagan's Justice Department, in which "majority rule" is apparently an ideological disguise for hierarchical, centralized elite domination. Yet Guinier never specifically identifies the elites in question or develops a critique of inequalities of wealth, status, or class.

The only certain and constant feature of Guinier's majority rule is that it is exercised by whites at the expense of nonwhites. Based on racially polarized voting statistics, she tends to identify whites as a politically cohesive group, downplaying the obvious partisan, class, ethnic, and ideological cleavages. For example, her account of Representative Solarz's race for a seat in New York's "Latino district" labels him the "white" candidate, even though residents are quoted as calling him "this Jewish person." While evidence of racist attitudes is plentiful, it simply does not follow that the country is or could be ruled by a "white majority." Indeed, the prevalence of gridlock, in Washington especially, raises questions as to whether the country can be ruled at all.

Thus the "disaggregation" of the white majority, which Guinier identifies as a central aim of her project, seems too crude and sweeping a program to address the broader problems of a politics in which race relations may be a unique rather than a typical issue. Perhaps, as Justice Thomas seems to believe,[32] there are important issues on which "minorities" do not hold highly distinctive views, and (whether represented by minorities or not) can have their preferences satisfied by government as often or as seldom as most whites do. Neither Guinier nor Thomas offers decisive empirical evidence on this point. While Guinier's call for cross-racial coalitions is entirely welcome, it is doubtful that issues of procedural reform would suffice to animate such coalitions and unclear what substantive issues she would have such coalitions address.

Indeed, her procedural proposals would alienate many liberals because of her focus on group interests and divisions, which cumulative voting could make even more intense and divisive. Thus, Shuck argues that any form of PR elevates reified group interests over freely chosen individual ones, and hence is inconsistent with liberal-individualistic principles. Moreover, PR, he holds, promotes political fragmentation and narrow, ideological, or parochial electoral strategies, undermining the goal of "effective and responsible governance."[33]

Beitz, however, identifies a certain form of PR—the single transferable vote (where voters rank-order their preferred candidates in a multimember district)—as the most individualistic of all election systems. Here constituencies are self-defining, wasted votes are minimized, and "the distribution of opinion in the legislature will reflect that found in the electorate at large, undistorted by filtration devices like primaries or the political judgments of party elites."[34]

Other critics have observed that PR guarantees neither that all useful ideas will be heard, nor that policy—as opposed to legislative membership—will faithfully reflect the distribution of preferences, nor that representatives of the different groups will be willing and able to engage either in dispassionate republican discourse or in effective liberal bargaining. In many countries, PR has been associated with political fragmentation and stalemate. Some argue that it also supports the rise and growth of extremist movements by guaranteeing them a modicum of legislative seats, where in a winner-take-all system they will be absorbed into and contained by middle-of-the-road parties. Beitz replies that empirical research has shown that historical, cultural, and social factors play a much larger role than electoral rules in shaping a polity's party system.[35]

A related criticism of Guinier's analysis is its neglect of the political role of (nongovernmental) institutions. On the one hand, her voters and politicians are autonomous individuals, free to define their own identities, take their own stands on issues, and associate politically as they please. On the other hand, they are lumped involuntarily into groups not of their own choosing, based on circumstances of race and gender, but also on geography, that is, the intersection of personal residential choices with the economics of housing markets and the politics of districting struggles. Missing are the implications of connections based on one's position in the economy. Also missing is the corresponding political role of organized economic interests. Those connections and activities not only shape our politics to a large extent; they also suggest possibilities for restructuring our system of representation at least partly along functional rather than geographic lines—possibilities Guinier, unlike Grady, does not entertain.[36]

Even if Guinier's analysis is theoretically valid, her legal proposals may not be feasible. Whatever the theoretical merits of such a system as cumulative voting, its specificity and unfamiliarity identify it as, at best, a possible experiment—not as a constitutional requirement. In Guinier's view, courts should consider its suitability, taking its "disruptiveness" into account, as a *remedy* in specific cases where the existing system has been found to violate minority rights.[37] But, in fact, courts have been extremely wary of imposing such unorthodox experiments.[38] If cumulative voting for representatives seems too radical, such ideas as cumulative voting *within* the legislature—advanced as a way of letting minority representatives register the intensity of their preferences—are even more so. Guinier's concern that minority representatives may be marginalized and lack effective influence is well taken, but she does

AUGUSTANA UNIVERSITY COLLEGE
LIBRARY

not develop her proposals for special legislative voting rules clearly enough to allow a confident assessment of their feasibility and impact.

Although fighting her nomination by labeling her as "radical" and "undemocratic" may have been something of a cynical rhetorical ploy, Guinier's political vision does seem to have elements that go well beyond "purely procedural" ideas that all would accept as fair. Even her call for moving "from power politics to principled politics" may be pregnant with radical implications, insofar as it seems to subvert the conventional distinction between politics and law, and even to question the legitimacy of ordinary pluralist politics itself. Yet her critique and proposals are less radical than Grady's, for she would make relatively modest changes in the electoral system—she does not advocate a quota system, much less full-scale PR—while leaving the socioeconomic system essentially intact.

In the end, while Guinier's ideas clearly deserve serious discussion both in academic and in political forums, she recognizes that their speculative character makes them unlikely prospects for adoption by the courts—especially today's courts. She also recognizes that there are problems both in principle and in practice with undue reliance on litigation as a vehicle for political reform.

In order to form a sound judgment on the appropriate judicial role in these matters, it is vital to use a rich, realistic description of the ways the electoral system and the legislative process actually function. It should be clear from chapter 1 that the theories and empirical findings of modern social science, unconfined by the assumptions of traditional jurisprudence, have figured significantly in the breakdown of the once-axiomatic barrier between law and politics. These findings have also fueled ongoing debates in democratic theory, for example, between pluralists and elitists, advocates of "strong," "unitary," and other alternate forms of democracy, and so on.[39] The upshot is that neither with nor without judicially imposed reforms could we expect to win general scholarly assent today to the proposition that the current workings of the "political branches" faithfully reflect the "will of the People." Meanwhile, opinion surveys and voter turnout statistics show high levels of popular discontent with the current system,[40] and activists of many stripes attack it on diverse grounds.

Some draw on republican thought in decrying the parochialism, passionate vulgarity, and corruption of modern campaigns. Others invoke democratic ideas in lamenting the manipulations of professional managers and rich contributors, the concealment or misrepresentation of candidates' agendas and voting records, and the undue influence in government of unelected lobbyists and bureaucrats. All parties will complain on occasion of opponents' electoral gerrymandering, favoritism toward incumbents, heavyhanded majority steamrolling, or minority obstructionism and gridlock in the legislative process. And, of course, all decry partisan opportunism and selfishness while claiming for themselves the virtue of true public spirit.

Radicals, meanwhile, often argue that systemic flaws are not aberrations but are part of the basic design: the system never aimed at representing the masses, but only at creating an illusion of representation. One sort of radical—a deconstructionist, perhaps— might say that even with the best of will, any scheme of representation will be seriously flawed and incomplete. But to representation there is no alternative, even in principle. For if I insist on acting on my own behalf, the inherent limits of self-knowledge, unpredictable changes in human needs, desires, and situations, and the nonexistence of a truly objective vantage point mean that I cannot act with certainty. I must struggle even to adequately represent myself!

The more complex the process and the associated norms, the harder it becomes to assess the quantity and quality of representation a particular person, group, idea, or interest is receiving, whether from a particular representative or from the system as a whole. For example, my representative may cheerfully and effectively engage in "casework" on my behalf (intervening and solving problems with administrative agencies), even if I voted against her and despise her policy agenda. Moreover, I may feel well and truly represented both on the "recognition" level and in policy making by one for whom I cannot vote because I live outside her district.

Normally we leave such judgments entirely to the electoral process; since one can be a fine representative in some sense without being very good in others, voters may have difficult choices to make. Surveys show that American voters tend to put personal character first, party affiliation second, and stands on specific issues last in deciding whom to support. To modify the categories somewhat, it seems plausible that the typical voter cares greatly about "character" and descriptive similarity (the image of a confidence-inspiring role model, and the sharing of one's demographic traits such as race, gender, ethnicity, or religion), cares secondarily about ideological stances, and is not very well informed about candidates' specific past or likely future behaviors.[41] If so, the voter has better prospects for being descriptively than behaviorally represented; the goods the representative delivers may be largely symbolic.

The Constitution, offered by Publius as designed to prevent tyranny of the majority, today is praised as a guarantee that the majority's will is done. These inconsistent claims cannot both be true, and it is possible that both are false. Certainly they cannot be evaluated in the abstract, from behind a "veil of ignorance" about our culture and social structure, for the consequences of federalism, bicameralism, territorial districting, and so forth will differ according to where, how, and among whom we live.

In a day when most districts had homogeneous electorates, the system could produce a suitably diverse legislature—leaving aside, of course, the situation of the disenfranchised—whose individual members had relatively strong mandates and few cross-pressures. Today more members will represent a diverse coalition of minorities, with special advantages going to minorities rich in one or more of the following: wealth, education, political activism and cohesion, geographically concentrated numbers, or protected status under the 1965 Voting Rights Act. The fairness or unfairness of this state of affairs is nowadays subject to regular dispute and litigation, in connection with decennial redrawing of congressional district boundaries.

Note, however, Beitz's point that even if the electoral system *could* ensure that all votes had equal influence and that the composition of the legislature as a whole would faithfully reflect the composition and will of the whole People, this still would not guarantee that the outputs of the legislative process had that same character. For one thing, not all legislators have equal influence. Congress, for example, has power, scarcely subject to judicial or other control, to make rules for its own proceedings.[42] These rules have always permitted certain members, for example, the speaker, committee heads, and so on, to wield special powers not possessed by others; it is difficult to imagine a nonanarchic alternative. Any nonrandom way of distributing such powers among the members is liable to give advantages, intentionally or not, to some groups more than others. For example, the seniority system long favored representatives from the South, who were likely to serve longer because of the weakness there of the Republican party. While recently-elected minorities may, as Guinier points out, have only marginal influence, arguably they share this plight with the vast majority of their peers.

It is not only the internal power structure of Congress that can yield inequalities in representation. Despite the plenary power of Congress to control its own proceedings, from the outset the president, his subordinates, and powerful outside interests have played major roles in setting the legislative agenda and influencing subsequent action. Today's textbooks identify the president as "chief legislator." Indeed, the capacity of Congress to make policy, save in the most episodic manner, is very much in question. Certainly, floor debate seldom appears to be the site of major decisions; most of the real work is done behind the scenes by "iron triangles" of lobbyists, bureaucrats, and powerful committee members. As the classical distinction between law and politics has blurred, so too has that between politics and administration. It becomes difficult to articulate the ways in which Congress is more, or differently, representative than is the bureaucracy.

At any given time, ordinary citizens are apt to feel, with good reason, that they have little access to or influence over these decisions. Given the size of the country, the complexity of public policies, and the unequal distribution of political resources, it is hard to see how it could be otherwise. Indeed, no human agency can provide time enough for everyone to participate. Deliberation and debate can hardly go on *ad infinitum*, even in the United States Senate—filibusters, gridlock, and all.

Representation in Constitutional History

Insofar as he who makes the electoral rules can call the policy tune, it is striking how little the Constitution binds us on this subject and how much "the People," in establishing the Constitution, left to their future representatives to decide.

Clearly, the Founders were not committed to universal suffrage and did not see voting as a necessary condition for being adequately represented. With the republican notions of indirect and virtual representation current at the time, representation required neither direct popular participation in decisionmaking nor literal fidelity on the representative's part to the views and desires of those represented. Thus it was possible to aver that "the People" had ratified the Constitution, even though by some estimates fewer than 5 percent of the population had taken part in choosing the delegates to the ratifying conventions.[43]

Not only was representation not limited to voters, it was not limited to persons. Madison, for example, writing in defense of bicameralism, argued that "property," as well as persons, ought to be represented.[44] Hamilton showed equally clearly the influence in America of the British Whig idea that interests, not individuals, are the proper objects of representation.[45] Interests tended to be geographically centered, explaining the organization of Parliament according to *place* rather than population. Places, in the Whig-republican view, had objective interests which elected members were to discover and represent. In so doing, they served all their constituents, regardless of whether or how those constituents might have voted. Madison's vision, however, went beyond the imperatives and limitations of place: the task of representatives was to "refine and enlarge" the often narrow and passionate ideas of local or other factions into a rational and effective public policy for the entire community.[46]

Pitkin[47] distinguishes Burke's theory of "virtual representation" from that held by the American Founders. For Burke, society consisted of relatively few broad and fixed interests, largely economically defined and geographically based; while for Madison, it consisted of a multitude of factions, based on passion as well as on interest, resulting in a political structure far more fluid and subjective. Hence Burke thought expanding the suffrage was largely unnecessary, since members of Parliament enjoyed a "community of interest and sympathy in feelings" with most nonvoters and could effectively pursue the common interest on their behalf. For Madison, in contrast, the key point was that in an extended republic the multiplicity of factions would obstruct the formation of tyrannical majorities, while constitutional checks and balances would permit the national welfare to emerge as a by-product of governmental inaction. To this reader, however, Madison's position seems equivocal or transitional between republican and liberal views, while the similarities between Burke's views of the social and political structure and those of conservative Americans such as Hamilton[48] or even Calhoun[49] are very striking.

Of course, our current ideas are different, both as to who or what is represented and as to how. On the modern liberal understanding, political rights, like all rights, are personal. Democratic theory holds that individuals have an equal right to be heard, to participate in choosing representatives, and to affect political outcomes. Members of Congress, as the Supreme Court put it, represent persons, not trees or acres.[50] Modern "democratic pluralism" addresses the role of groups through "freedom of association" and the legitimation (contrary to Madison's condemnation of "faction") of interest-group activity.

Yet the individualist presumption that all have equal access when all have equal personal rights, including the right to join or organize groups, does not address the persistent advantages and disadvantages possessed by different groups due to inequalities of property and education, race and gender prejudices, and so forth. Unless such obstacles are directly imposed by the state, it is difficult for the law even to recognize them, much less remove them. Instead, as Grady and Guinier argue, constitutional liberties and democratic pluralism legitimize the status quo and its associated inequalities.

Nor does a purely individualist theory of representation always square well with the notion, also popular today, of politics as a "marketplace of ideas." It is worth noting that the latter notion has been articulated and employed especially by courts—themselves supposedly forums of principle rather than of politics. In an important sense, courts in their ordinary decision making are supposed to represent and uphold a body of ideas—the substantive and procedural rules of law—rather than the desires of litigants or of other, outside interests.

To put it another way, legal texts represent ideas (in the literary sense of representation) and courts uphold or represent (in a peculiarly legal sense) the texts. But because the legal texts are created on the People's authority, the courts still are representing the People in this work—albeit in a quite different way than applies to legislative voting. In the classical separation of powers model, courts apply general rules (public policy, the will of the People) to problems brought before them by individual litigants, while lawmakers, chosen through individuals' votes, transform individuals' ideas and demands into general rules.

In the legislative marketplace, vote trading and compromise are routine and legitimate. If the courtroom is also a marketplace, it is a special one where only principles are supposed to count. Nevertheless, its isolation from politics is surely incomplete. Its members are politically chosen, its reasons are publicly debated, and its proceedings are subject to a multitude of ultimately political constraints. That the path to reform may be slow and indirect is not a circumstance unique to the judicial process. The special safeguards of "judicial independence" cannot make the law totally nonpolitical, nor can they make judicial review totally illegitimate.

Nevertheless, as the previous chapter made clear, the notion of purifying politics by appealing to a discrete legal discourse that somehow stands outside and above politics is fraught with paradox. That is why critics could, with some plausibility, criticize the decision in *Baker v. Carr*[51] and its progeny as unwarranted judicial involvement with an inherently political question. At the very least, more representation for some entails less for others; to define equality in this context is not merely a difficult, but an inescapably political, task. Any ostensibly neutral standard of fair representation announced by a court is apt to remain bitterly contested.

Consider, for example, the ultra-orthodox argument of Allan Moore,[52] which, precisely by insisting on the sanctity of the law/politics distinction, would effectively inscribe in the Constitution a reactionary partisan agenda. Moore's thesis is that the Constitution contains no coherent, justiciable standard of fairness in representation. Instead, he asserts, the Constitution uneasily incorporates both democratic and republican elements—representation of persons according to population (as in the House) and of places or communities regardless of population (as in the Senate). Not only does the Constitution not impose (democratic) proportional representation as a general practice; it does not permit a legislature, let alone a court, to do so. Fidelity to the Constitution requires respect both for democratic and for republican principles and does not condone purely democratic solutions. Since there is no *principled* way of compromising or combining the two approaches, the courts have no role to play here.

Thus, although gerrymandering may indeed cause serious political harms, it does not violate any identifiable constitutional rule. *Davis v. Bandemer*,[53] which held that partisan gerrymanders may violate the equal protection clause, was wrongly decided. Not only *Bandemer*, but *Baker v. Carr*[54] and the entire line of one person, one vote cases it spawned should have been dismissed, as raising nonjusticiable political questions. For Moore the only judicially cognizable form of vote dilution is the *racial* gerrymander—a special case in light of the intent and wording of the Fourteenth and Fifteenth Amendments. This important exception aside, disappointed voters have no legal complaint: "Republican theory . . . assumes that the winner of an election can and will adequately represent *all* of her constituents, including those who may have voted for the opposition."[55]

On the surface, Moore's argument is neutral as between democratic and republican views of representation. The Court first erred in reading a democratic one person, one vote rule into the Constitution, and now can find no principled way of avoiding the "political thicket" of the partisan gerrymander. It is true that the Court shows no inclination to go all the way: "Indeed, if the democratic principle of equally weighted votes is truly a constitutional requirement, then the Supreme Court should invalidate district-based systems altogether . . . ."[56] On the contrary, the Court has repeatedly denied that proportional representation is a constitutional requirement, and has clung to the single-member district as the standard remedy for racial gerrymanders. To Moore, this moderate or compromising course does not earn the Court any credit; it merely highlights the unprincipled, politically expedient nature of the judicial involvement.

Under the surface, Moore's position is more radical in its way than that of, say, Lani Guinier. What he fails to acknowledge is that his alternative of judicial abstention would be no more faithful to the dual nature of the Constitution's representative scheme. On the contrary, it would tolerate the complete triumph of the republican "principle" over the democratic, as illustrated by the gross malapportionment that prompted actions such as *Baker*. Since judicial abstention always favors the status quo, it is not politically neutral but inherently conservative, in a partisan sense. In general, the prospect of nonpartisan legislated solutions to legislative malapportionment is laughably unreal, and constitutional amendment is scarcely attainable by the action of the systematically disempowered. In contrast, the rulings of Republican-appointed justices on racially motivated districting—whatever else we may say about them—at least do not seem calculated or likely to increase Republican electoral prospects.

Despite the history of expansion of the suffrage, Chief Justice Burger's declaration, quoted approvingly by Moore, that "the Framers . . . placed responsibility for correction of [representational] flaws in the people, relying on them to influence their elected representatives"[57] seems either naive or downright cynical. Surely we cannot take it for granted that the beneficiaries of an unfair system will make a general practice of reforming it, or pressuring their representatives to do so, on behalf of the currently un- or underrepresented. Even if idealism or partisan self-interest may *sometimes* prompt them to do so, "auxiliary precautions" are obviously useful for cases where they do not, and judicial review is one of the very precautions the Framers made available for such cases.[58]

Because the broader diffusion of political access and influence is the central criterion of democratization, it seems perverse to label "undemocratic" the use of judicial review for this precise purpose. Chief Justice Burger's statement may remind us that *in the best of all possible worlds*, people would win democratic reforms by their own unaided efforts and thereby gain fuller empowerment than they can from reforms bequeathed to them by others. In the real world, however, the powerless or handicapped outsider/minority does not often have that option.

Moore's thesis that courts must abstain because "[w]here there is no generally accepted principle, there can be no rule of law"[59] is a *reductio ad absurdum* of the political questions doctrine. Taken seriously, it proves that no case whatsoever is justiciable! After all, the typical legal controversy (purely factual disputes aside) pertains to which of several contending principles is valid and applicable to the case at hand. That the contending parties appeal to different principles, each of which has some plausible claim to validity and relevance, is absolutely standard. That both democratic and republican theories of representation have some constitutional basis does not make voting rights cases in any way unique.

Would Moore contend that the case of *Riggs v. Palmer*,[60] made famous by Cardozo and Dworkin, in which one party (who had murdered the testator) relied on the principle that wills must be construed literally, while the other (who sought to block execution of the will) relied on the principle that one should not profit from his own wrongdoing, was nonjusticiable? Or does he perhaps still adhere to the classical formalist view that all of the available valid principles are prioritized and reconciled by an objective logical structure, without which judging would indeed be impossible? But if so, why cannot the competing theories of representation be reconciled by legal reasoning? If the Constitution is somehow paradoxical or incoherent at its very core, on what principled foundation can *any* judicial action—even simple contract enforcement—rest?

At the opposite pole on the justiciability of political rights we find John Hart Ely, who, in his well-known book,[61] offered the reinforcement of representation as the primary function of judicial review in a representative democracy. To the charge that such efforts dragged courts into the partisan "political thicket," he replied that the political norms established by our Constitution provide no warrant for efforts of incumbents to block free expression, choke off the process of change, or injure minorities out of sheer dislike. Such actions violate political rights essential to democracy and not safely left in the incumbents' exclusive care. While "one person, one vote" may not suffice to insure fair representation—let alone equal political influence—for all, it is both judicially manageable and responsive to real, widespread abuses.

Ely's critics, however, were able to discern political biases in his theory. It was not as purely procedural as advertised, for no such thing is possible.[62] On the contrary, "one person, one vote" arguably endorses an individualist, egalitarian, majoritarian, and democratic theory of representation over the alternative communitarian, elitist, consensus-oriented, and republican theory that also pervades our traditions. Moreover, even if "one person, one vote" were truly neutral, it also opened the door to judicial consideration of other claimed abuses, such as racial gerrymandering, for disposition of which manageable standards have proved exceedingly hard to come by.

It seems clear that, if there is to be a distinction between political and legal questions, the adequacy of my representation by those currently in office must be first of all a political question, to be resolved by me in the privacy of the voting booth. All the same, it is equally clear that the fairness of the current voting rules, which cannot be addressed in that way, must be kept open to challenge. Often the politicians will be unwilling to respond; nor would it be desirable to require a constitutional amendment for each and every electoral reform. It was just such an impasse, after all, that produced the Dorr War. It seems implausible that a judicial ruling on the merits in *Luther v. Borden*[63] would have been disastrous for the Court or for the country. *Pace* Moore, the modern reapportionment decisions are generally accepted as having been good for both.

Still, a fully adequate theory of representation needs to address a scary range of issues. Based on the materials reviewed here, the relevant concerns include at least these: deterring abuses of power by majorities or minorities; helping as many persons and groups as possible to feel empowered and well represented; and aggregating their different preferences into coherent, effective, and stable policies that will be received as fair representations of the People's will.

If these be the relevant concerns, we must acknowledge that they scarcely, in themselves, supply anything like "manageable judicial standards." The concerns can be very controversial; for example, many would dismiss out of hand the notion of a feeling everyone is entitled to have. Moreover, the concerns are sometimes, like the interests they support, in tension with each other, making it impossible fully to satisfy them all. Finally, even taking the concerns one at a time, there are few obviously necessary conditions, let alone sufficient ones, for satisfying them. The pertinent facts are seldom easy to obtain or scientifically measurable.

Perhaps that is why the right of fair representation, like such similarly inchoate (although textually explicit) conceptions as 'a more perfect Union,' 'domestic tranquility,' and so on, has not been fully assimilated into constitutional law. Yet it is not hard to argue that 'due process' and 'equal protection' are just as inchoate on close inspection. The more important difference is that the institutional role of the courts and the nature of their everyday business have made it utterly impossible for them to escape from interpreting the latter provisions, while the former seldom if ever arise, and then only in unique cases that are tempting candidates for judicial abstention.

History shows quite clearly that our system offers at least three different avenues for egalitarian political reform, and that these avenues are, in the long run at least, more complementary than mutually exclusive. While we may generally begin with a presumption that representative institutions are tolerably fair, there are several ways of testing the presumption or seeking improvement.

The first, illustrated by the expansion of suffrage in the antebellum period, is a form of "ordinary politics," driven largely by the desire of competing politicians to enlarge their bases of electoral support. Even the Federalist party, for all its dislike of democracy, was led by self-interest to support democratic reforms and employ populist electoral tactics when circumstances made it seem profitable.

The second avenue for reform, illustrated by the advent of "one person, one vote," is constitutional politics of a preservative sort, that is, judicial review. As Ackerman, Ely, and others have argued, it is not only incumbent politicians who speak for the People. The People speak through the Constitution, and the courts, as well as other officials, are sworn to uphold it. If the courts can persuasively discern in the Constitution a mandate for a political reform, the country will accept it. As noted, today that mandate appears rather narrow, as it most often has in the past. It enables courts to respond to grave and widely recognized political injustices that seem entrenched against the first avenue of reform. Yet it surely does not extend to the courts an open-ended invitation to develop and enforce their own comprehensive theory of just legislation (that is, substantive due process) ungrounded in the constitutional text.

The third avenue, constitutional politics of the transformative sort, may take many forms, including popular agitation for constitutional amendment or even a populist uprising bypassing the power structure, such as Dorr's rebellion. Outside reform movements, moved by a mix of altruism and self-interest, played major roles in bringing on the suffrage-expanding Fifteenth, Nineteenth, and Twenty-sixth Amendments, whose direct beneficiaries, initially bereft of voting rights, could not have won those rights unaided. (Constitutional revision can also be initiated primarily from above; but such changes, for example, the Eleventh and Twenty-fifth Amendments, are apt to be very different in significance. Ackerman terms these cases "superlegislation," highlighting their technical character.)

Popular pressures can also, of course, induce officials to bring about major, transformative change even without constitutional amendment. In such cases, the line between ordinary and constitutional politics is blurred; this gives rise to the doubts about the changes' legitimacy with which Ackerman, Bickel, and others are so concerned.[64] Courts, of course, cannot act until someone brings a case before them. Elected officials can, but, given the pressures under which they operate, seldom do, initiate significant reforms in the absence of significant constituent pressures. Sometimes the politicians' response aims to preempt more radical developments or coopt movement leaders, yet such reform can be a large step forward.

Standing behind and linking together these different avenues of reform is an inchoate idea—what Bowles and Gintis[65] refer to as the inherent expansionary logic of the discourse of personal rights. Through the rhetorical imperatives both of "republican" and of "democratic" politics, what may begin as a selfish quest for special privileges will be voiced as an appeal to universalistic principles, and thereby made available for additional groups and uses to which the original claimants may have been oblivious or even downright opposed.[66]

While the record of reform, uneven and incomplete as it may be, is undeniable, radicals continue to argue that problems of race, gender, and/or class oppression cannot be successfully addressed within the system, since the system's individualism, tolerance, and "neutrality" are part of the problem. It is also true that not all change is necessarily progressive. Reaction can, in principle, be brought about either from above or from below, and with or without formal constitutional amendment. The gradual institution of Jim Crow regimes in the South after 1876 provides examples of every conceivable sort—even including black legislators voting to repeal black suffrage.

These concerns deserve serious consideration. A simple reading (?) of the Constitution itself, out of historical context, neither unequivocally supports nor unequivocally forecloses a multitude of possible changes, many of them radical indeed. That is why Frederick Douglass could at one date read the Constitution as proslavery, and later read it as antislavery.[67] That is why some justices could find the theory of laissez-faire economics in the Constitution, while to others it was clear that the Constitution endorsed *no* economic theory.

What does *not* follow is the extreme conclusion that the Constitution means anything and nothing, that it has no constraining effect whatever on constitutional discourse, let alone political action. Even Stanley Fish,[68] who pointedly denies that any text can be read simply, literally, and out of context, insists that interpretive discourse is a profoundly significant, action-constraining enterprise. A realistic account of our politics cannot be rendered without reference to the Constitution, to changes in its text and in our understanding of the text. It can be argued that we would be better off with a different Constitution. It can scarcely be argued that we would be better off with none at all, for we would not know how to proceed.

As James Lennertz points out, often our "[a]dversary system drives out the middle ground, reducing most things to matters of taste or to questions of [technical] expertise to be delegated to administrative experts."[69] The realm of *political principle* becomes narrow, endangered by cynicism on the part both of representatives and of the represented.

Of course, the lines between matters of taste, of principle, and of technical knowledge will always be themselves deeply contested. By and large, courts do not need to draw such lines (given the desuetude of the delegation doctrine) except in circumscribing their own jurisdiction, limited as it is to matters of legal principle. Subject to Congress's power (and that of the People) to limit this jurisdiction "from outside," the norms of judicial restraint always and already project the courts into a "political thicket," especially where voting rights claims are presented. Abstention, after all, is just as politically consequential as is intervention. Nevertheless, interventions may differ significantly in depth, duration, detail, and efficacy.

What the Constitution Says

Let us turn, finally, to examine the guidelines for representation actually found in the Constitution. As is well known, the electoral issue that preoccupied the Framers above all was the apportionment of legislative votes among the states. Even after watching—especially after watching—the quadrennial demonstrations of state pride at national party conventions, it is difficult for a mobile modern academic fully to appreciate the Anti-Federalist and republican attachment to one's state as a sovereign community—as, indeed, one's "country." States today (and their political elites) have less and less of the uniqueness and internal homogeneity that gave point to such sentiments two hundred years ago. The claim that those elected can represent the entire community fairly and effectively—including those who voted against them—has become harder and harder to credit.

At any rate, there is no current controversy over the basic, federal structure of the Constitution, save for sporadic murmurs of distaste for the electoral college. Should a candidate who did not win the popular vote ever again gain the presidency, the call for repeal of the electoral college will likely become overwhelming. Yet the equal representation of states in the Senate—and bicameralism itself, for that matter—seem as well-entrenched today as they are hard to justify.

Of course, the explicit, special entrenching provision of Article V ("no State, without its consent, shall be deprived of its equal Suffrage in the Senate") would make it especially difficult to change the Senate's constitution. Is it not a monument to the sagacity of the Framers that they chose this, along with the slave trade, to privilege above all else?

Beneath the peculiarity of the Senate lies a deeper set of questions: Why should Congress have two houses? Why should representation be based on geographical districts? Why should each district (in the House) have one representative? Why must districts be contiguous, let alone compact, in shape? The modern requirement of nearly equal population, derived from the one person, one vote standard, seems far easier to justify than these other ideas. The claim that they are simply safeguards against unfair gerrymandering of district lines calls out, of course, for a theory of fairness in districting. Since the existing boundaries are neither "natural" nor randomly drawn, every district is in a sense gerrymandered.

Of course, the Constitution expressly imposes only one of the above features of our current system: bicameralism. That device had two justifications: the threat of usurpation by a tyrannical majority, and the desirability, as Madison put it, of providing for representation of "property" as well as that of "persons." Neither of these arguments, I submit, makes much sense in our era of egalitarian sentiment and congressional feebleness. Better ones may be available, but the weight of tradition is such that we see no need to elaborate them.

As for districting, the Framers presupposed homogeneous local communities (minorities and women not being full members), low physical mobility, and a political system in which the preponderance of important policies would necessarily be locally made and administered. In that context the importance of physical proximity was obvious. Congress, in its wisdom, has chosen to entrench by statute a single-member districting system for the House of Representatives that perpetuates the same assumptions. While geography is obviously still crucial for organizing the delivery of basic services such as police and fire protection and garbage collection, its survival as the exclusive basis for organizing representation, especially at the national level, seems a product of inertia and incumbents' self-interest rather than of cogent political analysis.

The questions of second-greatest concern to the Framers pertained to the qualifications of representatives and their terms of service. As to qualifications, Publius argues that the reasonable limitations as to age, citizenship, and residence leave doors open "to merit of every description . . . without regard to poverty or wealth, or to any particular profession of religious faith."[70] The qualifications are in fact modest, and there is no indication that the states or Congress were seen as having residual power to impose additional qualifications. In particular, Publius denies that the "regulation of time, place, and manner of elections" includes any such power.[71] As for the power of each house to "be the judge of the . . . qualifications of its own members," this is most plausibly and safely read, as the Supreme Court has held, as only a power to determine whether an individual actually has the specified qualifications.[72]

Admittedly, Publius's assurances of inclusiveness must be taken in context, since he has earlier argued that "the idea of an actual representation of all classes of the people by persons of each class is altogether visionary." Instead, "landholders, merchants, and men of the learned professions" will understand and attend to "the interests and feelings of the different classes of citizens."[73] Yet these elitist predictions and sentiments are not matched by any corresponding restrictions on eligibility for office.

The matter is quite different with regard to qualifications for voting, since those are explicitly left to the states, which often had rigid property qualifications and other significant restrictions. Publius's defense of this arrangement seems weak and self-contradictory to the modern mind, like that of the three-fifths rule for counting slaves:

> The definition of the right of suffrage is very justly regarded as a fundamental article of republican government. It was incumbent on the convention, therefore, to define and establish this right in the Constitution. . . . To have reduced the different qualifications in the different States to one uniform rule would probably have been as dissatisfactory to some of the States as it would have been difficult to the convention. The provision made by the convention appears, therefore, to be the best that lay within their option.[74]

As to terms of office, Publius has a stronger case to offer. He presents eloquently the trade-off of accountability, which favors frequent elections, versus experience and stability, which favor longer terms of office. However, as to the number of terms an individual can serve, he argues that unlimited reeligibility is more conducive to accountability than term limits would be.

Publius offers this point only in the context of the presidency. Nevertheless, there must have been equally strong objections to the congressional term limits found in the Articles of Confederation, for the Virginia Plan's proposal to include a different version of term limits in the Constitution was quickly rejected by the convention. Given the typical career patterns of that era, it seems unlikely that this simply reflected the self-interest of would-be permanent congressmen. Perhaps the fact that the House was to be the only directly elected body made such limits cut too deeply into the Constitution's democratic aspect.

Another issue that attracted significant notice at the convention was that of the overall size of legislative bodies. Publius recognized that the smaller the district, the closer the bond between the representative and the constituency. However, the smaller the constituency, the larger the total membership of the body—which progressively makes operations more unwieldy and effective policymaking less likely.[75] Since total population is not stable, this issue cannot be resolved by settling on fixed sizes both for the legislative body and for the legislative district. The Framers opted for a maximum House size: "The Number of Representatives shall not exceed one for every thirty Thousand . . . ." This precise figure, interestingly, was substituted for forty thousand at George Washington's insistence—the sole occasion when the convention's presiding officer took a recorded, open stand on a matter of substance.

Today, of course, this maximum permissible size would yield a House of more than eighty thousand members. Years ago, Congress legislated a cap on that body's membership at 435, necessitating the decennial reapportionment struggles that the census now entails. Given the guarantee to each state of at least one representative, the result is a major departure from the principle of representation according to population: some states may have one representative for every four hundred thousand inhabitants, while other states have one for every eight hundred thousand. Meanwhile, the body is already much too large for effective collective deliberation aimed at consensus. Yet for all the ostensible smallness of our districts, far fewer than half of American adults can even name their representative in Congress.

Can we say in compensation, at least, that in our democracy all voices are effectively heard? To this observer, it appears that minority groups and their issues remain marginalized, while progressive ideas that in Europe or in Canada are mainstream cannot receive a serious hearing. At the same time, voices from the Stone Age retain a Calhounian "concurrent veto." Is the skewed nature of our politics (only) a byproduct of our culture and social structure, or is it enshrined in the electoral system—and in our jurisprudence—in a manner subject to constitutional dispute and reform? If the Constitution really had nothing to say on questions of fair representation, such a silence would be unfortunate, even ominous, for our polity's self-understanding.

Conclusion

Two considerations make this chapter necessary. First, the topic of representation brings the law/politics distinction into especially clear focus, as no other topic save executive prerogative (see chapter 4) does. What are the source and nature of political rights? How are they defined and protected in our representative system? Second, the political questions doctrine and the endless debate over judicial review compel close attention to the question: In what sense are the "political branches" more "democratic" than the judiciary?

Political rights are further discussed in chapter 8; the materials considered so far should be sufficient to indicate why I believe the following:

1. democratic theory, representation, and political rights are and long have been highly contested terrain;
2. a *constitutional* form of politics is, at minimum, one constrained by stable procedures, where authority comes from agreed-on principles rather than from force or the sheer will of a majority;
3. the Constitution, as it has so far evolved and been interpreted, provides incomplete and inconsistent answers to our most urgent questions regarding political rights and procedures;
4. to answer these questions by *exclusive* resort to the norms and methods of "ordinary politics" is unacceptable, since ordinary politics itself is often far from democratic;
5. it is proper in principle, and sometimes urgent in practice, for the courts to involve themselves in at least some of these questions;
6. the judicial contribution will be more successful to the extent that it is perceived as preservative, rather than transformative, of constitutional values;

7. this distinction allows much room for reform, for our constitutional history contains a deep transformative impulse—even a transformative mandate—toward democratic empowerment, equal dignity, and a more equitable system of representation;
8. the traditional system of legislatively drawn single-member districts is not constitutionally mandated and, from the standpoint of fair representation, is open to serious objections.

❖ *Part II* ❖

The Many
(Against Nationalism)

A standard text would focus at this point on the governmental powers jurisprudence of federalism, the commerce clause, and so forth. Yet the current relevance of these doctrinal questions is far from obvious. Indeed, until recently it seemed that the very idea of a national government constitutionally limited to the exercise of certain enumerated powers was quite defunct.

Despite renewed judicial interest in the outer limits of the commerce power,[1] the Court's decisions have been quite narrow; on the whole, the broad New Deal understanding of what the Constitution permits still seems secure. Even looking beyond the Court, the most radical "New Federalist" initiative now under discussion, the balanced budget amendment, would at most reduce the government's revenues, not its scope of authority. It is revealing how many of the supporters of this ill-advised and probably unenforceable measure are also backing an unprecedented nationalization of tort law. The two proposals seem contradictory when viewed through the lens of federalism; what unites them is the elitist social and economic agenda of the intended beneficiaries.

More pressing questions for constitutional theory emerge from the brittle fragility of today's public sphere: the aimless gridlock, recurrent abuses of power, widespread alienation from politics, and the bitter cleavages that divide Americans. Can reflection about the Constitution help to remind us what we are about as a country, what commitments we share, what we jointly care about enough to make personal sacrifices for? If not, then the Constitution may no longer be part of our solution. Even more chilling, there may no longer be a "we" for whom the Constitution could speak.

Constitutions as we know them must address questions of membership (the boundaries of the polity—who is speaking, and for whom), of scope (which decisions are confided to government, and which reserved for other authorities), and of governmental structure and competence (who makes the decisions, and how, and with what resources to carry them out). The challenge for us today is to address such questions in a way that unites and guides us by synthesizing our constitutional culture. That culture rests upon a multifaceted tradition, and its diverse strands reflect and foster conflicting *expansionary* and *exclusionary* tendencies.

The strands or facets I have in mind include, in particular, liberalism, republicanism, democracy, nationalism, and imperialism. These ways of thinking (and their adherents) are not discrete, self-contained, monolithic, or comprehensive; but neither are they always mutually supportive, or even always compatible. Each has its own assumptions and preoccupations; each urges us to expand the polity, its members, and its agenda in some respects and to hold it steady or contract it in others.

The central preoccupation of liberalism is the individual person, her well-being, and her rights. Liberalism arose and flourished with the decline of traditional, hierarchical forms of authority in an age of increasingly "masterless men."[2] It reached new hegemonic heights in America, where feudalism had never held sway.[3] Substantively, the first principles of liberalism are that the purpose of government is to secure equal individual rights and that the authority of government depends on the consent of the governed. Methodologically, liberalism seems to assume that the polity consists simply of individuals: there is no whole greater than the sum of the parts. The one dissolves into the many.

These premises quickly generate questions that have received much attention from liberal theorists: what motivates individuals to join together in civil society, yielding up much of their natural freedom? What do those motivations tell us about the kinds of arrangements to which those individuals would or should agree? How can society and/or the state be induced to respect and support the surviving (and the newly created) personal rights of its members?[4]

Liberal thought tends to address these questions without regard to the actual membership of the polity and the shape of its agenda. The parties to Hobbes's or Locke's social contract, for example, are generic persons, motivated by generic concerns. Rationality and tolerance (however hard-won or reluctant) are among their most salient traits. This depiction provides the parties no basis for denying membership to anyone willing to join, and it provides us no account of why the world should be divided into numerous polities rather than a single one.

Such questions were familiar to liberal thinkers, but the traditional answers were couched in terms of values that fit uneasily within the liberal framework if they did not contradict it outright: blood and soil, religious orthodoxy and tribal custom, ascribed (inherited) over achieved status, group identity over individual freedom. Liberals knew what stresses cultural diversity and sheer size might bring to a polity, yet they could not respond by resorting to frankly illiberal values. Instead, they put faith in the universal appeal of "the rights of man," "the rule of law," and the orderly, prosperous life these ideals could secure for all.

Thus, close inquiry into the identity of "the People of the United States" has historically received little attention in liberal discourse. It has been far more crucial for republican thought. Republicanism is not so much an abstract theory as a situated political culture—an appreciative orientation toward a specific polity, its unique constitution, and the virtues appropriate to its citizens. For republicans, in order to decide what we should do, we must begin by remembering who we are. Constitutional government rests upon shared values, responsibilities, and goals. Republicans may be open to territorial and economic expansion, to cultural and moral progress; but they are loath to admit members, ideas, or activities that may violate the integrity of the polity's core values. The many unite to form the one.

The tension between republicanism and democracy revolves around the idea of equality. Republicans stress the superior political virtues of the governing class and doubt the capacity of others to participate in self-government. Democrats are more optimistic, either about the innate qualities of the currently excluded and/or about the potential of education to prepare them for full participation. They embrace the liberal concept of 'universal rights,' but expand their content (enlarging political, social, and economic rights) and the ranks of their possessors.

Two further stands of our constitutional culture—nationalism and imperialism—share the particularism of republican thought, yet are theoretically distinct from it and may or may not accompany it in practice. Republicanism looks inward; nationalism and imperialism look outward. Nationalism today is the agenda of groups seeking recognition for a would-be nation or of a weak nation seeking enhanced respect. Imperialism is an aggressive, expansive foreign agenda for a nation-state (whatever its form of government). These "isms" can be practiced by any polity, including liberal democracies; yet they are not in themselves universalistic principles. The typical nationalist does not support nations in general, nor, *pace* Hegel, does imperialism advocate empires in general.

The world's division into nation-states has become a simple background fact. Nationalism does, however, have a history. For all its ancient antecedents, many writers see modern nationalism as significantly different, precisely because modern nations are different in their internal constitutions. An ethnically diverse republic with an industrial economy and mass political participation, for example, will have a political culture—including citizens' sense of their shared identity, mutual commitments, and relations to the stranger—very different from that either of an ancient Greek city-state or of a medieval absolute monarchy.

By definition, republicans believe in self-government, but both "self" and "government" can be variously understood. The English Revolution was especially interesting in the way that it both replaced King with People as locus of sovereignty—the republican move—and placed unprecedented emphasis on the equal rights of individual citizens—the liberal move. Latent tensions between these two ideas were held in abeyance by a lusty pursuit of the "wealth of nations,"[5] in which commercial, military, and missionary impulses were mixed. It is clear that the American Revolution too was accompanied and motivated at once by liberal, republican, nationalist, and imperialist ideas—as well as, to a novel extent, democratic ones.[6] Talk of the rights of all men ran alongside talk of *e pluribus unum*, America's unique mission, and our "infant empire."

Madison in *The Federalist* (no. 10) contested the maxim of classical republican thought that self-government was possible only in small polities, because large ones could be held together only through autocratic methods. His major concern was the structure of government, not the membership of the polity. He sought here to persuade readers to accept a stronger Union, not to join or to conquer a larger one. The safety and stability of a large republic, not its geographic or demographic bounds, were his primary themes; yet safety did have an external aspect.

Madison's famous argument that size and diversity were not liabilities, but rather assets against the paramount threat of a leveling majoritarian tyranny, was a clever response to the parochial fears of many Anti-Federalists, whose principles were more often republican and communitarian than liberal and individualistic. He did not, however, fully explain how a single polity—even a federal one—could successfully pursue both kinds of principles at the same time. As *The Federalist* (no. 51) famously recognized, liberty required the "auxiliary precautions" of a strong, independent executive and judiciary. The executive would be a check on unwise legislation at home and act with the requisite "energy" overseas. Courts would help confine the other branches to their proper places.

Territorial, population, and suffrage expansion were swift, and they brought pressures not easily containable within the bounds of Madison's Constitution (see chapter 1). In the 1770s, there was one independence movement. By the 1790s there were two parties, representing (among other things) a split between liberal-republican ("Federalist") and liberal-democratic ("Republican") tendencies. By the Civil War, that split (or its offspring) nearly produced two separate nations; with the victory of the Northern democrats ("Republicans") over the Southern republicans ("Democrats") expansion resumed in new forms. Modern developments have brought further changes, to the point that today, many see only incoherence: a demographic, cultural, institutional, and doctrinal "mosaic" that Moses for one would never have tolerated. What sort of polity does our Constitution now constitute, ordain, and establish?

The expansionary-*cum*-exclusionary logics of nationalism, imperialism, and republicanism have always been deeply threatening to liberal principles of individualism, freedom, and equality. Part II explores each of these tensions in turn. (As part III will argue, the discourse of personal rights has its own logic, partly reactive and partly autonomous.)

Chapter 3 considers our conception of American peoplehood and the implications of nationalism for our other commitments. Peoplehood and nationalism go to the very identity and role of the individual and the claims the polity can rightfully make upon her. They always threaten to subordinate individual to polity—and to discriminate between insider and outsider—in ways that liberal democracy can accommodate with extreme difficulty, at best. The difficulty increases as one proceeds up the expansive scale: with the siege mentality of full-blown imperialism, *every* nonconformist or "alien" becomes a threat to "national security."

Chapter 4 focuses on the "auxiliary precautions" of our constitutional structure and explores the *institutional* implications of nationalism and imperialism. It examines imperialism's constitutional locus—the presidency—and the ways that threats to "national security" enhance presidential power, while expansive claims of presidential power compromise the rule of law, the separation of powers, and civil liberties.

Chapter 5 returns to the broader debate over the scope of governmental powers and the public agenda, a debate informed and partly driven by conflicting liberal and republican conceptions of peoplehood. Liberals and republicans both can claim to favor sharply limited government; this convergence played an important facilitating role in the ratification debates. Yet the limits they favor tend to be different, and each side has had occasion to support selected expansions of the public agenda. Liberals support personal autonomy, but also national action on behalf of the exploited, oppressed, and outcast. Republicans support local autonomy, but also national action on behalf of law and order, moral virtue, and family values. Both often have supported economic growth, nationalist and imperialist foreign policies, and the associated expansions of executive power.

Despite incessant controversy over specific initiatives, the overall trend has been a pronounced growth in the exercise of national governmental powers and a concomitant relaxation in our constitutional jurisprudence of such powers—their outer limits and their relative priorities. Chapter 5 revisits the question of how the Constitution can stand above the fray to mediate and constrain controversies over what government may and may not do, keeping personal liberties secure in the process.

⁖ Chapter 3 ⁖

Peoplehood and Nationalism

For us, then, a people is primarily a spiritual individual.

—Hegel

America is not anything if it consists of each of us. It is something only if it consists of all of us.

—Woodrow Wilson

Liberalism in one country is impossible.

—after Trotsky

The People of the United States

*T*he constitution begins, of course, with the phrase, "We, the People of the United States . . . ." As a grade-school child, I found no mystery in this self-referential expression. It seemed obvious who "the People" were—unlike, for example, the witch mentioned in "the Republic for which it stands." On more mature reflection, a host of problems appear. In what sense does the People exist? Who exactly are its members? How can we know when the People have spoken and verify what has been said?

Some of these questions, pertaining to issues of validating particular laws or governmental actions, have already been broached under the headings of "constitutional politics" and "representation." Let us concentrate here on the more diffuse concerns of the nature and boundaries of peoplehood.

From the standpoint of liberalism, it seems clear enough that a People does not exist in the same sense that an individual person does. We can use the term *people* to refer to a group of individuals standing across the room, and we can point them out one by one; but *the People of the United States*, for example, cannot be identified or located in this way.

The problem is not simply one of imprecise extension. Most groups (such as persons over six feet tall, persons who hate spinach, or liberal Republicans) are of imprecise extent; while there may be doubt as to who exactly is a member, we do not ordinarily infer from this that the group's very existence is problematic. Ordinarily, indeed, no such issue arises at all: if a group proves to be a useful construct in our category system, that is all the "reality" it requires. On the other hand, although there are clearly many people within the United States at this moment—we might even have an exact count—their physical presence does not logically entail the existence of "an American People."

Liberal thought regards the individual as the basic element of political and social life. Within this framework, it is obviously tempting to regard groups as "nothing but" aggregates of individuals. It would follow naturally that only individuals really possess interests, rights, and duties. "Group interests" would be nothing more than the interests of the group's members, and organizations would be nothing more than convenient devices for coordinating their actions. Such groups exist insofar as and so long as their members wish it. This way of thinking works well across a wide variety of contexts. It is especially helpful in combatting the exploitation and false consciousness that can occur when one subgroup urges another to sacrifice its "partial" interests for the sake of a larger, ostensibly common interest.

Yet reductive individualism seems to come up short in connection with the concepts of the People and the state. Here we encounter entities—if such they are—that, in the name of "superordinate values," demand sacrifice and threaten coercion not just in special cases but as their basic, normal functions.

The search for ways properly to draw and maintain the line between "public" interests and "private" rights has been the core problematic of constitutional thought. But now: if the very concept of 'the public' is a mere fiction, what sense does it make to define the problem in this way? Does this not merely mystify us as to the identity of actual or potential oppressors by concealing the struggle for control among factions, classes, or individuals, each trying to appropriate to itself the legitimacy that flows from speaking as or for "the People"?

Some would cheerfully agree that, while individual persons exist, the People is just a way of talking. But this concession entails potentially serious costs. One concern, much pressed by republican and communitarian critics of classical liberalism, is the difficulty that a thoroughly individualistic theory will have in justifying any form of authority not convincingly based on the actual consent of the individuals over whom it is exercised—consent which, in the real world, is not easily demonstrated to have occurred.

The founding generation, or some of them, were able to take part in the ratification of the Constitution—but not all of those eligible actually played an affirmative role. The rest of us, naturalized citizens excepted, receive no such opportunity. The effort to infer implied consent from our everyday actions or failures to act is, to say the least, a project fraught with difficulty. Indeed, philosophers are far from agreed on the proposition that rational, purely self-interested individuals, if offered the opportunity, *would* in fact consent to the sorts of authority actually exercised by the modern state. But, since people are not always and only self-interested, why not appeal to a conception of the public good?

If the classical account of the social contract is unrealistic as an account of how the state actually originated, it is equally unhelpful as to how the articulate, cultured individuals who supposedly agreed to form the state could themselves have originated. (If the People is a fiction, is it really so clear that the individual person too is not a fiction?) All these points lend support to those who insist that the People is a genuine, collective entity existing outside of and prior to the individuals of any particular generation. As such, it can possess interests of its own. It can act; it can speak to us. It can strive to propagate its form of life through time and space. So, where Hobbes and Locke have "natural" individuals enter into peoplehood by a collective act of will, Burke and Montesquieu—not to mention Hegel—see peoplehood as equally natural, as coeval with or even prior to individual personality.

A third approach might hold, perhaps along utilitarian lines, that even if the People is a reification, it is entirely proper to identify interests that are "public" in that they are very generally shared, and to privilege those goods of the greatest number over interests confined to smaller groups. If any reasonable member of the society ought to agree to such priorities, what harm is done by calling this policy the will of the people?

Perhaps the most prudent course is to bypass the metaphysical chicken-and-egg conundrum by recognizing that both persons and peoples are never fully formed, but always under construction. In both cases, we can establish identity and mark the moment of origination only by resorting to some legal formality. This *action* is itself the solution to the problem. Thus, Derrida has written cleverly about the authorship of documents such as the Declaration of Independence and the Constitution, suggesting that a People can come into existence by the very performative act of speaking: "We, the People of the United States . . . ."[1]

The original Constitution, significantly, does not elaborate on the identity of the People speaking here. The use of the plural pronoun and verb form tells us only that some unspecified group of individuals is meant. To be an individual person is logically a necessary condition. Equally obviously, it is not sufficient to make one a member of the particular people who are establishing this particular polity. Some persons belong to another people; some, conceivably, may belong to none at all. The Articles of Confederation distinguished between "citizens" and other "inhabitants"; the Constitution appears to accord special "privileges and immunities" to citizens, beyond the rights possessed by all persons.

The original Constitution refers only twice to "the People" as such: in the Preamble, where they (we?) ordain and establish the Constitution; and in Article I, section 2, where they are named electors of the House of Representatives. The role of the People, then, while limited, is a fundamental one, focused on collective political action. "Persons," in contrast, appear in a variety of contexts. They file lawsuits, are counted, taxed, and imported as slaves. They run for and hold office; but authority flows from the People to the office, not to its occupant. ("Citizens" also appear, but only as citizens of constituent states or of foreign states, not of the United States.)

The people (no longer capitalized) appear six more times in the Amendments. "The people" retain the rights to assemble and petition the government (First Amendment); to bear arms and serve in the militia (Second Amendment); to be secure in their persons, houses, papers, and effects (Fourth Amendment); and other, unenumerated rights (Ninth Amendment). They also retain all powers not granted to the U.S. government or to the states (Tenth Amendment), and (in the Seventeenth) acquire the power to elect senators. All of these provisions are directly aimed at reaffirming that authority ultimately comes from the people and ensuring that they retain the ability to engage in effective political action, including, the Second Amendment implies, revolutionary action. (Recall that the Fourth Amendment was prompted by memories of sweeping, politically motivated police actions directed by colonial authorities against the people generally.)

In short, while private persons enjoy rights and immunities against undue action by the state, that is, negative or Lockean liberties, the people have rights, privileges, and powers to participate in political life and to hold government accountable, that is, positive or Tocquevillian liberties. After "citizenship" is nationalized by the Fourteenth Amendment, the voting rights extended by the Fifteenth, Nineteenth, Twenty-fourth, and Twenty-sixth Amendments are vested in different classes of "citizens." In the modern equation, then, members of the people = citizens = (except for the very young, the incompetent, and felons) possessors of political rights.

The history of our discourse about the people has taken many turns, revolving around two distinct though related issues: who exactly *are* the people (the membership issue); and what is the political *role* of the people (the powers issue). In fact, it must be recognized that from the outset, the concept of 'the people' has been not just flawed or vague at the margins, but has been essentially contested—a tool of political struggle. If 'the people' were a totally inclusive, tolerant category, no doubt its use would have had a totally different history—if indeed it had any political use at all.

In the account of Daniel Rodgers,[2] "the people" figures primarily as a rhetorical device for expanding participation in public affairs, in opposition to elitism and unresponsive government (Power to the people!). At the same time, populist rhetoric also works to maintain unity among the ranks in the face of apathy or dissent (Will of the people!), while simultaneously if often tacitly maintaining barriers of exclusion (against nonpersons or inferior orders of persons, as well as aliens).

Appeals to the people were used in a new, majoritarian sense by the Jacksonian Democrats: "The cry of the people's sovereignty was the rhetorical tool with which the partisans of mid-nineteenth-century democracy broke apart the deference politics and much of the political machinery of Madison's and Adams's day and inaugurated a new era of popular politics."[3]

The new popular politics was not just marginally or accidentally in tension with the constitutionalism of the Founders. It explicitly rejected their distrust of majority rule and the cumbersome checks and balances that distrust had motivated, and it advocated a more active role for government together with new understandings of individual rights—especially the crucial right of property. Much of the struggle was carried out at the state level, where the people's favorite forum was the constitutional convention. This forum, conspicuously free of the established forms and standards that bound legislatures and courts, was in that sense inherently illiberal. Not only that, it was also potentially undemocratic!

[N]othing limited a convention from disfranchising a part of the people who had called it into existence—as the popular party did in New York in 1821 in disfranchising most of the state's black voters . . . . Nor . . . did anything but prudence require a constitutional convention to submit its work to a vote at all . . . .[4]

By the midpoint of the century, with new holders of the slogan (women, free blacks, and slaves) demanding to be counted among the people, with men talking more and more seriously of a house divided into two sectionally rival peoples, the words had begun to turn double-edged and dangerous. . . .[5]

The rhetoric of a sovereign people, possessed of unitary will, and the rhetoric of partisan political mobilization were two sides of the same phenomenon. . . .[6]

The issues on which the words turned sharp and double-edged were most dramatically rehearsed in Rhode Island in the early 1840s.[7]

Rhode Island's so-called Dorr War indeed brought several crucial issues in American political life and thought simultaneously to a head: cleavages of class and race, complaints about limited suffrage and unfair legislative apportionment, extraordinary obstacles to constitutional reform, and the proper roles of national versus state institutions, courts versus "political branches," and government versus the people in resolving such issues. The role of this controversy in the Supreme Court's development of the political questions doctrine was treated in chapter 1. For present purposes, the significant point is that the Dorrite attempt to exercise direct popular sovereignty outside the existing forums was decisively beaten. The movement collapsed because it received no effective support from any established institution or political party, inside or outside Rhode Island. Whatever their sympathies for Dorr's specific demands, all preferred "the rule of law" to revolutionary violence—even if that made the demands impossible to obtain. (In fact, most of Dorr's democratic demands were soon to be accepted by the Rhode Island establishment.)

In the years leading up to the Civil War the idea of popular sovereignty became even more divisive in its implications, as the struggle over slavery triggered more self-conscious arguments about the scope of the term *the people* and about who had authority to answer that question. The *Dred Scott* decision[8] and Stephen Douglas's alternative, localist theory of "popular sovereignty" played central roles in the breakup of the Democratic party, the election of Lincoln, and the Southern secession. The more Americans fought over who the people were and what they believed in, the less they felt themselves to be one People at all.

The Civil War and the Fourteenth Amendment resolved some but certainly not all of our membership dilemmas. Indeed, Southern whites' (apparent) failure to ratify the Reconstruction Amendments willingly suggests that the new, second Constitution really *did not* speak for the whole people, but was imposed by one faction upon another. (Note that *no* specific super-majoritarian amendment rule of the Article V type can prevent this.) Insofar as legitimate authority is based on consent, it would seem that the losing side in *any* constitutional struggle, peaceful or not, either is no longer fully part of the People or is a part of the People become in a fundamental sense unfree, unless and until they (freely) accede to the constitutional outcome. And note: *however* fair the procedures that were used, why *should* I, certainly on liberal principles, accept a Constitution that I voted against? Granted that Whoever-It-Is has spoken, who cares? Must I accept Rousseau's proto-fascist claim that the People's decision proves me to have been mistaken about my own desire? Or is it simply that I have, save emigration, no realistic alternative?

Nor are those who vote "no" the only ones whose consent is open to doubt. Some persons will not have been consulted—some, for instance, because they are not yet born. They may or may not have been adequately spoken *for*. Others will have chosen not to speak—perhaps unsure whether they truly belong, or what they truly want, or what the public interest truly is. Others will have voted "yes," but with insincere intent, or misled by inadequate information or mystifying ideology. Any number of flaws can impair the judgment of individuals, and, *a fortiori*, the will of the People.

Granting *arguendo* that "fair," agreed-on procedures should be binding even when they produce utterly repugnant results, of course there is no absolute guarantee against false consciousness, factual error, fraud, coercion, undue vagueness, or other possible flaws in the genesis of a purported agreement. Nor can we ever guarantee that all who might and should have been consulted have in fact participated. Even so, it behooves us to count our blessings when confronted with issues such as these; an imperfect Constitution may be far better than none at all. Compare, for example, the cases of peoples who are offered no constitutional choices: peoples under a tyrant's sway; peoples without a nation-state (for example, the Kurds); or states so irreducibly multinational (erstwhile Yugoslavia?) that there is no one People over whom or in whose name they can rule. In cases such as those the difficulty is not over what kind of Constitution to have, but over the impossibility of having one.

Perhaps, indeed, the only thing that makes it possible for a People to exist and to speak is its very will to do so: a general will that there be *some* polity, preceding any perfected notion of what polity there should be. It is, in other words, the determination to form "a more perfect Union" that provides the constitutive starting point.

As Levinson has argued, commitment to membership in an inchoate union calls for a substantial leap of "constitutional faith," for the object and scope of one's commitment are necessarily far from clear.[9] Still, it will not do to exaggerate the unusual character of such a leap. After all, Parfit[10] has argued forcefully that one's personal identity—to which most of us feel the deepest commitment—is itself factitious. This *reductio* reminds us that, though we and our world can be very fluid, we are able to decide, plan, and adhere to plans. If an individual (so-called) can do this, so, perhaps, can a collectivity; our Constitution purports to open up and instantiate this possibility.

Admittedly, any Constitution is at best an effort to crystallize a provisional—albeit well-considered—collective judgment. We can err not only as to what is in our long-term best interest, but even as to what we mean *right now*. Nevertheless, when we take the trouble to resort to our cumbersome procedures for constitution-making and ratification and bring an affirmative result to fruition, we have an at least presumptively valid performance.

Objection, your Honors! Remember Beard! Remember Nedelsky! Remember Guinier! What if this "Constitution" is an elitist fraud—a prettied-up form of oppression? Shall we just go on piously talking of "the People" for want of a better idea?

Folks, the court is getting truly bored with this pseudo-dialectical game. "Lay down the law. Trash the law. Ask what we'd do without it."—*Ad infinitum*. We know that law is possible because, with all its imperfections, it exists. It is true that, on the one hand, some laws are more fair than others. Ordinary fairness, like other "political" matters, is a matter of degree. *Constitutional* fairness, on the other hand, has to be a nominal variable—either a law is constitutional or it is not. And, in principle, we can distinguish the two kinds of unfairness—even if we can also disagree and err in making such distinctions. This is the same faculty of judgment, in Kantian terms, that enables us to recognize—to ourselves become—a person. If we could not distinguish political questions, even in principle, from matters *of* principle, then everything would be up for grabs. Neither the people nor ourselves could exist. Nor, needless to say, could we create any other "spiritual individual," such as "governments, government agencies, political subdivisions, partnerships, associations, corporations, legal representatives, mutual companies, joint-stock companies, trusts, unincorporated organizations, trustees, trustees in bankruptcy, or receivers."[11]

The world as we know it depends far more than we usually realize on distinctions like that between ordinary and constitutional politics. And we in turn depend more than we may realize not just on other persons but on the people to which we mutually belong. Without *constitutional* politics and constitutional priorities, we would have nothing better than votes to hang our public choices on. How many would opt for absolute majority rule, with everything up for grabs? Do we trust each other that much? (Note that one must take care in speaking of persons as "belonging" to a people, because of the expression's proprietary connotations. To acknowledge the role the society plays in constructing personhood is useful in directing our attention to the question of the state's responsibilities to foster personal flourishing. However, the state is wont to act as if *it* were the People; and the claim that individuals belong to the state is outright fascism.)

Then again, why should we trust the Founders—or the judges—more? Constitutionalism takes our law as self-made by the people, not as handed down from on high. We have made law, we are told, to guard us from the factious passions and interests that could tear our world apart. But then, why confine the safeguard to factious passions? Cannot the law—or even the Constitution itself, which, after all, singled out the slave trade for extra-special protection—be passion's child?

Against unjust ordinary law, we have fundamental rights, a bicameral legislature, an executive veto, and judicial review to protect us. The Constitution does not in terms announce that "Laws of Passion are null and void." Yet it bars several types of law—bills of attainder, ex post facto laws, laws impairing the obligation of contracts, and so on—that are null and void precisely because they are passionate. The Bill of Rights and other amendments can be read as augmenting and extending this principle. Thus Sunstein, for one, recognizes the invalidity of laws based merely on "naked preferences" as a fundamental, if implicit, principle of our constitutional jurisprudence.[12]

But what could protect us from injustice written into the Constitution itself? A Higher Law outside the Constitution? No: merely our power to remake it. And has this so-called People enough life to speak to us? Has it coherent projects, priorities, and principles? Has it, perhaps, unjust passions? *Can it even recognize itself?*

Nationalism and Liberalism

The questions of what the people have chosen collectively to *stand for*, what to leave open for decision through ordinary politics, and what to reserve for private individuals to decide, are dealt with at greater length in other chapters. The questions of primary concern here pertain to membership itself: who are the people; what is the character of the boundary between members and nonmembers; and what implications inhere in the way that this boundary is drawn and understood? In other words, what kind of nation is the United States of America, and how does its form of nationalism compare to others? (The quick transition from nationhood to nationalism is quite deliberate. What would a nonnationalistic nation look like? Would it simply have no army, like Costa Rica?)

Nationalism in general and American nationalism in particular have been compatible both with expansionary and exclusionary, with liberal and illiberal agendas. On the liberal side, some readers find that the Constitution's very reference to "People" instead of "nation" reveals deep commitments to principles of individualism and decentralized power. Some, such as Bowles and Gintis,[13] discern in our constitutional discourse a progressive (if slow and unsteady), inclusive, and rights-expansive trend, traceable through successive "accommodations" between democratic and capitalist forces. We may also remark upon the absence from the (modern) Constitution of exclusionary elements that have played major roles in national movements elsewhere: ascriptive characteristics such as biological kinship, shared language, religion, culture, and so on. Instead, American nationhood is founded on voluntary, political ties.

From a liberal standpoint, it seems quite clear why biological and, as it were, tribal criteria are utterly inappropriate for a modern society. To exclude people based on attributes beyond their control and irrelevant to their potential as citizens would be unfair. It would also be impossible to implement without shattering the fabric of a pluralistic society.

It would be foolish, however, to pretend that Americans are and always have been unambivalent liberals. Today, of course, the United States confers citizenship automatically—and nearly irrevocably—on all persons born within its territory, and, in a discretionary manner, on law-abiding immigrants who swear loyalty to the Constitution. Yet historically, doubts and conflicts have repeatedly arisen with regard to acceptance of "discrete and insular minorities." Questions of full citizenship are still unresolved with regard to residents of Puerto Rico and even, some would say, the District of Columbia. Those with reservations about extending membership in a given case often have strong, authentically American traditions on their side. For example, today's communitarians, drawing upon the republican tradition, are uncomfortable with some aspects of our diverse and tolerant scene. They believe that nationhood rests on shared values as well as on political institutions, and are more supportive of measures such as strict controls on immigration from the third world, organized prayer in schools, or making English the official language.

While membership questions are, politically speaking, entirely up to the existing members to decide, it is also true that the members ought to decide them in accord with the basic principles to which they are committed. The day is long gone when, for example, residents of Chinese extraction could be barred from applying for citizenship. Denial of political membership may be less grave than denial of personhood itself (see chapter 6), but it is still a serious deprivation. Moreover, a community that excludes others on arbitrary or unworthy grounds also does itself significant injury, losing both moral integrity and opportunities for growth. Growth, in many dimensions, has been a crucial theme in our history.

As many writers have pointed out, the "nation" is neither a fixed nor an ancient concept; its modern meanings are variously traced back two to four hundred years. The most common early usages were not political, but referred to one's locality of birth (whether or not self-governing) or, sometimes, to organized groups of workers or students.

Eric Hobsbawm's historical study of nationalism[14] emphasizes the many, very different forms that the concepts of 'nation' and 'nationalism' have taken. A central focus of his approach is the contrast between (1) the liberal nationalisms of 1780 through 1870, which were reformist/revolutionary and inclusive in spirit and stressed the political voluntarism of popular sovereignty as a unifying principle, and (2) the defensive/conservative, separatist, often intolerant and extremist nationalisms that have become so visible more recently (especially in Europe), stressing homogeneous ethnicity, language, and/or religious background as defining the nation.[15]

Hobsbawm goes so far as to suggest that for liberal nationalism, nationhood is but a stepping-stone on the path to world unity—a path adumbrated both by liberal-individualist political ideals and by a free-market economic theory in which persons and firms, not nation-states, are the key decision makers and creators of wealth. He offers the United States as a leading exemplar of liberal nationalism: a polity defined by its principles, not by ties of blood or language, that anyone is and has always been free to join.[16]

Hobsbawm makes no effort to demonstrate, however, that the "liberal" nation-state system of midnineteenth century Europe actually *had* a supranational unifying dynamic. Indeed, it is arguable that, to the extent that such a dynamic can be discerned in Metternich's world, it was supplied not so much by bourgeois liberal-individualist principles as by monarchical-aristocratic social forces. The peaceable "expansiveness" of liberal nationalism within Europe, moreover, was juxtaposed with a wave of overseas colonial conquests, in which the benefits of freedom and democracy would (with all deliberate speed) be made available to the suffering, backward peoples of the world.

Nor does Hobsbawm acknowledge clearly enough that the "freedom to join" the American polity was, until recently, limited by law to those of proper racial background. Instead, he takes the line that the process of democratization everywhere posed new challenges for liberal nationalism, since the newly enfranchised classes had different perspectives and loyalties from the established elites.

The argument here appears to be the familiar one that petit-bourgeois, worker, and peasant citizens are less tolerant, less liberal minded than their betters, and that their insecurities drive nationalist discourse in new directions. They tend to respond favorably to chauvinistic ethnic, linguistic, and religious appeals, and, in the case of minorities, may even enlist in separatist national movements that threaten the state's integrity.[17] While there may indeed be important variances in tolerance according to measures of class and education, Hobsbawm of course cannot demonstrate (and does not claim) that democratization is responsible for slavery, racism, or imperialism.

According to Benedict Anderson,[18] modern political nationalism is an American (in the larger, hemispheric sense) invention, whereby local colonial elites transformed administrative subdivisions of the Spanish and British (and other) empires into independent republics.

Out of the American welter came these imagined realities: nation-states, republican institutions, common citizenships, pop-

ular sovereignty, national flags and anthems, etc., and the liq-
uidation of their conceptual opposites: dynastic empires,
monarchical institutions, absolutisms, subjecthoods, inherited
nobilities, serfdoms, ghettoes, and so forth.[19]

Anderson stresses the role of local writers and printers in the
growth of the new "imagined communities," which were from the
outset "conceived in language, not in blood."[20] The literate, empowered citizens of the new nation-states had new attitudes toward
their rulers. In particular, government's function was not to pursue
its own interest, nor even that of the nation. Though social scientists and historians today speak easily of "the national interest,"
"for most ordinary people of whatever class the whole point of the
nation is that it is interestless. Just for that reason, it can ask for
sacrifices."[21]

Anderson's point here seems to be the Lockean one that the people are prior to the nation or, in other words, the civil society is
prior to the state. Indeed, neither the Declaration of Independence
nor the Constitution uses the term nation to describe the United
States. The Declaration speaks only of the People, while the Constitution refers several times to the Union which the People are resolved to establish. Yet insofar as the nation can legitimately ask
for sacrifices, one might hold that it does, precisely to that extent,
have interests—no matter how the demand is rationalized.

Liah Greenfield[22] traces the idea of a nation from a community of
blood or of opinion to a unique, sovereign people. While there are
several types of nation and of nationalism, all, Greenfield holds,
share a common core function: "Nationality elevated every member
of the community which it made sovereign. It guaranteed status.
National identity is, fundamentally, a matter of dignity. It gives
people reasons to be proud."[23]

Greenfield's typology includes three forms of nationalism:
civic/individualist-libertarian, civic/collectivist-authoritarian, and
ethnic/collectivist-authoritarian.[24] The differences, of course, are
profoundly significant—even ominous. Collectivist and ethnic nationalism have superior payoffs in status; they allow one to become
part of a whole far greater than oneself.[25]

This concern, however, has limited relevance to the American
case. American nationalism grew out of the British liberal tradition; the new nation was united by mutual consent, not by force.
That is, it was a *constitutional* polity. As Shaftesbury wrote in 1790,
"Absolute Power annuls *the publick*; and where there is no *publick*,
or *constitution*, there is in reality no *mother*-Country, or Nation."[26]

American nationalism diverged significantly from its British forebear, however. In place of a fascination with traditional ways, Americans substituted a love of equal liberty and self-government. The revolution came about because Americans "were better English than the English."[27] Indeed, "the logical consummation of the inherent tendencies of English nationalism, its fulfillment, absurd as it sounds, was the absolute sovereignty, self-government, or independence of every individual; in other words, complete atomization and political anarchy."[28]

In this environment, collectivism could make no headway. Even the word *nation* itself was seldom used, compared to *people*. Moreover, "It is indeed a singular feature of the political language of revolutionary America that the word "people" in it is used, as a rule, in the plural."[29]

Another key feature of American national identity was its universalism. The cherished traditional rights of Englishmen now became, in Paine's words, "laws of nature and of nature's god,"[30] open in principle to all who would claim them.

This universalistic ideology supports Greenfield's claim that nationalism, as such, is not inherently particularistic.[31] Yet it is also entirely consistent with claims of American exceptionalism vis-à-vis the outside world. Indeed, how could there be a nationalism that did not somehow distinguish one's nation from all other nations?

Greenfield recognizes three political factors (she does not focus on economic and social changes) that posed major threats to the unity and stability of the new nation. The first factor, federalism, she identifies as a product of the libertarian principle itself—

> the inherent and, in the framework of American nationalism, legitimate secessionist impulse which was confounded with the view, never seriously challenged, that the right of self-government was vested in the individual states. . . .[32]

> But at the same time the Constitution bound the states together in the shared loyalty to itself and thus by default created a unified inclusive polity—a nation in the American sense. Reverence for the Constitution, as earlier love of liberty, became the core of the American national identity.[33]

The second disturbing factor, democratization, was also inherent in the original scheme, insofar as the early restrictions of political rights along lines of class, race, and gender proved indefensible. Ironically, the Jacksonian preference for decentralized government was undermined by the new demands for government action that their own democratic movement unleashed.[34] In the long run, the traditional understanding of the proper scope and role of government, especially with regard to economic issues, was abandoned.

What most decisively undid the uneasy federal compromise, however, was the third divisive issue: slavery. Greenfield seems to regard this dimension of conflict as coincidental rather than inevitable, for she views slavery as an aberration—a lapse from the egalitarianism of the liberal creed.

> [O]ne could not *champion* slavery and uphold the ideal of equality in liberty at the same time. This was not simply inconsistent, this was schizophrenic. . . . It would be wrong to see the secession as in any way a result of Southern nationalism (namely the result of a specific Southern identity, loyalty, and consciousness). Southern nationalism and secession were both responses to the unbearable inconsistency between American national ideals and slavery.[35]

The defense of slavery, Greenfield holds, prompted novel ideological departures.

> Presenting slavery as a social ideal did not at all imply that Southern ideologists turned enemies of liberty. On the contrary, with the exception of slavery, nothing was so dear to their heart. . . .[36]
>
> [I]n the emergent Southern consciousness the group and rights of the group as such were consistently substituted for the individual and the rights of the individual. This was the fundamental alteration wrought in the American ideology, which underpinned other alterations. Racism was only a variety of collectivism, and authoritarianism was made possible only by it.[37]

Greenfield errs here in two respects. First, she does not fully appreciate the duality of the original American national impulse. Where the liberal strand—which she emphasizes—stressed individual autonomy and social pluralism, the republican strand—which she relegates to the margin—always stressed the importance of homogeneous local communities as centers of self-government. The exclusion of strangers, and especially racial or religious minorities, was not a lapse, but was (for many) an integral part of the original vision, closely bound up with Anti-Federalist and republican distrust of central authority.

Second, Greenfield underestimates the tensions inherent within *any* form of "civic/liberal-individualist nationalism." Like slavery, she apparently regards the modern problems of intolerant mass conformism, chauvinist militarism, and the national-security state, as well as ethnic separatism, as lapses from the mainstream tradition:

> There appeared a tendency to reify the nation and see it as a living organism or a collective—and higher—individuality. . . . This organic theory . . . , novel in America, was opposed to the traditional constitutional view. . . . [T]he nation represented an "Idea," but the "Idea" of the American nation was individual freedom.[38]

In her recent book, *Liberal Nationalism*,[39] Yael Tamir argues forcefully that liberalism and nationalism, if properly understood, are mutually compatible. Liberalism, she holds, can and should incorporate a right of all individuals to adhere to and preserve the culture of their choice; nationalism can and should incorporate a respect and tolerance for the right of members of other nations to do likewise.

Tamir's observations on the importance of national attachments and the cultural particularity both of personal and of national identities as we know them, and her associated critique of the versions of liberalism that insist on neutrality among conceptions of the good, are well taken. Yet, as she recognizes, most of today's so-called nation-states are actually multinational, and "one nation, one state" is not a realistic vision for the world of the future. Thus, "Alienation rather than a deprivation of rights is to be acknowledged as the main problem affecting members of national minorities. . . . This tension is endogenous to any liberal national entity and cannot be resolved."[40]

Instead of secession, Tamir's hopes for peace and justice among nations focus on the wealth of overlapping, crosscutting affiliations within and across national boundaries; on the increasing importance of supranational organizations; on the combination of two distinct rights recognized by liberal nationalism—the right of self-rule (to participate in the politics of one's nation-state) and that of self-determination (to have a secure public space for the cultural life of one's not necessarily coterminous nation); and on poorly specified "consociational" constitutional arrangements.

However constructive these forces, ideas, and arrangements sometimes can be, the remaining practical and theoretical problems are formidable. In particular, the effort to preserve and to protect one's culture is not infrequently felt to require interference with that of others. Moreover, some cultures are themselves frankly hostile to liberal values. Tamir does not tell us how her version of liberal nationalism would assess such policies, aimed at preservation of the national culture, as Quebec's law requiring all businesses to post signs exclusively in French, or France's quota for foreign songs on the radio. Nor does she discuss American laws, regulating a variety of "offensive" utterances and behaviors, which are also defended in terms of shared community values. Arguably such policies are anathema to liberalism, yet crucial to cultural nationalism.

Conclusion

On the whole, the distinctiveness of the "liberal" form of nationalism—including the American case—remains to be established. As Appleby puts it in her study of liberalism and republicanism, "[N]ineteenth century evolutionary theories placing Anglo-Saxon culture in the forefront of evolving civilizations fused easily with the Hegelian idea of the nation as the highest expression of civilization . . . ."[41]

However distinctive American nationalism might be on the political level, moreover, none of the writers discussed here adequately explores the economic dimensions of nationalism.[42] Hobsbawm notes capitalism's tendency to penetrate and weaken national boundaries, creating a progressively integrated world economy. Yet he overlooks the ways in which those same boundaries help firms to avoid or to minimize tax and regulatory burdens, to protect them against foreign competition, and to maintain divisions among workers in different nations.

Clearly, the nation-state must deal with capital both as input (a vital source of revenue, but a powerful threat to its own autonomy) and as output (the wealth of the nation and public satisfaction with the economy as crucial objects of its own policies). These complex and ambivalent relationships have major effects on the workings of modern law and politics and can both blur and exacerbate the differences between more and less liberal systems.[43] Thus, capitalism played crucial roles in the rise both of the New Deal regulatory aspect and of the cold war national security aspect of the current regime.

Hobsbawm, Anderson, and Greenfield all emphasize the progressive elements in American nationalism and treat its shortcomings as incidental. Certainly a contrary case can be made, that *any* nation plagued by internal divisions and/or by external threats—and especially one driven by an expansionist agenda—will have difficulty adhering consistently to liberal-constitutionalist norms. Such problems are apt to be frequent if not constant, for the very recognition of a "we" already necessarily constitutes a "they," and the distinction is hardly an incidental one. Inevitable contact with the "other" will bring calls to reinforce or rework the drawing of lines. Absorption of new members by democratization, immigration, or conquest will bring calls for distinction between core or first-class members and others.

The record of governmental abuses aimed at strangers and dissidents (for example, the treatment of native Americans and African slaves, the Federalists' Alien and Sedition laws; the Jacksonian suppression of Dorr's Rebellion; Lincoln's wartime violations of civil liberties; and the repression of labor, civil rights, and leftist movements in this century—not to mention acts of war overseas) is too full to dismiss as isolated aberrations. It testifies to the "sacrifices" that can be demanded at any time in the name of higher values or "compelling interests" of the nation, such as maintaining or expanding the Union, its tranquility, defence, and the general welfare.

The ultimate question is whether or how far liberalism and nationalism are really compatible at all. By leaving the nation's membership wholly unspecified, the Constitution deferred, largely to the processes of "ordinary politics," some of the gravest and most delicate questions a polity must face. How far our civic culture, disciplined by constitutional amendments and occasional judicial interventions, has provided appropriately liberal solutions is of course debatable, though it would be hard to argue that our solutions have been prompt, decisive, or always principled. However, if the Constitution *had* defined the People of the United States, it might well have done so in ways that excluded a great many of today's loyal and productive citizens.

Some insist that liberalism cannot be a viable doctrine or practice unless elaborated within a context that tells us what we agree on and what differences we are asked to tolerate. It is obvious that encountering difference can, in some situations, lead to most illiberal—or simply untenable—outcomes. The Framers may have contemplated admitting Canadians (even Francophones) to the Union; in 1812, many did so. Native Americans and Hispanics, Asians, and

Africans have proved more difficult to absorb. It is hard to see what constitutional language could have greatly facilitated the resolution of the cultural, social, and economic tensions involved.

Certainly, though, constitutional or legal line drawing does not make the stranger disappear. The urgent lesson of history is that, so long as it is felt that there are dangerous outsiders both beyond and within the nation's boundaries, liberty, inclusiveness, and tolerance will have their limits. In that sense liberal constitutionalism in a multinational world is, if not impossible, always fundamentally at risk. *Pace* Madison, liberalism within one country is more tested, and thus more at risk, the larger and the more diverse the country grows.

Chapter 4

The Myth of
Presidential Prerogative

Perhaps it is a universal truth that the loss of liberty at
home is to be charged to provisions against danger, real
or pretended, from abroad.

—James Madison

When the President does it, that means it can't be illegal.

—Richard Nixon

*T*he focus of this chapter is the impact of nationalism and imperialism on the powers of the presidency and the implications of
that impact for the rule of law, the separation of powers, and the liberties guaranteed by the Bill of Rights. Its theses are two: that our
constitutional thought and practice have failed to deal adequately
with these issues and that the doctrine of presidential prerogative,
or inherent powers, is flatly incompatible with the Constitution's
core principles.

In an earlier study I carefully reviewed the history of presidential
national security powers from the constitutional convention through

---

An earlier version of this chapter was published in Morton Halperin and Daniel
Hoffman, eds., *Freedom vs. National Security* (New York: Chelsea House, 1977).

the presidencies of Washington and Adams.[1] I concluded that, already by 1800, it was clear that international conflict and sharp domestic debate over foreign policy pose severe challenges to the integrity of constitutional controls over executive action. To a dangerous extent, the rule of law and civil liberties were dependent on the personal qualities of presidents and their chief advisors, rather than on stable, structural safeguards. If this was true in the Federalist era, it is true *a fortiori* in the nuclear age of *pax Americana*, "bipartisan foreign policy," secret bombing of Cambodia, and Iran-Contragate.

There is no need here to retrace the whole history of the presidency or of American foreign policy. It suffices, I think, to observe that, whereas the legislature was established to consider and enact general policy guidelines, the executive's functions were to implement those policies and respond to unexpected developments—especially emergencies. Anyone entrusted with the latter responsibilities may be tempted at times to act outside or even against the law, whether in the service of ultimate national values, factional agendas, and/or personal self-interest.

The Constitution purports to provide powerful checks against abuses, but the record shows that it is generally easier for presidents, endowed with the advantages of "vigor, secrecy, and despatch," to stretch their powers than it is for others to confine or reduce them. Congress, in particular, is inhibited from doing so by several factors. The more parochial experience and perspective of individual members, along with executive control of information, give rise to doubts as to its relative institutional competence. Many members have ties of party loyalty to the president and/or ambitions to someday hold that office, which deter them from challenging presidential action or weakening the powers of the office. Finally, vigorous action overseas is most often highly popular with constituents. The courts, meanwhile, are inhibited by the concerns associated with the political questions doctrine.

The expansive tendencies inherent in our nation since its founding have already been noted. The type of expansion most pertinent here is imperialism: the projection of influence beyond national boundaries, sometimes to the point of outright territorial annexation. No mandate for imperialism or "manifest destiny" is spelled out in the Constitution. Indeed, as late as 1857 Chief Justice Taney could still doubt whether the power to acquire new territories was textually granted.[2] Yet there was no gainsaying the Louisiana Purchase, the Mexican War, or the internal stresses these had brought.

The pursuit of happiness, and especially of property, had brought expansion. Expansion may have avoided or deferred some political conflicts, but it also engendered others—most conspicuously, that over the slave or free status of new territories and states. A number of other issues played out at the constitutional level as well, especially issues pertaining to federalism and the separation of powers. In fact, repeated episodes of war and severe domestic strife have fueled a long-run trend toward a system that approaches elective monarchy. Though facilitated by secrecy, stretches of executive power have often had strong congressional, judicial, and/or public support.

Nevertheless, they have not gone unnoticed or unopposed. Over the course of our history, competing views on the extent of presidential powers have repeatedly surfaced and clashed. In simplified terms, two radically different theories are at stake.

The "rule of law" theory stresses the constitutional principles of limited government, separation of powers, checks and balances, and the accountability of government to the people, and applies these principles across the board. Accordingly, this theory holds, in rough outline, that

- the President's foreign policy and national defense powers are not different in source and nature from his other powers;
- presidential powers are limited to those granted by the Constitution or delegated to the president by Congress;
- emergency does not create new powers, but only a new context for the exercise of existing powers;
- presidential action, even when properly authorized, is subject to the powers reserved by other branches of government;
- presidential action, even when properly authorized, is subject to the constraints imposed by the Bill of Rights;
- courts can adjudicate issues arising in these domains just as they review any other issues.

The "prerogative" theory holds that, if the Constitution is not to become a suicide pact, legal niceties must often yield to the exigencies of national interest, which the president is uniquely positioned to determine and address. Accordingly, this theory argues that

- the President has sweeping, unwritten powers stemming from the nation's inherent need for "vigor, secrecy, and despatch" in the conduct of defense and foreign policy;
- these powers increase substantially in times of war or other perceived emergency;
- when the President exercises these powers he does not need congressional authorization;

- Congress cannot constitutionally enact limits on the exercise of these powers;
- courts cannot question or limit such presidential actions and must issue supportive orders when asked to do so.

My reading of the Constitution and the historical materials associated with its framing shows clearly that the Framers proceeded from the rule of law perspective. The fear of unlimited governmental power was central to that perspective, and the key to limiting that power was subjecting it to the restraints of a written Constitution. Whatever disagreements or unresolved questions there may have been about the precise extent of specific powers and limitations, these were and are to be resolved within the framework of the Constitution and its fair interpretation—not by appeals to extraconstitutional, prerogative powers of the government. The same premise guided virtually all of the relevant debates and decisions, whether executive, legislative, or judicial, of our nation's first century. Only recently have the dual claims that emergency knows no law and that emergency is our chronic condition begun to gain a certain currency.[3]

The Supreme Court's contribution to the debate between these theories does not amount to a comprehensive, systematic, and consistent body of law. Its decisions have been sporadic, narrow, and heavily flavored by the idiosyncrasies of each particular fact situation, with all its sensitive political overtones—not to mention the idiosyncrasies of individual justices. While most of the decisions pay explicit homage to the rule of law axioms, certain pronouncements, chiefly in time of grave emergency—and especially *dicta* (that is, statements of little or no precedential value because not strictly needed to decide the case at hand)—have veered sharply toward the prerogative side. Despite the gaps and ambiguities in the caselaw, though, we can see that the judicial approach to cases involving the national security powers has been shaped by four primary concerns: (1) text, (2) context, (3) separation of powers, and (4) personal rights.

First, the textual concern refers to the nature and scope of the power asserted, and the ease with which that power can fairly be inferred from the text of the constitution, statutes, or judicial precedents.

Theorists like to distinguish between powers allegedly "implied" by a specific legal text and powers allegedly "inherent" in the fact of national sovereignty or the nature of the executive function. Some hold that while implied powers must exist if constitutional government is to be viable, inherent (unenumerated) powers have no place in such a governmental system. One may question the clarity and usefulness of the distinction, in light of the broad interpretations to which certain constitutional provisions are subject. For example, anything said to be "inherent" in the executive function could equally well be said to be "implied" by the clause designating the president as chief executive. Both approaches can appeal to the impossibility of anticipating and providing in advance for every contingency; both entail very similar if not identical dangers. As Madison put it, "[P]owers inherent, implied, or expedient, are obviously the creatures of ambition; because the care expended in defining powers would otherwise have been superfluous."[4]

At any rate, the record shows that advocates for the executive branch prefer to rely upon explicit grants of authority. Implicit grants are second best, and "inherent" powers are least often appealed to. The judicial discomfort with claims of inherent power is even more striking: courts clearly prefer to decide cases on other, textual grounds, referring to inherent powers at most only in *dicta* or in passing. The reason, of course, is that judicial expertise and legitimacy are much greater when, in John Marshall's words, "it is a Constitution we are expounding."[5] However much judges may differ over the norm of "strict construction," all must find it awkward to act judicially when there is *no* text to construe.

Courts are also more apt to accept claims that comport with the "plain meaning" or "fair implications" of the relevant text than those that do not. Yet whether a particular claim passes this test is often a difficult and divisive question. On the Madisonian view, the burden of persuasion in such cases ought to lie upon the government. However, it is not today a canon of constitutional law that all grants of power are to be given the narrowest plausible reading. As we shall see, in the national security realm the contrary approach has often prevailed; the desideratum of effective government has been more salient than that of limited government.

As early as *McCulloch v. Maryland* (1819),[6] the Supreme Court held that the implied powers of Congress should be generously construed, because Congress is expressly empowered to do everything "necessary and proper" to accomplish its enumerated powers. Since the executive and judicial branches have no equivalent textual mandate, the initial tendency was to hold them quite closely to the powers expressly granted by the Constitution or delegated by congressional statute. Over the years the pressures of war and other emergencies, as well as the ambitions cited by Madison, have prompted repeated claims for the expansion of executive power via looser interpretation of the legal texts. Given the ambiguity inherent in language and the high priority generally placed on national security concerns, it is not surprising that some such claims have met with success.

In principle, the expanded authority desired by the executive could always have been obtained by constitutional amendment, and often simply by statute. In practice, of course, this was not always a politically realistic option. But even where feasible, it is generally costly in terms of the political effort required, and usually painfully time-consuming as well. Thus, it is tempting to act immediately, relying for subsequent justification upon claims of implied or inherent power.

Second, the contextual concern refers to the urgency of need, in the actual context, for the power asserted, and the apparent costs to the nation of a decision adverse to the government.

A decision to proceed without seeking express authority can often be backed up by pointing to the urgency of the situation and the risks attendant upon delay. When the Constitution was framed, legislative sessions were brief and communications slow. Crises were apt to arise during congressional recess, and the Framers provided that on such "extraordinary occasions," the president "may"— not "shall"—convene them into emergency session.[7] The implied presidential power to identify an emergency and to respond unilaterally, if the situation in his judgment requires it, meets an important need. Unfortunately, it also creates the opportunity and temptation to treat any given problem as an emergency, thus circumventing the normal constitutional separation of powers.

Judicial review does not seem a particularly promising remedy for such abuses. For example, in the 1827 case of *Martin v. Mott*,[8] the Supreme Court showed a disposition to accord the greatest deference to presidential determinations that an emergency exists. In the 1863 *Prize Cases*,[9] it accepted subsequent congressional approval as an adequate substitute for a prior declaration of war, even though President Lincoln had prosecuted the Civil War unilaterally for many months, without calling Congress into special session. In such cases courts are vulnerable to charges of partisan bias, hard-pressed to demonstrate special judicial expertise, and easily moved by "the potentiality of embarrassment from multifarious pronouncements by various departments on one question."[10] Yet there have been notable exceptions to this pattern of judicial deference.

Third, the separation of powers concern refers to the extent to which the claim of power is in derogation of the powers of other departments of the government.

A claim of implied power which is essential to the effectiveness of the body claiming it can sometimes be accepted with minimum impact on the constitutional system as a whole. Thus, the judicial and congressional contempt powers and the investigative powers of Congress are recognized, though they are not spelled out in the Constitution.

A claim of implied power concurrent with the acknowledged power of another branch is more disruptive; it is suspect to the extent that it can be viewed as a usurpation of the other branch's power or an invasion of its autonomy. Nevertheless, such power sharing is sometimes held to have a structural if not a textual constitutional basis, especially in the areas of defense and foreign policy. Moreover, it is conceivable that Congress could delegate some of its power to the executive branch, much as the president could delegate his power to subordinate officials. The substantive and procedural limits on such delegation are an important area of inquiry, since, to the extent that delegation is made easy, the power may become exclusive in substance while remaining concurrent in form.

Finally, a claim of implied, exclusive power which denies significant powers to other branches is the most suspect of all. An example is executive privilege—the claimed power of the president to withhold information needed by other branches to perform their legitimate functions. Even this power has been recognized by the Supreme Court to a limited extent.

Fourth, the Bill of Rights concern refers to the impact on individual rights of a proposed extension of governmental power.

In principle the Bill of Rights is a restraint upon actions taken in the name of national security, just as upon any other governmental action. The usual judicial approach is to "balance" the public interests involved against the personal rights affected by the action. In the national security realm, two peculiarities appear.

The first is a reluctance to deal directly with conflicts of this type. As early as *Marbury v. Madison* (1803), the Supreme Court asserted in *dicta* that foreign policy decisions "respect the nation, not individual rights," and hence are political decisions, immune to judicial review.[11] The difficulty is that "pertaining to or motivated by foreign policy concerns" and "affecting individual rights" are not mutually exclusive categories. While a national security concern does not necessarily insulate a case from judicial review, on a few occasions the Court has simply refused to take litigants' Bill of Rights issues seriously and thus upheld the government's action without even a perfunctory exercise of the traditional balancing.[12] More often, it has found another basis for invalidating the government's action (for example, absence of statutory authority) and thus avoided the Bill of Rights issue.[13]

The second peculiarity of national security cases is that when balancing does occur, courts are profoundly affected by the gravity—indeed the mystique—of the alleged governmental interest involved. Although foreign and defense policies or even acts of war may sometimes serve quite narrow interests, such as bringing jobs to constituents of "the Senator from Boeing," rescuing a few hostages, or securing the rights of U.S. investors in a "banana republic," national security qualifies by definition as a public interest of the most "compelling" sort, and courts seldom feel free to question the basis for the assertion that national security is at stake. Often the facts are classified; their assessment, at any rate, calls for "political" and not "judicial" expertise.

A striking example is *New York Times Co. v. United States*,[14] in which the solicitor general assured the Supreme Court that the nation would suffer grave harm if publication of the Pentagon Papers continued. Although the government did not prevail, a majority of the justices were willing to accept this assurance without seeing the papers in question. Years later the former solicitor general revealed that, at that point, he himself had had very little time to study the papers and was acting on White House instructions. The grave threat to national security he had portrayed to the Court was, to say the least, vastly exaggerated; no visible harm had attended the papers' publication.[15]

That the requested injunction was nevertheless denied reflects the special regard shown by the Court in this era for the "fundamental" rights of free speech and press—especially in the face of threatened "prior restraints." Other rights, such as trial by jury or property rights, have been more favored in other times or contexts. Such priorities, though they can be defended in principle, are subject to historical change.

Even more ephemeral are judicial reactions to the status of the private litigant (citizen or alien, pillar of the community or despised political dissident) and the official litigant (popular or disgraced, reelection candidate or lame duck). These "political" aspects of a case are not supposed to count, but there is reason to believe that they sometimes do. In contrast to these mutable factors, the privileged status of the national security interest appears to be almost a given—even in an age where "crisis" has become a routine phenomenon.

With these background concerns in mind, we can summarize the relevant Supreme Court decisions on the allocation of governmental powers in terms of four doctrinal questions:

1. What can the president do absent congressional authorization?
2. To what degree can Congress regulate or limit the actions of the president?
3. Which of its powers can Congress delegate, on what terms, and by what methods?
4. What is the role of the courts in assessing the constitutionality of presidential and congressional acts?

The President Acting Alone

The Constitution says surprisingly little about the powers of the president with regard to national security affairs. Article II initially vests in him "the executive power"; this can be read either as a summary of the specific powers that follow or alternatively as an independent grant of additional, unspecified powers. It charges him to "take care that the laws be faithfully executed." Beyond this, the only pertinent provisions are these:

> The President shall be Commander in Chief of the Army and Navy of the United States, and of the militia of the several States, when called into the actual service of the United States. . . .

> He shall have power, by and with the advice and consent of the Senate, to make treaties, provided two-thirds of the Senators present concur; and he shall nominate, and by and with the advice and consent of the Senate, shall appoint ambassadors . . . .

> [H]e shall receive ambassadors and other public ministers.[16]

The Supreme Court has accepted the more generous interpretation of the executive power clause, and over the years the presidency has established itself as active military leader and sole representative of the nation in foreign affairs, with substantial powers to act on its own, particularly in wartime.

Two seminal cases expanding presidential power beyond the specific grants of the Constitution and laws are *In re Neagle*[17] and *In re Debs*.[18] Notably, the decisions also augmented the security and power of the judicial branch itself.

In 1890, *Neagle* held that the president had power to assign a U.S. marshal to protect a Supreme Court justice whose life had been threatened. Though beyond the scope of his express statutory duties, the Court held that the marshal was acting under "a law of the United States" in that he was performing a duty fairly inferrable from the Constitution. The president's unwritten powers extend to providing "all the protection implied by the nature of the government under the Constitution," such as protecting the mails and the national forests against robbery or suing those who defraud the United States. (Query: What further protections, and for whom, are "implied by the nature of government" under the expanded New Deal dispensation?)

In 1895, *Debs* extended the reasoning in *Neagle* still further. Here the president intervened in an Illinois labor dispute, in the face of vehement protests by the governor. Ignoring applicable federal criminal laws, he sought an antistrike injunction for which there was no explicit statutory basis. The Court held that the federal laws preempted the governor's authority and that the president's action, avowedly to protect interstate commerce, was in aid of congressional policy. (The vitality of *Debs* after the *Steel Seizure Case*, discussed below, is doubtful.)

More in point are cases dealing directly with the realm of foreign affairs. Early presidents gained much power in this area through direct give and take with Congress.[19] More recently, courts have acknowledged unilateral presidential powers to recognize foreign governments, employ open or secret overseas agents, gather and control information, terminate treaties, and negotiate "executive agreements." While these developments have large implications for the integrity of the constitutional allocation of powers, the most significant judicial decisions occurred in cases where the rights of private parties were allegedly affected. Two such cases arose from the executive agreements signed by Franklin D. Roosevelt in connection with his diplomatic recognition of the Soviet Union.

In *United States v. Belmont*[20] and *United States v. Pink*,[21] the issue was whether the agreements, not ratified by the Senate, took precedence over state laws in determining the ownership of Russian assets held in American banks. The Supreme Court held that executive agreements were binding and took precedence over state laws, just as a treaty would. Yet the Court acknowledged that such agreements, like laws and treaties, are limited by the constitutional rights of individuals, and it emphasized that in its view no constitutional rights of Americans were at stake.

Though military and foreign policy matters are often lumped together today under the "national security" rubric, the Framers dealt with them separately. The original understanding of the commander-in-chief clause focused on the need for civilian control of the military. This power, Hamilton wrote, "would amount to nothing more than the supreme command and direction of the military and naval forces, as first general and admiral of the confederacy."[22] As late as 1850, the Supreme Court avowed that "the power of the President . . . was simply that of a military commander prosecuting a war waged against a public enemy by the authority of his government." His actions by themselves could not annex territory or determine whether the nation was in a state of war or peace.[23]

Subsequent presidents, especially Lincoln and the two Roosevelts, persuaded the Court to adopt a somewhat broader conception. Though Theodore Roosevelt's claim that in wartime the president can do "whatever the needs of the people demand, unless the Constitution or the laws explicitly forbid him to do it"[24] is not the law, presidents today are widely held to have the powers, without specific congressional authority, to employ military force—at least when U.S. territory or forces are under attack, to create executive offices necessary to prosecute war, to issue regulations affecting industry and labor in wartime, to requisition property in a theater of war, to establish procedures for military government of occupied territory, and to end hostilities by armistice.[25] Under *Haig v. Agee*,[26] they may also deny or revoke passports on the basis of "substantial reasons of national security and foreign policy."

The president has power to create a system for excluding loyalty and security risks from government employment, but only if the procedures conform to due process—or so the court seemed to say in a case rejecting summary dismissal of a Defense Department employee.[27] Nor can the president suspend habeas corpus, seize property outside the war zone, or do warrantless surveillance of citizens who are not agents of a foreign power.[28]

The overall thrust of this line of cases is that, while the president has broad power to act unilaterally in the interest of national security, the Court may restrain him where the exigency does not appear severe, where the action impinges directly on legislative power, or especially where it impinges on fundamental constitutional rights.

Congressional Limitations on the President

An unqualified version of the prerogative theory, giving presidents essentially unlimited and illimitable freedom of action, has found favor with recent administrations. Every president since 1973 has questioned the constitutionality of the War Powers Resolution of that year. Gerald Ford, in vetoing a revision of the Freedom of Information Act, argued *inter alia* that the Act was unconstitutional because it gave the courts a role in determining what national security information could be kept secret. Spokespersons have argued that Congress cannot constrain the president's power to engage in electronic surveillance of foreign embassies. Constitutional objections have also been leveled at the process of legislative oversight of intelligence activities. Proposals to legislate changes in the security classification system, with its associated secrecy agreements, have been similarly questioned.

These claims are striking, because the Constitution makes it abundantly clear that Congress can regulate the president's actions as commander-in-chief and as conductor of foreign policy. The powers of Congress specifically include:

> To lay and collect taxes, duties, imposts and excises, to provide for the common defence and general welfare of the United States . . . .;
>
> To borrow money on the credit of the United States;
>
> To regulate commerce with foreign nations . . . .;
>
> To establish an uniform rule of naturalization . . . .;
>
> To define and punish piracies and felonies committed on the high seas, and offences against the law of nations;
>
> To declare war, grant letters of marque and reprisal, and make rules concerning captures on land and water;
>
> To raise and support armies, but no appropriation of money to that use shall be for a longer term than two years;
>
> To provide and maintain a navy;
>
> To make rules for the government and regulation of the land and naval forces;
>
> To provide for calling forth the militia to execute the laws of the Union, suppress insurrections and repel invasions;
>
> To provide for organizing, arming, and disciplining the militia, and for governing such part of them as may be employed in the service of the United States, reserving to the States respectively, the appointment of the officers, and the authority of training the militia according to the discipline prescribed by Congress.[29]

In addition, the Third Amendment provides that soldiers can be quartered in private homes only "in a manner prescribed by law," while the president's foreign policy power is limited by the Senate's advice and consent roles in treaty making and executive (including ambassadorial) appointments.

If the Constitution provides no textual basis for the claim that Congress cannot interfere with the president's national security powers, neither has the Supreme Court ever endorsed it. Indeed, it has seldom been directly asked to do so. The only cases in which statutes have been voided for invading the executive domain involved the president's pardon power,[30] his power to remove certain officials in the executive branch,[31] or his power to veto legislation.[32]

None of these rulings aimed at protecting the president's national security functions. The foreign policy ramifications of the deportation decision involved in the *Chadha* "legislative veto" case[33] (where respondent claimed to fear political persecution if deported to Britain) played no role in the Court's reasoning. While the sweeping *dicta* in the opinion suggest that the Court might also be inclined to overturn the "legislative veto" aspect of the 1973 War Powers Resolution, there are substantial obstacles—especially the political questions doctrine, see chapter 1—to bringing that question before the Court.

In addition, defenders of the War Powers Resolution could make substantial arguments for distinguishing the cases. First, the functional relationship between a congressional declaration of war and a warlike presidential action justified by emergency is quite different from the relationship between ordinary legislation and administrative action taken pursuant to that legislation. In the former case, it is impossible to see how guidelines could be successfully legislated in advance. Second, the unusually broad latitude that Congress has for delegation of its power in the national security sphere—see below—arguably requires and permits special measures to prevent the delegated power from being utterly usurped.

In a series of cases involving the president's power to fire alleged security risks from government employment, the Court consistently ignored the claim that this power could not be limited by Congress, focusing instead on the issue of what Congress had in fact authorized. Yet in holding certain dismissals unauthorized, the Court implicitly rejected the broader claim of inherent, illimitable presidential power.[34]

More frequent than cases of congressional inaction have been cases where Congress had prescribed specific executive behavior but the executive branch chose to act differently. Generally the Court has reasoned that until Congress acted to meet a particular threat to the nation's safety, the president could proceed on his own; but once Congress acted, the president was bound by the legislation.

The first such decision was *Little v. Barreme* (1804).[35] Here Congress had authorized the seizure of ships bound to French ports, but the navy had seized a ship coming *from* a French port. The Court held that, whatever might have been the president's power in the absence of legislation, he was bound by the enacted policy, which clearly did not authorize the seizure.

The ability of Congress to limit the president's actions or even to reverse them extends to diplomatic activities as well. *La Abra Silver Mining Co. v. United States* (1899)[36] involved an American company's claim against Mexico, which the president had sponsored successfully before an international arbitration board. Rumors of fraud led Congress to investigate, and Congress directed the government to sue the company, with a view to returning the award to Mexico. The Court held that Congress "undoubtedly" had power to intervene in what the president had done, just as it could abrogate treaties by statute at any time. In a later case involving deportation of aliens, the Court reiterated that where Congress had established specific procedures the president was bound to follow them.[37]

One way Congress can limit the president's power is to provide for judicial review of specific types of presidential action. Three modern cases in which judicial review was held inappropriate turned on congressional intent. *Chicago and Southern Airlines v. Waterman Steamship Corp.*[38] involved the awarding of overseas airline routes; *Knauff v. Shaughnessy*[39] involved the deportation of aliens; and *Department of the Navy v. Egan*[40] involved the denial of a security clearance to, and subsequent dismissal of, a defense employee. In all three cases, despite *dicta* on the sensitivity of the issues and the special role of the executive branch, the Court made it very clear that Congress could provide for judicial review if it wished.

The leading case on Congress's power to limit the president's actions as commander-in-chief is the *Steel Seizure Case, Youngstown Sheet and Tube Co. v. Sawyer.*[41] In 1952, steelworkers went on strike during the Korean War. President Truman, persuaded that a prolonged strike would jeopardize the war effort, ordered the secretary of commerce to seize and operate the mills. Since no statute authorized the seizure, the government relied upon the president's powers as chief executive and commander-in-chief. Despite the *In re Debs* precedent, the Court held that only Congress could authorize such a seizure of property. In a concurring opinion which has come to be regarded as definitive, Justice Jackson stressed the fact that Congress had laid down specific procedures for dealing with labor disputes. He distinguished three very different situations:

1. When the president acts pursuant to an express or implied authorization of Congress, his authority is at its maximum, for it includes all that he possesses in his own right plus all that Congress can delegate. In these circumstances, and in these only, may he be said (for what it may be worth) to personify the federal sovereignty. If his act is held unconstitutional under these circumstances, it usually means that the Federal Government as an undivided whole lacks power. A seizure executed by the president pursuant to an Act of Congress would be supported by the strongest of presumptions and the widest latitude of judicial interpretation, and the burden of persuasion would rest heavily upon any who might attack it.
2. When the president acts in absence of either a congressional grant or denial of authority, he can rely upon his own independent powers, but there is a zone of twilight in which he and Congress may have concurrent authority, or in which its distribution is uncertain. Therefore, congressional inertia, indifference or quiescence may sometimes, at least as a practical matter, enable, if not invite, measures on independent presidential responsibility. In this area, any actual test of power is likely to depend on the imperatives of events and contemporary imponderables rather than on abstract theories of law.
3. When the president takes measures incompatible with the expressed or implied will of Congress, his power is at its lowest ebb, for then he can rely only upon his own constitutional powers minus any constitutional powers of Congress over the matter. Courts can sustain exclusive presidential control in such a case only by disabling the Congress from acting upon the subject. Presidential claim to a power at once so conclusive and preclusive must be scrutinized with caution, for what is at stake is the equilibrium established by our constitutional system.[42]

Justice Jackson concluded that the steel seizure clearly fit into the third category: Congress had ample authority to limit the president's exercise of the war power, especially when it turned inward and affected constitutional rights.

In sum, there is *no* precedent invalidating a congressional regulation of the president's national security-related actions.

Congressional Delegation of Powers

Two questions arise in connection with congressional attempts to delegate power to executive officials or executive claims that Congress has in fact delegated such power: (1) Are there decisions that the Constitution forbids Congress to delegate? (2) If delegation is permitted, how and when must it be accomplished?

On the first question, the Supreme Court has spoken emphatically. Whatever restrictions may apply to delegation in other spheres, the power to delegate where national security is concerned is very broad. *United States v. Curtiss-Wright Corp.*,[43] a 1936 case often cited as declaring broad, inherent presidential powers in this field, is in fact an authority only on the matter of delegation.[44] In the *Steel Seizure Case*, Justice Jackson described the *Curtiss-Wright* holding as follows:

> [Curtiss-Wright] involved, not the question of the president's power to act without congressional authority, but the question of his right to act under and in accord with an Act of Congress. The constitutionality of the Act under which the president had proceeded was assailed on the ground that it delegated legislative powers to the president. Much of the Court's opinion is dictum, but the *ratio decidendi* is contained in the following language:
>
>> "When the president is to be authorized by legislation to act in respect of a matter intended to affect a situation in foreign territory, the legislator properly bears in mind the important consideration that the form of the president's action—or, indeed, whether he shall act at all—may well depend, among other things, upon the nature of the confidential information which he has or may thereafter receive, or upon the effect which his action may have upon our foreign relations. This consideration in connection with what we have already said on the subject, discloses the unwisdom of requiring Congress in this field of governmental power to lay down narrowly definite standards by which the president is to be governed. As this court said in *Mackenzie v. Hare*, 239 U.S. 299, 311, 'As a government, the United States is invested with all the attributes of sovereignty. As it has the character of nationality it has the powers of nationality, especially those which concern its relations and intercourse with

other countries. *We should hesitate long before limiting or embarrassing such powers.'" Id.*, at 321–22 (emphasis added).

> That case does not solve the present controversy. It recognized internal and external affairs as being in separate categories, and held that the strict limitation upon congressional delegations of power to the president over internal affairs does not apply with respect to delegations of power in external affairs. It was intimated that the president might act in external affairs without congressional authority, but not that he might act contrary to an Act of Congress.[45]

It is worth adding that Justice Jackson's careful reading of *Curtiss-Wright* does not make that decision unproblematic. First, the *Curtiss-Wright dicta* are historically unsound, in that they do not at all coincide with the Framers' intent.[46] Second, they are analytically unsound, in that in cases where individual rights are affected by a national security decision, the distinction between internal and external affairs simply breaks down. Moreover, in a constitutional system predicated upon the sovereignty of the people and the separation of powers, to equate limits upon presidential power with limits on the government, and those in turn with limits upon national sovereignty, is gravely fallacious.

That a court may think some arrangement wise or unwise of course does not automatically determine its constitutionality. These *dicta*, like those in some of the other cases discussed, have worked great jurisprudential mischief, as executive officials understandably yielded to the temptation to rip them from their original context and cascade one claim of prerogative upon another. Unfortunately, not all judges have been as careful as Justice Jackson in their reading of these precedents.

Even if Congress does have broad power to delegate decision-making authority, it remains to determine in each case the second question—whether it has actually done so. Most of the important delegation cases have involved executive claims that a certain authority was delegated *by implication*. In general, the Court has shown sympathy to such claims, not insisting that the congressional sanction be timely, specific, and clear. Congressional authorization can be retroactive; it can be read into the appropriation of funds to carry out an activity, or the authorization or funding of a general program under which, to the knowledge of Congress, the activity was carried on.[47]

In several cases where personal rights were implicated, the Court interpreted delegations more narrowly, taking the view that "the clearest language would be necessary to satisfy us that Congress intended that the power given by these acts should be so exercised."[48] For example, though it had upheld various aspects of the World War II Japanese internment program, the Court in *Ex parte Endo*[49] ordered the release of an interned citizen whose loyalty had been established, declining to read authority for such detentions into the relevant legislation. It also held, in *Duncan v. Kahanamoku*,[50] that civilians could not be tried in military courts, even though Congress had authorized martial law. In response to a claim of presidential power to dismiss any government employee on security grounds, the Court found in *Cole v. Young*[51] that Congress had authorized such dismissal only from truly sensitive positions. Later, in *Kent v. Dulles*,[52] the Court struck down on similar grounds a State Department regulation denying passports to Communists.

More recent decisions, however, have shown more solicitude for executive power than for personal rights. *Snepp v. United States*[53] held that Congress had implicitly authorized not only binding, lifelong secrecy and prepublication clearance agreements for certain government employees, but also government seizure of the profits from any publication not so cleared, even if no classified material was disclosed. Snepp's First Amendment claims were summarily dismissed in a footnote. As the dissenters noted, the action of the majority in granting respondent's conditional cross-petition, and then disposing summarily of the case without seriously considering petitioner's constitutional claims was, to say the least, unorthodox.

In *Haig v. Agee*[54] the Court abandoned the spirit if not the letter of *Kent v. Dulles*. It held that revocation of a passport on security grounds was implicitly authorized by Congress in that, though the State Department had publicly claimed to possess such a power (while seldom if ever exercising it), Congress had failed to prohibit such actions. In *Dames and Moore v. Regan*[55] and *Regan v. Wald*,[56] the powers delegated to the president by the International Economic Emergency Procedures Act were held to include, respectively, the power to suspend pending court claims and to prohibit certain expenditures for travel to Cuba. Though neither power was expressly granted, the Court asserted that the breadth of the statutory language and the ostensible *un*clarity(!) of the legislative intent warranted these holdings. In *Department of the Navy v. Egan*,[57] the power to deny a security clearance and, accordingly, employment without a hearing was likewise upheld on the ground that Congress had not explicitly provided otherwise—even though the statute did appear to provide for hearings in any case of "adverse action."

In sum, the modern Supreme Court has been receptive to claims that Congress has delegated its authority in the national security domain. Where the allegedly authorized action impacts severely on personal rights, the Court has been willing—at least until very recently—to overturn presidential actions that lack a clear mandate from Congress. Nowadays, however, it seems that only clear evidence of specific congressional intent to *withhold* the authority in question will compel a ruling against the executive claim of delegated power. Increasingly, judicial deference to the "political branches" means deference to the Imperial Presidency.

Judicial Restraint

The Court's hesitancy to enforce firm limitations in the national security domain stems in part from the political questions doctrine, discussed in chapter 1—that on certain occasions the nation must speak with one voice, and that some issues, not resolvable by legal reasoning or judicial order, must be left to the political branches. This doctrine traces back to the *dicta* in *Marbury v. Madison* discussed above; the most thorough modern discussion is in *Baker v. Carr*.[58]

The first application of the doctrine to national security matters came in 1829, in *Foster & Elam v. Neilson*,[59] where the Court held that it was bound to accept the president's interpretation of a treaty. In a similar vein, the Court in *Oetjen v. Central Leather Co.* refused to consider whether a seizure of property by the Mexican government, recognized as valid by the executive branch, was legal. The Court declared,

> The conduct of the foreign relations of our Government is committed by the Constitution to the Executive and Legislative—'the political'—Departments of the Government, and the propriety of what may be done in the exercise of this political power is not subject to judicial inquiry or decision.[60]

According to Corwin, the political questions doctrine requires judicial deference to the following "political" determinations:

> whether a certain newly constituted community was a qualified belligerent at international law; what was the correct boundary of a certain country; what country was the sovereign of a par-

ticular region; whether a certain community was entitled to be considered as a "belligerent" or as an independent state; who was the de jure, who the de facto ruler of a certain country; whether a particular person was a duly accredited diplomatic agent to the United States; how long a military occupation of a certain region should continue in order to fulfill the terms of a treaty; whether a certain treaty was in effect; and so on.[61]

Nor will a dispute between the "political" branches necessarily entail judicial intervention. In *Goldwater v. Carter*,[62] a senator argued that the Senate's consent is necessary for presidential abrogation of a treaty. However, the Senate as a whole had taken no action to challenge the abrogation, and a majority of the Court held that the case in this posture was not justiciable, though they could not agree as to which specific doctrine—standing to sue, ripeness, or "political questions"—justified their abstention.

It should be stressed that the Court has never held that all cases potentially affecting foreign relations are nonjusticiable. On the contrary, many such cases, including those requiring interpretation of treaties or executive agreements, present straightforward, justiciable legal issues, as the Court recently noted in *Japan Whaling Association v. American Cetacean Society.*[63]

The Court's ability and willingness to hear most national security-related cases is consistent, however, with a pattern of great deference in its ultimate disposition of those cases. The explicit basis for judicial deference sometimes pertains (as in most of the above cases) to positions which the government has already announced and which the Court could not contradict without causing serious embarrassment to our foreign policy.

Another line of cases emphasizes that governmental action can depend on information that, in the Court's view, is properly kept secret in the interests of national security. Examples include a presidential finding that there was imminent danger of invasion[64] and a finding that the international situation justified the seizure of telegraph lines.[65] Nor would the Court review findings justifying invocation of the Trading with the Enemy Act[66] or findings justifying deportation of aliens.[67] In the most widely quoted of such cases, *Chicago and Southern Airlines v. Waterman Steamship Corp.*,[68] the Court declined to review a finding regarding the award of an overseas airline route, holding that Congress had not provided—though it could have—for judicial review. Without referring explicitly to the occasional use of "private" companies for intelligence purposes, the Court offered the following declaration:

The president, both as Commander in Chief and as the nation's organ for foreign affairs, has available intelligence services which reports are not, and ought not to be, published to
the world. It would be intolerable that courts, without relevant
information, should review and perhaps nullify actions of the
executive taken on information properly held secret. Nor can
the court sit in camera in order to be taken into executive con-
fidences. But even if the courts could require full disclosure,
the very nature of executive decisions as to foreign policy is political, not judicial. Such decisions are wholly confined by our
Constitution to the political departments of the government,
executive and legislature. They are delicate, complex, and involve large elements of policy. They are and should be undertaken only by those directly responsible to the people whose
welfare and lives are in peril. They are decisions of a kind for
which the judiciary has neither aptitude, facilities, nor responsibilities, and which has long been held to belong to the
domain of political power not subject to judicial intrusion or
inquiry.[69]

The preceding discussion has already shown that these *dicta* are
too sweeping: "executive decisions as to foreign policy" are not automatically immune to "judicial intrusion or inquiry."[70]

A specific area in which the Court has exercised especially great
restraint involves the rights of aliens to enter or remain in the
United States. The Court has long held that the government has inherent power to exclude aliens, and that its exercise is not a deprivation of the "liberty" protected by the Bill of Rights.[71] Moreover,
Kleindienst v. Mandel stated that "the courts will neither look behind the exercise of that discretion nor test it by balancing its justification against the First Amendment interests of those who seek
personal communications with the [visa] applicant."[72]

Others who can expect only limited protection from the courts include enemy aliens (especially in regard to their property) and prisoners of war.[73] These cases are in tension with the more recent
holding, in *Plyler v. Doe*,[74] that alienage is a suspect classification
for purposes of equal protection analysis. Yet *Plyler* is unlikely to affect the doctrine that aliens simply have no right to enter the country or to remain in it, whatever their rights may be while inside the
country.

These cases aside, the Court's abstention from review of "political" decisions does not apply to acts that infringe upon constitutional rights. Normally the Court balances the governmental

interests against the personal rights involved. The war power is subject to the "applicable constitutional limitations";[75] in the 1934 *Blaisdell* case the Court stated:

> Emergency does not create power. Emergency does not increase granted power or remove or diminish the restrictions imposed upon power granted or reserved. The Constitution was adopted in a period of grave emergency. Its grants of power to the Federal Government and its limitations of the power of the States were determined in the light of emergency and they are not altered by emergency. . . . [E]ven the war power does not remove constitutional limitations safeguarding essential liberties.[76]

There has never been a decision to the contrary. To be sure, in performing the constitutional balancing the Court has usually given great weight to governmental findings of fact, and it has been reluctant to overturn actions taken in the context of emergency, especially in wartime.[77] Moreover, the Burger and Rehnquist Courts have been even more deferential to the government than was the Warren Court in applying the applicable principles to the case at hand.

Yet decisions still valid today make it clear that governmental findings and decisions pertaining to national security are not necessarily binding. Thus, the subjection of civilians to military justice was held unconstitutional both in the Civil War and in World War II.[78] *Kennedy v. Mendoza-Martinez*[79] held that a statute stripping citizenship from draft avoiders who fled the country was a denial of the liberty protected by the due process clause. *United States v. Robel*[80] held likewise for a statute making it a crime for members of Communist organizations to work in defense facilities. In the same cold war era, *Lamont v. Postmaster General*[81] held unconstitutional a statute requiring citizens to file a written request in order to receive "communist propaganda" by overseas mail, on the ground that the government had not shown a danger sufficient to warrant interfering with First Amendment rights.

Even when persuaded that the asserted state interest is sufficiently compelling to justify curtailing fundamental personal rights, the Court has insisted that the policy be narrowly drawn so that its impact does not exceed what is essential to serve that interest. Thus in *Aptheker v. United States*,[82] the Court held that a statute denying passports to all members of "subversive organizations" was void for overbreadth; it would suffice to apply the ban only to those whose travel might reasonably be expected to harm the national security. Likewise, in the *Robel* case, a sweeping ban on all defense-related employment for all members of "communist organizations" was held overbroad.

Under the *Blaisdell* doctrine, civil liberties apply in emergencies as well as in normal times. Under the *Steel Seizure Case*, the constraints that fundamental rights place upon congressional action apply with at least equal rigor when the president, for some valid reason, acts on his own. If the Court has sometimes felt obliged to defer to executive actions that violated fundamental rights, in so doing it acted unfaithfully both to the Constitution and to its own best precedents.

Conclusion

The prerogative theory, a product and adornment of absolute monarchy, has no valid place in our constitutional law. Neither the constitutional text nor the record of "original intent," fairly read, can support it. Yet this theory has repeatedly surfaced in times of real, perceived, or manufactured crisis, providing encouragement and support for expansions of presidential power at the expense of checks and balances as well as personal freedoms.

This heretical theory is ultimately sustained not by respectable constitutional logic and historical research, but by the felt imperatives of patriotism, party unity, and personal ambition. "National security" all too often refers not to genuine, palpable, widely shared public goods, but to the foreign and domestic interests of powerful factions and individuals. How many of us can recite the more than two hundred times presidents have resorted to acts of force overseas without declaration of war and explain how the people as a whole benefited from each? *Uncritical* acceptance of appeals to national security is tantamount to nationalist hysteria.

Insofar as the Presidency has successfully claimed primary responsibility for determining what national security requires, this dynamic has brought us to the point where implicit trust in the president can be depicted, by Oliver North and his ilk, as a patriotic duty. Such an ideology is not and cannot be confined for long to a distinct realm of "foreign affairs." Thus, in arguing Richard Nixon's very broad claim of "executive privilege" to the Supreme Court, his counsel could identify only two differences between the powers of the president and those of a king: the president does not serve for life, and his office is not inherited.[83] The Court ruled against Nixon but did not expose the fundamental absurdity of his argument.

Neither Congress nor the Court has so far been able to consistently or decisively reject the prerogative theory, lest the Constitution prove to be a suicide pact.[84] The public, for its part, seems more often to crave a monarch than to fear one. While adhering to the Constitution cannot itself guarantee our safety and prosperity, neither can we save the nation by abandoning its defining principles. The problem, it would seem, is not in our Constitution but in ourselves.

‰ Chapter 5 ‰

Compelling
Governmental Interests

The law is just—drools & dregulations to me.

—after Patti Smith

A genda setting is the very heart of ordinary politics. Representatives and voters, parties and interest groups form and exchange ideas about what government should do and how it should do it. Time and resources are limited; priorities must be set.

Constitutional politics can only affect agenda setting from the margins, lest ordinary politics be confined to trivia. Yet a constitution that has nothing to say about the nation's agenda cannot be constitutive of its ordinary politics. Constitutional government is limited government, and mere prohibitions are not enough: we expect the Constitution to express some vision of the public interest and the governmental responsibilities that flow therefrom.

What are the limits on the powers granted to government? Do some of our goals and its functions have priority over others? Where we are in severe disagreement over the agenda, are *all* matters up for majority vote, or can we sometimes look directly to the Constitution (and its authoritative interpreters) for answers? Or does the Constitution sometimes enjoin us to make *no* collective decision, leaving the matter instead to private resolution?

It appears that liberals and republicans may wish to answer these questions somewhat differently. Adopting a classical liberal focus on the priorities of individual liberty and group pluralism/tolerance, we avoid seeking consensus on all but a very few matters, limiting the scope of permissible public projects and requiring loyal citizens' agreement/conformity with those only to a very limited extent. But if we instead presuppose a republican consensus (or need for one) on a wider set of virtues and projects, then (a) we draw limits to our tolerance; (b) we demand more active commitment from citizens; and (c) we expect to find in the Constitution a more full-fledged vision of the principles for which we stand. It will not be enough to obey laws of the thou-shalt-not variety and politely leave each other alone; we must also be civic minded, work together, and sacrifice to build that shining City on the Hill.

Such choices clearly cannot and should not be controlled by a text alone; they must be suited to the possibilities we find in the world, as well as to our aspirations. At any given conjuncture one key question must be: How much manipulation and coercion would be required to enforce general participation in a communitarian, republican vision? And another: How much government do we need in order to justify having any at all? On one hand, how many people will fail to attain a "private" life worth living under the aegis of a minimal, liberal night-watchman state? On the other, what becomes of "public" life—how many will lose all sense of purpose and belonging—if there is no business at hand save the private pursuit of wealth, pleasure, and status? Yet again: How much do we allow the government to do *for* us, and how much do we insist on doing ourselves?

From one viewpoint, a jurisprudence of governmental powers would have to be partisan. The country's agenda is (aside from power for its own sake) exactly what parties fight about. Now, today's party conflict is not primarily constitutional in its level, and the ramshackle two-party system does not neatly track the republican-liberal dichotomy I have been using. Instead, the party of market freedom and family values has a vision of who we are and what we are about that narrows the public sector, marginalizes a great many citizens, and channels public benefits to relatively few, without acknowledging that it is doing so. The party of welfare rights and multiculturalism tries to decide what we are about without deciding who we are (that is, without excluding anyone) and in the process promotes a more activist government, seen by critics as beholden to "special interests," without providing much sense of community or reason (aside from immediate material needs) for remaining together.

Both parties claim to believe in human dignity. One believes that dignity trickles down from having a prosperous middle class, free competition, and ample social mobility; the other, that it trickles up from having a safety net at the floor. These days, it seems that neither side knows how to talk to the other or has much motivation to do so. The negativity of most campaigns and the level of (non)voter apathy suggest that neither side's vision is capable of mobilizing the people at large. More and more of us perceive the government as "them," not "us"—implying that there *is* no People, no prospect for general dignity, security, or welfare. The public space is ailing. Is the Constitution part of the solution or just more fodder for ordinary politics?

Governmental Powers Jurisprudence

The Constitution does make clear that an action can be unconstitutional in two distinct ways: first, that it exceeds the powers granted to the governmental agency in question; or, second, that the action, while of a type that is authorized in principle, would violate someone's personal rights.

For a long time federal courts were concerned almost exclusively with questions of the first type. The post–Civil War amendments and the modern expansion of the national government (especially the executive bureaucracy) made possible the explosive growth of personal rights jurisprudence that is the focus of part III. The topic of this chapter is the concomitant transformation (or should one say collapse?) of governmental powers jurisprudence.

As noted in the introduction to this part, constitutional controversy over (nonrights-based) limits on federal power has become very uncommon. The most obvious textual bases for such controversy have been eroded by the extremely generous readings now given to congressional power under the necessary and proper clause and the commerce clause, as well as to presidential powers under Article II, section 1. In addition, the Court's abandonment of the "delegation doctrine" since the New Deal makes it difficult to argue that a power belonging to Congress has, improperly, been exercised instead by the president or by the bureaucracy.

Any effort to revert to earlier understandings of these matters would encounter grave obstacles, both intellectual and political. One indication is the impact of the Court's holding in *Chadha*[1] that "legislative veto" arrangements violate the constitutional plan—that instead of delegating broad rulemaking authority, subject to legislative veto, Congress must itself enact policy, subject to presidential veto. In the aftermath, Congress continues to make frequent resort to "legislative veto" provisions; presidents sign and comply with the bills. Both branches find the procedure very convenient, even essential. Given the size and complexity of today's policy-making work load, no one seems to know how Congress could actually govern in the original sense. It is far too small to *represent* vast and fragmented constituencies in the manner originally calculated, yet already too large to *deliberate* effectively in the classical manner on the bulk of pending policy details. Current proposals for constitutional revision fail to address the structural legislative weakness.

This is not to say that measures further aggravating the imbalance between legislative and executive power should escape strict judicial scrutiny. For example, Congress's recent grant of a presidential power to veto individual line items in spending bills is unprecedented and dangerous. If this is constitutional, where *will* the line be drawn—at a measure authorizing the president to tax and spend as he sees fit until further notice, and then adjourning Congress until the following year?

As for federalism, it is too soon to say with confidence whether the Court's 5-4 decision in *United States v. Lopez*[2] will be a real watershed, or a short-lived aberration like *National League of Cities v. Usery*,[3] or something in between. *Lopez* held that a federal statute criminalizing gun possession within a school zone was not a valid exercise of the interstate commerce power. If it were, the majority said, the commerce power would have no limits at all. While insisting that the commerce power must have limits and that this statute's nexus with interstate commerce was too tenuous, the majority seemingly disavowed any intent to revisit the constitutionality of the major New Deal regulatory innovations or the 1960s Civil Rights Acts. In itself, the decision thus seems fairly narrow. It does, however, remind us of the political and interpretive tensions attendant upon the modern expansion of governmental functions, accomplished without the benefit of constitutional amendment.

It also reminds us of the legerdemain involved in resting modern civil rights legislation on the commerce clause instead of the Fourteenth Amendment. It would be far more honest and legitimate to overrule the *Slaughterhouse Cases*[4] and the *Civil Rights Cases*,[5] and thus allow Congress effectively to enforce the "privileges and immunities" and "equal protection" guarantees—and, by the same token, to disallow the resting on the commerce clause of measures whose real impulse obviously has far less to do with regulating commerce than with other aims.

At the present juncture, at any rate, the jurisprudence of federalism and of separated powers appears to have little scope or vitality. The doctrine of a government limited to enumerated powers, meanwhile, has none at all. One does not hear proposals to augment Article I with references to the new, modern objects of government spending and regulation, or Article II with new guidelines for the management and accountability of the bureaucracy. Constitutional law books seem not even to notice the chasm between (1) a textual grant of three narrow powers to define and punish crimes and (2) a federal criminal code spanning thousands of pages and distinct offenses. (Moreover, grants-in-aid to states are sometimes conditioned on their modifying their own criminal laws, relying on the very tenuous distinction between permissible "inducements" and impermissible "coercion."[6]) In lieu of a vital jurisprudence of powers, we count on ordinary politics and on rights jurisprudence for our protection. Some say we are already everywhere in chains. Two questions arise: How did this come about? and What are the consequences?

My very concise history of powers jurisprudence begins, once again, with the stresses that territorial, economic, demographic, and democratic expansion placed upon the evolving system. The early understandings of limits on national and presidential powers, formulated by the Marshall and Taney Courts, were heavily infused with republican notions about the role of homogeneous local communities and the limited substantive agenda of the national government. Many of these ideas became unsustainable in the expansion-driven crisis that led to the Civil War. After decisions such as *Dred Scott*[7] and *Ex parte Merryman*,[8] the position of Taney's Court itself became precarious. The stronger presidency that war created was largely ratified by a chastened Court,[9] while federalism was reformulated by constitutional amendments whose jurisprudence, revealingly, focuses heavily on court-enforced personal rights.

The politics of the postwar era (Ackerman's second regime) was dominated by new issues associated with the rise of industrial capitalism. Social and economic development and conflict brought new interest groups and popular movements with new demands for governmental action. For a time, innovative policy responses met with stiff, if selective, resistance from "activist" judges, who blended an expansive property rights jurisprudence with sometimes crabbed readings of the powers granted to Congress to tax, to regulate commerce, or to delegate power to regulatory agencies.

There are many accounts, differing in approach and in emphasis, of the rise and fall of *Lochner*-era jurisprudence.[10] *Lochner*[11] was the notorious 1905 decision invalidating a state law that set maximum hours for labor in the baking industry. Most commentators see the case as mistakenly reading a (classical liberal) theory of laissez-faire economics into the property rights ("liberty of contract") guaranteed by the Constitution. Gillman,[12] however, reads the case as grounded first of all in a (classical republican) theory of governmental powers: that government must act for the public benefit, not for that of any particular, politically favored interest, such as workers in a single industry or even, perhaps, labor as a class. It is important to note that both the rights and the powers doctrines presupposed that law could and should stand above, or be neutral as between, competing social and political interests. They also presupposed that there are things the government simply may not do, no matter how much it (and/or the majority of citizens) want to.

By 1937, events had made such ideas untenable. Intensified class conflict, the crisis of the Great Depression, and the New Deal's electoral triumph brought a decisive mandate for effective action. While a new, Realist jurisprudence made belief in "neutral" property rights or "impartial" public policy hard to sustain, social scientists and reformist politicians argued that expert administrators were competent to solve the pressing problems, if only allowed to do so.

Fatefully, New Dealers chose not to seek enabling constitutional amendments. Instead, the charge that "nine old men" were preventing a willing and able government from dealing with a genuine national crisis, based on nothing but their own reactionary political agenda, was backed by a threat of legislation to increase the Court's size and enable further, transformative Court appointments. In the end, the Court gave way. Its theory of property rights was supplanted by a highly deferential approach to review of economic regulations. Its readings of the commerce power, the taxing and spending powers, and the power of Congress to delegate policy making to executive agencies became, to all intents and purposes, plenary. The existing jurisprudence of governmental powers was, in other words, effectively abandoned.

The Prioritizing Turn

The proverbial "switch in time that saved nine" called for rethinking the rule of law and the Court's role in the new order (Ackerman's third regime). The primary response was a refreshed and expanded jurisprudence of personal rights. Thus, by far the most common sort of constitutional controversy in recent years has involved a clash between a recognized governmental power on one side and a personal right on the other.

In such cases several approaches are logically available to a court. It can hold that either the power or the right is absolute and not subject to limitation for the sake of the opposing value. It can *balance*, in situational context, the importance of the personal right against that of the competing public interest. Finally, it can engage in a two-step analysis, in which the right and the power are first abstractly categorized, and then the weight or priority appropriate to each *category* is theoretically determined.

The last option requires a bit of explanation. In the most familiar form of categorical analysis, "fundamental" rights (as opposed to ordinary ones) can be overridden only when this is essential for the attainment of "compelling" (as opposed to ordinary) governmental interests. In contrast, ordinary rights may be restricted whenever a legitimate public purpose provides a "rational basis" for doing so. This idea is usually traced back to the 1938 *Carolene Products* footnote[13] or perhaps to the wartime *Japanese Relocation Cases*.[14]

Kathleen Sullivan[15] has explored in some depth the question whether two-step review and balancing are significantly different. As she notes, the Court has been eclectic in the tests employed, shifting from categorization to balancing even within the same area of law. Some justices have on occasion advocated hybrid, sliding-scale approaches, blurring the distinction even more.

Sullivan rejects the hypothesis that case outcomes depend directly on the method used. Over history, each method has been used both by judicial activists and by advocates of judicial restraint; each has been employed to reach both pro-government and pro-individual outcomes. If there is a systematic pattern, it is that justices who reject the results reached in a given line of cases tend also to reject the analytical method used in those cases.

It does not follow that the choice of method makes no difference at all. Rather, Sullivan argues that the choice may be relevant in two different ways: institutionally, as it bears on the way that judicial action is perceived and evaluated; and pragmatically, as different rhetorical burdens make it easier or harder to justify a given result depending on the method used.

The institutional argument is, of course, two-sided. On the one hand, the categorical approach has the advantages of formalism.

Courts can confine themselves to examining the relevant legal texts, avoiding the need for empirical research on the concrete interests at stake in the case at hand. Such research, after all, raises questions both about judicial *competence* in this field and about the *legitimacy* of the court acting as a "superlegislature" and revising a judgment the people's representatives have ostensibly already made.

On the other hand, balancing has the competing advantages of pragmatism. Where categorical judgments rest on inevitably crude and often outdated generalizations, balancing permits and even requires a careful look at the actual effects the court's holding will have. To blindfold justice may guard against improper bias, but it can also yield unwarranted insensitivity. Accountability, moreover, is furthered when the litigants and the court must go beyond reciting sterile formulae and acknowledge the real-world impact of the legal positions they take. As Sullivan argues, to shoulder this responsibility may sometimes affect the case's outcome.

Sullivan concludes that neither approach is inherently superior. The best course depends on the nature of the case at hand and the state of existing law. Her examples clearly show that both approaches can be used in unpersuasive ways to reach unfortunate results.

An example of foolish categorization is Justice Scalia's repeated insistence that "laws of general applicability," which do not discriminate on their face against a protected class, do not warrant strict scrutiny. The major difficulty is that formal "applicability" has little to do with real-world relevance. Superficially "general" formulas (for example, "any city whose population exceeds two million," "any person with an SAT score above 999," or "anyone sleeping in the park") can be highly selective in their impact. Formalism obscures the fact that such selectivity, whether or not calculated and deliberately disguised, may be highly unjust. Perhaps we, and Scalia, should be more concerned about laws so very general in applicability that they provide inadequate guidelines for executive implementation. This was, of course, the point of the moribund "delegation doctrine."[16]

Scalia's theory of degrees of scrutiny reminds us how far the classical understanding of the legislative function has eroded. It is an attenuated offspring of the older idea, found in Locke and Rousseau, that, for liberty's sake, all laws must be of general application and their implementation in particular cases reserved for other branches of government. Measures lacking general applicability were not proper "laws" at all. Rather than receiving stricter scrutiny, they were simply void.

The critique of formalistic notions of "neutrality" played a part in the broad retreat from this way of thinking. Only a few textually mandated exceptions remain fairly intact. A law singling an individual out for punishment would, of course, be a bill of attainder. Laws benefiting favored individuals or groups may also be vulnerable to challenge under constitutional provisions that limit spending or takings of property to "public uses."[17] On the other hand, although Article I, section 8 empowers Congress to make "an uniform rule of naturalization," no one involved in the *Chadha* case[18] questioned the constitutionality of private bills for the relief of single individuals. How can a "private bill" (however traditional) be a "uniform rule"?

Theodore Lowi[19] attributes the vagueness of much modern legislation and the demise of the delegation doctrine to the theory and practice of "interest group liberalism," which, he holds, prefers an elitist politics of case-by-case bargaining to an open one of debate over just and effective general rules. Lowi advocates revitalizing the delegation doctrine as a crucial step in restoring democracy and the rule of law. It seems implausible, however, that a few judicial rulings would have any more effect on the practice of sweeping delegation than they have had on the "legislative veto." The veto is, after all, an easily recognized category of legislation, whereas delegation is always a matter of degree and not so amenable to clearcut rules.

At any rate, the weaknesses of categorization as a judicial methodology must be set off against those of its counterpart. In the abstract, balancing seems less predictable in its outcomes and offers less guidance to those who wish to obey the law. It has the flaws that Lowi attributes to modern legislative policy making. In practice, moreover, balancing has often been used to dismiss the seemingly modest interests of individuals as obviously outweighed by those—perhaps equally modest, but shared by multitudes—of society as a whole. This sort of calculus, uniformly applied, would soon swallow up individual rights entirely—at least as far as minorities or dissidents are concerned.

Thus, civil libertarians devoted much effort to a search for alternatives to the all-too-predictable "bad tendency" test initially applied in free speech cases. The "clear and present danger" test produced only modest improvement, and the more recent *Brandenburg*[20] formula is similarly vulnerable to abuses in times of real or perceived crisis.[21] If the most liberal Court we have ever had was unable to reject the utterly groundless claim that Japanese-American citizens as a class were a threat to national security,[22] perhaps courts should not be in the business of balancing.

T. Alexander Aleinikoff, in the course of his powerful critique of balancing as a judicial practice,[23] offers some interesting guidelines as to how courts should assess the weight or legitimacy of the interests relied on by government. With regard to judicial competence, he notes that balancing has often seemed rudimentary in its evidentiary basis and manipulative in the selectivity of the interests examined. Moreover, by undertaking to weigh interests that have an explicit constitutional basis (for example, the defendant's right to free speech) against interests that do not (for example, the plaintiff's right to a good reputation or the public interest in controlling littering), the court goes beyond *constitutional interpretation* and engages in a form of superlegislation. This poses a question of legitimacy: whereas a failure in legislative (or executive) balancing might justify a judicial remand for reconsideration, it does not obviously justify an independent—and final—rebalancing by the judiciary.

Aleinikoff believes that courts can perform their proper function, to "provide a forum for the affirmation of background principles and for ratification of changes in those principles—changes the amendment process could only sporadically produce,"[24] without being drawn into decisions that subvert the distinction between constitutional and ordinary politics in that they "examine similar variables in similar ways."[25] Rather than balance social values against constitutional rights, courts should account for social values in their description of the right itself, reminding us that basic rights are indeed of value not just to individuals but to society at large.[26] He argues that judges in the nineteenth century were able to do this successfully, although the specific values to which they most often appealed (property rights, freedom of contract, and federalism) would require supplementation and revision today.

The problems with balancing identified by Aleinikoff are serious. The question is whether alternative approaches provide a real improvement or merely disguise those problems, while raising the added difficulties discussed by Sullivan. Critics of formalism will eagerly point out that any set of categories or any definition of rights or powers is built on a balancing of values—unless it is utterly arbitrary.

On the surface, for example, the jurisprudence of governmental powers entails no judgments about priorities: either the constitution grants the power in question or it does not. Yet, when government relies on an implicit grant of power, the necessary and proper clause, or the like, it is in effect asking the court to recognize that the action in question is essential or extremely valuable to pursuit of another, already acknowledged goal. To determine the importance or value of an action as a *means* is not quite the same as deciding on the relative importance of a set of *ends*. Still, the argument does involve judgments about priorities, for the means take on urgency from the importance that the end is deemed to possess.

The significant distinction is between *ad hoc*, context-sensitive forms of balancing, which explicitly identify and evaluate the concrete interests at stake in the specific case at hand, and "definitional" forms of balancing, which label the competing interests and thereby assign them to pre-established categories with relative priorities that have been weighed in advance. Thus Stephen Gottlieb, one of very few who has explored the "compelling governmental interests" doctrine in great detail, disagrees both with Sullivan and with Aleinikoff, classifying compelling interests analysis as itself a form of balancing, rather than an alternative to it. Gottlieb does not oppose balancing *per se*, but has two primary concerns about the way courts have carried out this form of analysis: the weakness of their methodology for identifying and weighing the interests involved, and the asymmetry of their treatment of rights and interests.[27]

A significant point he makes in passing about the compelling interests approach is that the term *governmental interests* is an unfortunate misnomer. The logic of popular sovereignty tells us that government is purely an agent and can have no valid interests of its own, over and against those of citizens. If individual rights can ever be overridden, it can be done only in the name of collective interests of the people. Thus, *compelling public purposes* would be a far better term.[28] But how can such interests be identified?

Gottlieb holds that, in principle, the effort can proceed from the constitutional text, from "penumbras" of provisions in the text, or from means/ends analysis of such provisions. There is a large problem with the entire enterprise, however. While the Constitution confers many responsibilities and possibilities upon different governmental institutions, it does not identify any of them as especially "compelling." Therefore, the notion that fundamental rights may be overridden only by compelling public or governmental interests gives to rise to major interpretive challenges.

Gottlieb is on very firm ground in his critique of the Court's compelling interest jurisprudence. As he observes, not only are constitutional interests not explicitly prioritized in the text, but there is always a large gap between the generality of the interest textually confided to government and the specific program or action sought to be justified. The Court has not been clear and consistent as to whether its judgment of "compellingness" pertains to the general interest itself or to its application to the case at hand.

Thus, while it often has been said that the protection of national security is a compelling interest, it is not the law that *any* appeal to national security, no matter how remote or implausible, will override *any* competing claim of personal rights.[29] Likewise, while it has been said that governmental efficiency and expense are not compelling interests, it does not follow that there is *no* level of harm to these interests that could conceivably justify *any* infringement of an otherwise fundamental right.[30] At some level of governmental disruption or insolvency, after all, other, more obviously compelling interests would also be jeopardized.

In general, then, the Court's previous identification of a general interest as compelling or not compelling does not fully control the outcome of later cases in which that same interest may be implicated. Courts must decide whether and to what extent the relevant interests (including but not limited to those asserted by the government) are actually at stake. (Courts typically then go on to weigh those interests separately against the competing rights claims advanced by the other party, whereas Gottlieb and Aleinikoff hold that all the values can and should be weighed in one context-sensitive step.) Gottlieb thus has good grounds for viewing compelling interest analysis as a form of balancing, even though the balancing is not purely *ad hoc*, but (as Sullivan argues) constrained by the precedential weight of earlier categorical pronouncements.

Gottlieb's most devastating point is that such pronouncements typically are *ipse dixits*, unsupported by elaborate argument or textual analysis. The balancing is performed inside an impenetrable "black box."[31] Once an interest is deemed compelling or not compelling, moreover, later courts feel free to rely on that judicial assertion as sole authority for the point.

Some of these pronouncements may seem self-evident to most. Victory in wartime is a compelling interest; curtailing public debate on important issues is not. Others are far more controversial: Gottlieb will not be alone in thinking it nakedly partisan for some justices to term "maintaining political stability" a compelling interest.[32] A third subset of these judicial pronouncements is simply mystifying.

To me the best example is Justice Powell's opinion in *Regents of the University of California v. Bakke*,[33] where the state medical school relied on four distinct interests to support its affirmative-action program: reducing the historic deficit of minority enrollment, countering the effects of societal discrimination, improving care in underserved communities, and obtaining the educational benefits that flow from student diversity. Justice Powell announced that the first two could not be deemed compelling state interests, in the absence of a finding that the school in question had previously discriminated. The third might indeed be a compelling interest, but the program in question was not demonstrably tailored to its pursuit. The fourth, however, was compelling, because of its link to academic freedom and the "robust exchange of ideas" safeguarded by the First Amendment. Justice Powell went on to hold, however, that even this interest could not justify the quota-like design of the program and the harm it inflicted on innocent white applicants.

Gottlieb criticizes Justice Powell primarily for undervaluing the interest in remedying past discrimination.[34] To me, however, the most troublesome feature of his opinion was Powell's singling out, as the most compelling feature of the affirmative-action plan, the one asserted interest that was of value primarily to *white students*. The other asserted interests have a far more clear, direct, and substantial grounding in the equal protection clause than a "diverse student body" has in the First Amendment; and they surely played a larger role in the university's decision to adopt the affirmative-action plan. Justice Powell's compelling interest analysis not only did not support the affirmative-action plan, it added insult to injury.

While the details of compelling interest analysis are of quite recent origin, Gottlieb traces its roots back to the civic-republican focus on community values and goals.[35] His approach to harmonizing those values with personal rights begins with the insistence that protecting personal rights is itself a preeminent public interest. The values he finds central to the overall constitutional scheme—and not just to the Bill of Rights and later amendments—are life, liberty, property, equality, and democracy. All or nearly all other legitimate public interests, he holds, are derived from these.

Gottlieb argues that the task of identifying and prioritizing public interests is essentially the same as that involved in identifying and prioritizing personal rights. Thus the same interpretive techniques and the same norms of judicial restraint are applicable in each case. An asymmetric approach, which condemns broad or creative readings of personal rights while accepting broad or creative readings of governmental powers, is indefensible in principle. It bespeaks a statist bias that has no constitutional warrant and was surely not intended by the Framers.

As Sullivan[36] points out, there are strong objections to Gottlieb's case for symmetrical treatment of rights and interests. In particular, his claim that to every compelling interest there corresponds a fundamental right raises several related questions. Is it not the case that constitutional interests belong to the public, while constitutional rights belong to individuals? Is it not the case that the interests expressly confided to government generally give it *discretionary* powers, rather than expressly imposing on it *mandatory* duties? Is it not the case that virtually all of our explicit constitutional rights are negative liberties *against* state action, rather than positive liberties *requiring* state action? Should courts not be more deferential to the way that government conducts discretionary activities than to the way that it performs mandatory duties? Would not a judicial order requiring government to develop, initiate, and fund a certain program trench far more deeply upon the separation of powers than an order to refrain or desist from a certain action?

Gottlieb's answer appears to be that the traditional maxims appealed to here are not compelled by the text. They express a controversial constitutional vision and should be reexamined in light of the imperative of treating rights and interests symmetrically. Judicial deference should be sensitive to all the circumstances of a case—not to a categorical distinction between rights and interests. The task is not to weigh two incommensurables against each other, but to find the outcome indicated by the overall "hierarchy of values," or "theories of priority of value."[37]

For Gottlieb, the Constitution requires neither a distinction between collective interests and personal rights, nor one between negative and positive liberties, nor the familiar "state action" doctrine (rights are restrictions only on *governmental* action). Yet it does not follow that all interests are on a par: "Not all compelling interests are equal."[38] Indeed, protection of life, liberty, and property are paramount among them. Courts can and should intervene to assure that paramount interests prevail; yet judicial deference is proper when textual ambiguity or factual uncertainty make the case a close contest between "values of comparable magnitude."[39]

Whatever one may think of the symmetry argument (and there is no mistaking its radicalism), it is a herculean task Gottlieb here poses for constitutional theory—and a task he has not yet undertaken in a systematic way. Apparently, he thinks it would involve a utilitarian calculus in which "the benefits of a particular definition of rights are weighed against the costs of that definition."[40] Yet such an approach seems inconsistent with Gottlieb's core emphasis on personal rights, for it permits the costs incurred by one person to be outweighed by the benefits accruing to others. At any rate, to agree that the weighing must be somehow anchored in the Constitution does not show us how to carry it out, given the deeply contested—

and not necessarily always mutually consistent—meaning of the superordinate values Gottlieb identifies.

Suppose that we are resolved to be both serious and "realistic" about respecting personal rights. How can we rationalize imposing on them limitations not explicit in the language that proclaims those rights?

It is quite tempting to argue that such limitation is unwarranted, that constitutional rights are absolute. On the surface, this would relieve the courts of the need to prioritize public interests. In practice, though, we would have to expect courts to look for ways of narrowing the definition of fundamental rights, so as to avoid imposing on the public agenda the apparent costs of making them sacrosanct. (This concern appears, indeed, to be integral to Aleinikoff's antibalancing project.) In the end, we might wind up with an "absolute" right to free speech—but only so long as the speech is harmless. If it has serious harmful consequences, we could call it "conduct, not speech." Justice Black, the closest we have had to a judicial "absolutist," employed this and other limiting stratagems on numerous occasions.[41]

The second possibility is to insist that the rights granted are implicitly limited by (other) public interests. "The Constitution . . . is not a suicide pact,"[42] and there are times when personal rights must yield. For reasons similar to those Sullivan presents, there is no reason to expect any systematic difference in outcomes between these two approaches, although rhetorical patterns will certainly change.

How could we—and courts in particular—identify the interests that overtrump personal rights? Is there a political theory of public priorities implicit in the constitution? Or is this quest rather at the heart of the functions reserved to the "political branches"? Shall the identification of an interest as compelling be seen as a potential violation of judicial restraint—or as driven by that very norm? For example, does the felt inappropriateness of judicial second-guessing of national security-related actions follow from the compelling nature of that interest? Or is this intuitive reluctance precisely what identifies that interest for a court as compelling? To pursue this matter, my method will be partly textual and partly empirical.

What the Constitution Says

Justice Scalia believes that linguistic, rather than functional, analysis can solve the problem—a hope dismissed by Gottlieb as unrealistic. Still, one can try to glean as much aid as possible from the text. For example, a formalistic approach might seek to prioritize interests by drawing inferences from the sequence of interests/powers in the Preamble, Articles I and II, and elsewhere, and/or from the exceptions explicitly inserted where rights are guaranteed:

> The privilege of the writ of habeas corpus shall not be suspended, unless when in cases of rebellion or invasion the public safety may require it.[43]

> No person shall be held to answer for a capital, or otherwise infamous crime, unless on a presentment or indictment of a grand jury, except in cases arising in the land or naval forces, or in the militia, when in actual service in time of war or public danger . . . .[44]

So, let us start by looking at the objectives specified in the Preamble and consider what agreements, procedural or substantive, are logically or practically entailed by our joint commitment to them. While the Court has called the Preamble "precatory," rather than legally binding, it can do no harm to start at the beginning. Indeed, it is the only way I know to read a document seriously. We should, however, not forget Barber's point that the Preamble—and the document as a whole—is not guaranteed in advance to support a coherent reading that will satisfy all our wants.[45]

For each clause of the Preamble, I shall indicate both the general aim or value and the more specific, immediate concerns/issues the Framers appear to have had in mind. Of course, there is no single account of "the Framers' intent" that can command universal assent. The Framers were neither single-minded as individuals nor unanimous as a group, and there has from the outset been ample room both for questions and for criticism regarding the nature of their project. My strategy here is to draw eclectically from a fairly broad range of sources, in search of points that (1) can be advanced with reasonable confidence in their historical accuracy, and (2) tend to support a reading of the Constitution that could still be constitutive for us today.[46]

To form a more perfect Union: this clause pertains primarily to federalism, as an improvement over the Confederation. The aim: a more effective, respectable government. Specific concerns: trade war among the states, independent foreign policies, and the Confederation's lack of tax power.

To establish justice: this pertains to the rule of law, as opposed to arbitrary power or factional tyranny. The aim: security of fundamental rights, especially property. Specific concerns: Edmund Randolph's keynote address at the constitutional convention cited the need for barriers against the "excesses of democracy" in certain states. These included laws interfering with collection of debts by American and overseas creditors, issuance of paper money, and so forth. Beyond these concerns of the creditor class, the clause can and should be read to express disapproval of other governmental violations of personal rights—including slavery!

To insure domestic tranquility: this pertains to a secure and peaceful civic order. The aim: a government able to pass and enforce laws binding on individuals within the states, in cases where state power proves insufficient to avert turmoil. Specific concerns: Shays's rebellion, Indian attacks, and slave uprisings. (Standing alone, this clause could support a general power to define and punish crimes. Read in the context of the whole federal design, and the very specific crime-related powers identified in Article I, I think it does not.)

To provide for the common defense: this pertains to providing a respectable military capability. The aim: to deter foreign attack and respond to attack if necessary. But isolationism is not a constitutional policy: the "infant empire" envisioned by many was referred to in chapter 3. Specific concerns: British retention of forts in the Northwest Territory, harassment of shipping, and impressment of seamen; Spanish denial of access to the Mississippi River; hostile Indian tribes.

To promote the general welfare: this pertains to economic prosperity. The aim: behind substantial tensions between landed rural interests and urban financial/trade interests, there appears to have been a unifying vision of a "commercial republic," enjoying increasing wealth, distributed in a manner consistent with "domestic tranquility." Specific concerns: the depression of the 1780s, national debt, currency shortage; expansion/unification of a national market and better access to overseas markets. (The government's role in "internal improvements" would prove highly controversial.)

To secure the blessings of liberty: this pertains to the legitimacy and stability of the new political system. The aim: to maintain national independence, maintain a republican form of government, and safeguard personal rights via the devices of federalism, separation of powers, and so on. Specific concerns: all of those mentioned above. It was hoped that a government commanding the people's support and organized for effective action could address all of these successfully.

Now, does it make sense to prioritize these aims or interests in sequence? Much depends on whether we focus on the broad aims or on the specific concerns. To prioritize the former, we might use a philosophical method, analyzing the relationships among our conceptions of justice, security, and so on. This approach is characteristic of historical-aspirational readings of the Constitution, such as Bruce Ackerman's or Sotirios Barber's, and also of less historical, more analytical moral-philosophical readings such as Ronald Dworkin's. There are also those who insist that we must simply identify the relationships the Framers saw among these concepts; yet it is not at all clear why we should feel bound by those nontextual beliefs if we believe the Framers were mistaken. The distinction between a general concept voiced in the Preamble and specific conceptions of that concept held by the Framers is important. Since this is *our* Constitution, our understanding of the former need not be confined to the terms of the latter.

To focus on the Framers' specific concerns embroils us in a separate controversy over the thrust and value of their concrete political agenda—which filiopietists have read as wise, pragmatic patriotism and Beardians have read as an evil, elitist conspiracy.[47] Both of these readings seem simplistic today, and more moderate, nuanced assessments, such as Nedelsky's,[48] are now available. But again, whatever we make of the motives of the Framers cannot logically determine our view of the Constitution and what it means to us today.

It is clear enough that neither appeals to logic nor appeals to history will unite us around a single, canonical reading of the Constitution. The country has never been thus united, and it is hard to see how a large, free country with a diverse population ever could be. But if so, in what sense was the "more perfect Union" to be united? Surely this was the heart of the Framers' immediate constitutional project—the primary change they sought, as an essential means to any and all of the rest.

The obvious starting point is the commitment to membership, to speak as "We, the People." Shared, liberal beliefs about the social contract, popular sovereignty, and the rule of law tell us that membership entails participatory rights and duties: in exchange for a role in making the rules, members recognize the legitimacy of duly authorized governmental actions and the reciprocal rights of other members. They do so in the expectation that others will join them in striving to realize or to maintain the goods indicated in the Preamble. In other words, union is a means—not an end in itself.

The next step in our reading takes account of some further background beliefs that reflect the civic-republican elements of the

Framers' thought. In particular, republicanism sees conditions of justice and tranquility both as good in themselves and as essential for constructive, public-spirited debate about what the remaining community goals consist of or require. When many citizens see government as unjust or incompetent to provide for their basic security, the legitimacy of the constitutional regime comes into question. A healthy "ordinary politics" is impossible in times of revolutionary upheaval. The new Constitution, responding to the crisis perceived by the Framers and detailed by Publius, aims to (re)create the conditions for a healthy ordinary politics.

Where republican theory suggests that only a stronger, more just Union will bring tranquility, a liberal voice might add that justice and tranquility are not just goods but *rights*. If we escape the blinkers of anachronistic historiography, this duet appears more as a sympathetic chorus than as a debate. One might almost say, after Jefferson, that "we are all republicans; we are all liberals."[49]

As we discussed in chapter 2, however, the Framers were by no means all *democrats*. Their vision of politics lacked the emphases on inclusiveness and active participation that are so important to modern democratic thought. In an era when each decision was a novel, constitutive precedent, politics could not be ordinary in the modern sense[50] and elitist traditions provided strong resistance to democratic ideas. The regime was supported and stabilized by the consensual frame already agreed upon and the procedural safeguards against "tyranny of the majority" built into the Constitution.

Yet the founding generation also held conflicting conceptions of justice, tranquility, and liberty, or of how best to attain them. These differences were to become the focus of political struggle and would oblige *all* sides to reach out for additional support. The emergence of a political party system helped to introduce an enduring expansive, democratizing impulse into our politics.

As Sotirios Barber[51] incisively argues, it is competing conceptions of "defense" and "welfare" that are the very stuff of ordinary politics. While one could hope that concerns about justice and tranquility would surface only infrequently, regular debate over foreign and domestic policy issues seems inevitable. "Liberty" is also in constant contest insofar as governmental inaction is always an option and larger government always a threat. If this ordinary politics is properly constrained by constitutional safeguards and supported by a modicum of public (especially elite) wisdom and virtue, its results, it is hoped/promised, will secure the blessings of justice, tranquility, and liberty. That is, a diffusion of security and welfare, along with due restraint on government's invasions of the private sphere, should ensure citizens' continuing respect for the rights of others and general confidence in government.

The substantive questions of *how* to provide for security and welfare cannot be answered fully in advance, at the constitutional level. Such an attempt would leave no room for pragmatic adaptation to changing circumstances—or for any recognizable form of ordinary politics. Thus the constitutional project is largely devoted to specifying—or more accurately, to constraining—the procedures whereby such substantive decisions shall be made. Given our frequent, deep disagreements over the agenda and our relatively broad support for the inchoate idea of the rule of law, a focus on procedural criteria of political fairness as the core of our shared, constitutional understanding is a tempting solution.

So suppose that the criteria, the "rules of recognition" for when and what "the People have spoken" are primarily procedural—even if *some* outcomes might be unacceptably repugnant regardless of the procedures followed. The axiom of popular sovereignty directs attention in particular to procedures entailing public consent and/or accountability of government to the governed.[52] To say this is not to deny that procedural arrangements have substantive consequences. Far less is it to posit as a theoretical premise that we can find some set of procedures which any rational person, regardless of circumstances, ought to accept as fair, neutral, and binding. The claims of Publius and the Federalists were far more concrete: the new Constitution would be greatly preferable to both of the available alternatives—the Articles of Confederation or disunion.

The Articles of Confederation had declared the following set of goals and priorities: confederation and perpetual union; state sovereignty and reserved powers; friendship, common defence, secured liberties, mutual and general welfare. The Articles then proceeded to provide for:

privileges and immunities of free citizens (paupers, vagabonds, and
    fugitives from justice excepted)
justice (fugitives from)
full faith and credit
power to recall delegates
their qualifications and voting rules
congressional immunity
no nobility
centralized foreign policy and defense

limits on state taxes
common treasury
boundary disputes
private land disputes
currency
postal service
executive committee (establishment, powers, procedures)
budgeting
borrowing
armed forces
adjournment
keeping and publishing journal
new states
assumption of debts
binding observance
amendments.

Now, in comparison to the Articles, notice the following:

1. The Constitution forms a "more perfect," yet no longer an expressly "perpetual," Union.
2. The Constitution adds establishing justice and insuring domestic tranquility as explicit goals.
3. The Constitution is far more detailed about the structures and procedures of government and the separation of powers.
4. The Constitution entrusts more functions to the national government and, unlike the Articles, does not limit that government to the powers *expressly* delegated to it.
5. The Constitution, unlike the Articles, can be amended without unanimous state consent. Yet the amendment procedure remains very cumbersome.
6. Article V makes two aspects of the Constitution especially hard to amend. If rights are trumps and compelling public interests are overtrumps, these two ultraprivileged features (metatrumps?) rank higher still. They are the equal representation of states in the Senate, and the immunity of the slave trade from federal regulation prior to 1808.

These changes, as a whole, bespeak a dual emphasis on the Framers' part: a stronger Union and containing the "excesses of democracy." In reading *The Federalist*, we obtain a very clear sense of the weaknesses of the Articles and the dangers facing Americans: foreign aggression, interstate rivalry, and class struggle. The concrete advantages of a stronger Union, beyond avoiding or suppressing these problems, are understandably less clear. The best understanding of the Framers' conception of the goals announced in the Preamble comes from the specific powers granted to government.

The sixth point above, by the way, reinforces the claim that, when it comes to prioritizing public interests in particular, a rigid resort to literal "Framers' intent" techniques of interpretation, as opposed to "aspirational" or "evolving standards" techniques, leaves much to be desired. The historical shifts and situational sensitivity of mainstream thinking on such questions are clearly very marked.

Moving now from the Preamble to the body of the Constitution, how do the granted powers—and their sequence—relate to the aims and concerns identified above?

1. The overall frequency distribution of the Preamble's aims seems fairly equal. Liberty has more than its proportional share if the provisions pertaining to separation of powers and internal administration are placed under this heading. (Liberty is of course the express rationale for the separation of powers and for giving each branch control of its internal operations.) Tranquility has fewer than its share of mentions, largely because it is, on the whole, less a direct product of federal governmental action than a byproduct of avoiding unjust actions and achieving the other aims.

2. The sequencing of the grants of power within each Article has no apparent pattern. Powers pertaining to justice, defense, or welfare are not necessarily grouped together; and the seemingly most momentous powers, such as the war power, do not necessarily precede lesser ones such as the copyright clause.

3. The three branches are listed in order, according to the relative magnitude and scope of their powers as well as the closeness of their accountability to the people. The branches of government differ in obvious ways in the aims for which they are chiefly responsible. The powers of Congress are the most numerous and diverse, bearing most heavily, it seems, on welfare (taxing, spending, commerce, etc.), union (commerce, currency, weights and measures, capital district, etc.) and defense. The executive branch has special responsibilities in the areas of defense and justice; otherwise, its duties are largely administrative (originally, these were assigned to it largely in the name of liberty; today, they bear heavily on welfare). The courts are focused on justice above all.

4. The consequences of all this for the enterprise of balancing governmental powers against personal rights are far less obvious.

The text will not bring us to easy agreement on which of the Constitution's aims are primary. A liberal might hold that justice, welfare, and liberty are the primary goals, while union, tranquility, and defense are means. A republican might see more intrinsic value in unity and tranquility and also hold that the responsibility of government, especially national government, for increasing welfare is quite limited.

Nor, surely, will all agree as to which governmental actions are most conducive to each of the primary goals, for example, enforcing civil rights versus punishing crimes to establishing justice, or better education versus deregulating the economy to promoting the general welfare, or cutting taxes and spending versus election finance reform to securing liberty. Even if there *were* consensus on such questions, moreover, so that certain governmental powers were deemed privileged by their generally close relationships to certain vital goals, it still would not follow that any exercise *whatever* of such a power must take priority over *any* fundamental right, no matter how severely that right is infringed upon by the action in question. Nor, of course, would such a schematic prioritization of governmental powers help us resolve disagreements over which purpose actually was the primary basis for a particular governmental action.

It appears correct, therefore, that categorical analysis cannot avoid balancing, but only disguise it or make it willfully insensitive to the realistic values at stake. To escape from balancing, the courts would have to declare rights absolute, or decline to enforce them at all. And again, even absolutism would leave courts with the need to define the right at stake—with all the temptations for covert balancing *that* task entails.

Additional politically volatile issues beset judicial review of state, as opposed to federal, government actions. Before identifying government interests as compelling, they must be identifiable as government interests *tout court*. As noted above, it has become difficult to identify powers clearly outside the reach of Congress. State constitutions, however, have their own particular grants of power. Some limit spending to ill-defined "public purposes," but states in general are held to possess a "plenary police power" over "public health, safety, and morals" that is nowhere granted to the national government.

The traditional adage that states have power to legislate on behalf of "public morals" deserves to be but has not yet been effectively challenged as contradictory to our ideals of tolerance or, more specifically, to the establishment clause. Instead, there have been fitful and largely unsuccessful efforts to invoke against it the recently developed right of privacy. This governmental interest, termed "unfocused" by Nagel,[53] is at least as nakedly partisan on the republican side as is the one person, one vote rule or the "wall of separation" between church and state on the liberal side. Critics of the undue liberalism of the Warren Court seem oblivious to this ongoing rightist bias in American jurisprudence.

Most of the issues mentioned in the preceding paragraphs are staples of contemporary politics. If we regard them as issues of ordinary politics, the courts should not undertake to resolve them. If they are constitutional issues, courts do have a role to play, even if no branch of government can finally resolve them. But have we any principled way of making this distinction? Can courts authoritatively determine which kinds of issues they are?

One role that both liberal and republican thought accord to courts is maintaining the boundary between the public and private realms. It follows, at minimum, that courts can—indeed must—undertake to distinguish public from private interests. What is the core idea behind this distinction?

First, certain decisions must be made collectively, because the consequences of incongruent private decisions are, all agree, intolerable. For example, recognition of others as members of the polity is not a matter left to each citizen or to each local government to decide. Instead, Congress can make "an uniform Rule of Naturalization," and citizens are entitled to have their "privileges and immunities" respected throughout the Union. As Gottlieb argues, the safeguarding of all fundamental rights is more than a personal privilege; it is in an important sense a "compelling public interest," which government surely has power—if not always a judicially enforceable duty—to pursue. Likewise, paying taxes and obeying other valid laws is not voluntary, but a duty for all to whom they apply. Otherwise, the public could not rely upon the effective operation of government. Within constitutional limits, government is empowered to define and regulate the public agenda. Indeed, that is its *raison d'être*.

Second, certain other decisions must not be made collectively, because all agree the consequences would be, for some or many of us, intolerable. Thus, it is undisputed that Congress may not establish a national church, the police may not adopt torture as standard procedure, and citizens may not be denied the right to vote on account of race. For the sake of union, justice, and tranquility, religious faith, confessing to crimes, and political participation—unlike paying taxes or obeying speed limits—are matters for voluntary, private decision.

Third, at the margin are certain matters deeply contested as to how they should be regulated. Some insist on various collective actions, while others may strongly oppose any such action. On issues like these, even agreeing to take a vote tends to prejudge the question as a public one; to take *no* collective action is the way to leave it private. (A neat paradox arises, by the way, if we adopt a constitutional amendment barring future public action. In this case, at least, privacy is obviously a public artifact. But then, the social contract that created the very public sphere was itself, until the ratifying moment, a private undertaking.)

Initially, the question posed may be whether government *should* act: shall we enact a national health insurance plan, or let the market system solve our problems? Yet, if any law is enacted, opponents may well challenge it as outside the scope of governmental power. Again paradoxically, they may well appeal to a branch of the government—an arm of the public—to protect their sphere of privacy.

Thus arises the paradigm "hot" constitutional case: can government ban abortions to protect life, or is ending a pregnancy a matter of personal choice? Can a school board decree a moment of silence at the start of the school day, or is this tantamount to coercing prayer? Can government interfere with factory closings that would bankrupt a community, or is this simply the owner's absolute property right?

In laying such questions before a court, litigants deliberately seek to elevate the issue from one of ordinary to one of constitutional politics. They ask the court: Does the Constitution decide the question? The court, in turn (depending on whether it sees itself as discoverer or as creator of law) will ask: Can we/should we develop a constitutional answer, or must we/should we leave the matter to ordinary politics?

From the court's point of view, the institutional need is for a *principled*—not a flagrantly partisan—decision. Of course, to recognize the case as a hard one is to recognize room for dispute about what—if anything—the Constitution says or implies. One argument might hold that the very contested nature of the issue makes it unfit or unripe for resolution at the constitutional level. But this is to say that all politics is ordinary politics and that judicial review, unless it attains to total scientific objectivity, is completely illegitimate.

It is simply not the case that the only alternative to an outmoded and bankrupt legal formalism is an unfettered and inadequately democratic ordinary politics. Nor can it be wise to make constitutional amendment the only way of deciding what to regulate and what to leave to the private sphere. The issues arise constantly, and amendment is far too difficult and too permanent a way of resolving most of them.

In most cases, the pragmatic methods of ordinary politics will be suited to deciding what we *should* do. In others, judicial review may be the best way to determine what we *may* do. Sometimes the question is whether there is a profound objection to having *any* public policy on the matter at hand. But of course, privacy is not the only constitutional value of which a policy may run afoul. On most matters government is free to make policy, so long as it adheres to proper procedures and respects personal rights. Whether the court likes the policy is irrelevant, if it falls within the responsibilities that the people have bestowed on government.

Obviously, no canonical account of those responsibilities is available today. Indeed, the Constitution itself seems to encourage endless partisan conflict between advocates of Nozick's minimal, night-watchman state;[54] of Rawls's intermediate, market with safety-net state;[55] of Dworkin's more egalitarian welfare state;[56] and even of Stone's state in which trees and rivers, as well as persons, would have rights.[57]

Conclusion

The Constitution permits and invites debate on many matters, but the rule of law and the separation of powers are core principles to which liberals and republicans alike are committed. That is why the "prerogative" doctrine is a heresy, and why the abdication and overdelegation of power by Congress pose major threats to the system. If it is hard for courts to restrain the executive, however, it is even harder for them to force an unwilling Congress to act. Thus it is not surprising that the constitutional dimension of the struggle between the liberal and republican agendas has come to be mediated largely by rights jurisprudence. It was so already in the *Lochner* era but, as chapter 8 argues, that era's rights jurisprudence was fundamentally flawed.

The liberal constitutional teaching is that there must be at least enough law to provide basic mutual security and, the post-Civil War amendments remind us, equal respect and concern. The republican teaching is that it is not enough to let individuals go safely about their private business. It also seems necessary to constitute and nourish the polity as a specific public project, geared to more than the mere survival or even the individually defined welfare of its members. Otherwise, many will find insufficient reason to accept the burdens that living together requires.

Now, to the extent that a polity is thus individuated, it is also set off from other communities and placed in potential opposition to them. And, to the extent that some members have reservations about or feel marginalized by the projects and commitments chosen, they become second-class or semivoluntary members. So how can such a polity be sustained without violence? The bottom line is that it cannot: the notion of a totally nonviolent state is an oxymoron.[58] Nevertheless, there is a tremendous difference between a constitutional polity and Hobbes's Leviathan.

Tolerance in matters fundamental to individual identity, the pursuit of self-defined and self-defining individual projects, is essential if either individuals or the community are to thrive. Likewise, a measure of unity and sacrifice in support of community-defined and community-defining projects is essential not just for collective welfare but for that of individual members, for the individual and her identity do not exist before and outside that of the community.

There is clearly no objective, neutral measure of what is "fundamental" or "compelling" for the individual or for the polity. When we have debate about where to draw these lines, for the "public" to draw them is already to make autonomy a matter of collective grace. But, on the other hand, if the people cannot define the public realm, the Constitution, the state, the People itself cannot exist. As Derrida argues, the people is not prior to the state but (re)constitutes itself in the process of (re)founding the state.[59]

Fortunately, in our tradition the People in so doing has not been oblivious to the rights and welfare of individuals. On the contrary, the Constitution, from Preamble to amendments, clearly identifies those interests as fundamental. While the scope and shape of state action have always been controversial, we have also found it not just useful but essential to make, and argue over, constitutional rules about the limits of state action. We have not left everything to the pragmatic judgments, the "naked preferences,"[60] and the lurking violence of "ordinary politics." Is there reason to doubt that we were wise?

Part III

The One
(Against Positivism)

*R*ights, we have seen, are crucial in mediating the tension between liberal and republican visions of our polity. The jurisprudence of powers, by recalling the aspirations that guide the people's agenda and by ensuring that government is adequate to its tasks, guards against the atomization and aimless drift that can result from excesses of liberal individualism. Rights jurisprudence, for its part, guards against the republican excesses of exclusion and intolerance. It might also, if political and property rights were better formulated, help to ameliorate the evils of irresponsible government and widespread economic dependency that afflict the current regime.

The chapters in this part develop some ideas about the place of personal rights in our constitutional system—the significance of such rights, how to make sense of claims for or against particular rights, and the consequences of certain specific doctrinal peculiarities within our jurisprudence.

To avoid misunderstanding, let me stipulate at the outset that my primary concern is not philosophical rigor but my best understanding of political soundness. A valid deontological argument must also be consequentialist: the real meaning of a polity's rights discourse lies in its actual impact on citizens' lives. The phrase *against positivism*, therefore, does not announce an elaborate theoretical argument. It simply declares a refusal to accept that my

rights are, by definition, only what some "duly constituted authority"—or, for that matter, some self-appointed prophet of "political
correctness"—has declared them to be. Nor are they given by a natural law on which all rational beings must agree. Rather, as Von
Jhering put it, rights are won by historically situated struggle: "All
the law in the world has been obtained by strife."[1]

What rights we should struggle for today is, loosely speaking, a
pragmatic question, in much the same sense that the Legal Realists
were pragmatic. Some see the Realists as positivist, because they
were sometimes heard to say that "we are under a Constitution, but
the Constitution is what the Court says it is,"[2] or "the prophecies of
what the courts will do in fact, and nothing more pretentious, are
what I mean by the law."[3] But the Realists were by no means at a
loss to criticize what judges said when the results clashed with
their visions of a good and just society. Nor did Realist judges always shrink, as a vulgarly consistent positivist would, from trying
to expound those visions and persuade others to accept them.

There are critics today, of various political stripes, who argue
that struggling for rights is a misguided and even pernicious effort.
Because enforcement can be fraught with uncertainties, apparent
victories may prove largely pyrrhic. Even worse, some say, the
prevalence of rights talk focuses our politics on selfish and inflexi-
ble private demands, driving the trends toward atomization and po-
larization from which the polity suffers. They call instead for a
spirit of compromise and a renewed focus on the public good.[4]

While the critics' concerns are well taken, their extreme conclusion does not follow. Our constitutional politics indeed needs to be
principled, rising above self-interest in any narrow, shortsighted
sense and, hopefully, appealing to a vision of community that most
if not all will respect—and even embrace. It also needs to respect
each individual in ways that pure majoritarianism could not, even
if everyone really had an equal say.

Bear in mind that the *political* criteria for saying that "the People [of the United States] have spoken" cannot be identical with the
criteria for saying that "Americans are one people"—a cultural sort
of claim. Peoplehood in the cultural sense is essentially inner: it
goes to states of mind of various individuals, whether they regard
themselves as American, and what that term means to them. The
answers could well be a matter of degree and of overlapping rather
than identical assessments.

In the political realm, however, we are concerned with *authoritative actions*, and the criteria must be strictly operational. Legally,
the final answer to a dispute over governmental authority must be

yes or no, and, as Macedo and Habermas differently argue, its jus-tification must be publicly accessible and persuasive.[5] I do not mean, of course, that if authority exists it must be absolute; that would leave no logical space for rights to operate. By the same token, that a right exists does not automatically make *it* absolute either. Powers and rights are designed with a view to their possible conflict and mutual limitation. To abandon rights would leave us far more defenseless against abuses of power than we are today. Critics, of course, remain free to waive their own.

My arguments are based on an eclectic synthesis of informal em-pirical observation, conventional political and moral wisdom, de-ductive analysis, and legal precedent. While none of the above, taken alone, can be decisive, neither can any safely be ignored. An "is" does not always determine a specific "ought," but our norms ought to be grounded in what is the case. Because constitutional rights are personal rights, conventional morality or political con-sensus cannot automatically prevail over deeply felt individual needs. Otherwise judicial review would be superfluous.

Yet majority opinion deserves *prima facie* respect in a democra-tic polity. Judges are not free simply to impose their personal philosophies upon the body politic. Rather, their task is to remind the polity of the fundamental principles upon which its integrity and legitimacy depend. Of course, the implications of those princi-ples can change as circumstances do. When the needs, desires, and values of persons change, shopworn precedents may require recon-sideration. Yet change must be justified in light of enduring princi-ple if constitutional integrity is to be maintained.

These maxims are open textured: they do not obviate the need for judgment, but indicate the kinds of judgment that are called for. If my more specific claims are less than conclusive, it is hoped that they point toward arguments that deserve careful response: argu-ments that the dignity of all persons in our society can and should be made more secure.

Personal rights are means to the flourishing of persons. A prin-cipled approach to personal rights, therefore, must begin with an inquiry into the concept of 'personhood' itself. In chapter 6, I con-sider what is at stake in that inquiry, its history, and how it should proceed. I argue that it is necessary and possible to be both princi-pled and realistic—both legally and politically sound—in this en-deavor. I suggest some general guidelines for a viable constitutional jurisprudence of personhood.

In chapter 7, I consider further the methodologies available for deriving from a concept of personhood a jurisprudence of personal rights and their relative priorities. After exploring some important philosophical theories, I argue for a "politics of rights" approach to understanding and strengthening our rights jurisprudence.

In chapter 8, I review and critique the Supreme Court's modern development of fundamental rights jurisprudence. I identify some major problem areas in our current constitutional jurisprudence that my suggested approach makes salient. Certain rights that our jurisprudence has mistakenly denied, ignored, or underemphasized are fundamental: they should be recognized, clarified, expanded, and upgraded in priority.

Chapter 6

Personhood and Rights

This is a very personal document!

—Irvan Taube

*M*ost of our fundamental concepts have large, celebrated bodies of literature devoted to their elaboration. One might be tempted to think that any concept that has not received so much attention could not be equally fundamental.

The view taken here is that the concept of a 'person' is absolutely central to our political thinking. It has received relatively little close attention, primarily because there have been relatively few historic occasions for dispute about its meaning. Yet those occasions amply demonstrate both the fundamental nature and the difficulties of the concept of personhood.

Personhood in World History

For primitive peoples, animistic beliefs denied any sharp separation between man and nature. Spirit(s) could be found alike in

This chapter originally appeared, in different form, in the Fall 1986 issue of *Polity*, Volume XIX, #1. It is adapted/revised from a later version that appeared in David Freeman, ed., *Political Concepts*, copyright 1994 by Kendall/Hunt Publishing Company, with permission.

rocks, ponds, trees, animals, and man. Such a culture does not appear to have the concept of personhood as we know it. Rather kinship, however understood, is the basis for social recognition and interaction. Many tribes and clans around the world have named themselves "the people," often explicitly regarding other human groups as animals or beasts and deeming them proper targets for cannibalism, ritual sacrifice, or slavery.[1]

This seemingly straightforward kinship principle leaves open important issues about both the boundaries and the implications of social membership, which can be resolved in various ways. Even the most primitive cultures known to us have elaborate rules on these matters. Sometimes certain animals are claimed as kin. Then there is the question of outsiders marrying into the tribe: exogamy may be forbidden, permitted, or even required. Another issue is the exact moment at which tribal membership commences for the young. For example, in many societies with high infant mortality, the ceremony of recognition is not performed until some set period of time after birth. If the infant dies before then, no funeral is held.[2] A final issue is that the privileges attendant upon membership may be very unevenly distributed, and in some cases may be meager indeed. In short, to be a person is simply to have a place.

The classical world, with its higher technology, cities, and written languages, encompassed many different peoples. The ancients had a more extended concept of 'human kinship' than did more primitive tribes, and a more scientific understanding of the uniqueness of our species. To Greeks, Romans, Hebrews, or Chinese it was evident that such qualities as rationality and the knowledge of good and evil made moral and political concerns uniquely and universally human. But kinship still counted very heavily, and, lacking the egalitarian bias of modern thought, the ancients drew far-reaching conclusions from the observation that some humans seemed more rational, not to say more virtuous, than others. Whole classes of humans, such as children, women, foreigners, or heathens, might thereby be relegated to second-class status (or worse) in political, social, and religious institutions.[3]

Mere membership in the human species thus still guaranteed very little in social-political terms. In Rome or in China, even after the birth ceremony, children were subject to extremely broad parental authority, including the possibility of infanticide. It does not follow that children were not viewed as persons, or else they could not have inherited parental property. In general, elaborate religious and legal systems assigned to every person a place, based on birth rather than on personal qualities or choices, with relatively little prospect for mobility.

According to Marcel Mauss,[4] both the primitive and the classical worlds viewed the individual as nothing more than a bearer of a set of roles assigned to him/her by the community. One who played those roles well earned praise; one who failed or rebelled against the assigned role earned censure. There was, in a sense, no one behind the role one played—very little scope for individual choice, and very little attention to the question of who might do the choosing. In fact, the term *person* is derived from the Latin *persona*, which denoted a disguise or mask!

The decisive event, for Mauss, was the advent of Christianity, with its overriding emphasis on individual salvation as opposed to this-worldly, collective concerns. For Christians, introspection and self-cultivation assumed a new importance. On judgment day, every person stands alone before God; life in this world must be lived accordingly. (Hinduism, Buddhism, and Daoism, it might be argued, paralleled Christianity in their overriding concern for spiritual enlightenment and their devaluation of worldly strivings. But, instead of ascribing to each individual a unique personal soul, these creeds posited the separateness of the self as a dangerous illusion that needed to be transcended. Thus, even if the quest for enlightenment was largely up to the individual, it did not entail a conception of the person similar to that entailed by Christianity.)

So long as the world was God's *imperium*—or that of an Emperor designated as His spokesman—the political implications of this conceptual shift in Western thought were modest. Man's duty still was basically to obey God and King. Somewhat new was the notion, slowly and variously emerging, that if the King should depart from the will of God (or the law of nature), his command should not be obeyed.[5] But until the Protestant Reformation, God's will and natural law were declared by the church, not by the individual. Authority and hierarchy were divided between church and state. That a man had two masters did not make him free.

The Reformation radically decentralized theological authority, while the Renaissance witnessed a trend toward secularization in the artistic, economic, and political spheres. In the fullness of time, there emerged a concept of a person not created by or subject to arbitrary power, whether divine or communal. Instead, the person was conceived in theory as existing alone, in a state of nature, and endowed with the capacity to decide which, if any, allegiances and associations he/she chose to form. This person, according to Hobbes, Locke, and Rousseau, had natural attributes of freedom and equality that had not been recognized before. One was free and responsible for the creation of one's own identity and status. In this perspective, only consent can give one person legitimate authority over another.[6]

In tandem—and in tension—with these ideas came the rupture between King and People, the claim of popular sovereignty, and the insistence that *both* King and People were bound by the laws they together had made. As noted in chapter 3, these themes supported a new, more legitimate form of authority alongside the new concept of 'freedom.'

Against this background we can appreciate many nuances in the Declaration of Independence's axiom that all persons are equally endowed with certain fundamental, inalienable rights, including the rights to life, liberty, and the pursuit of happiness. For us, to be a person is to be a recognized member of human society, entitled to develop and pursue one's own conception of the good life, so long as one respects the equal rights of others to pursue their own perhaps very different conceptions. Nonpersons, in contrast, by definition can have no rights of their own, because they are incapable of engaging in this form of life in community with others.

Personhood in Liberal Philosophy and Politics

This perspective may give the impression that personhood is simply an empirical or scientific fact: one either does or does not possess the capacity indicated above. In reality, however, it is a moral-legal-political judgment made through social-political processes. This becomes very clear when we reflect that our society has granted legal personhood to ships and corporations, while denying it to the human fetus and, for a time, to slaves. It is these controversial cases that best illuminate both the importance and the difficulty of the concept of personhood for our own polity.

Philosophically speaking, the easiest case for recognizing personhood is self-reflection: "I think; therefore I am." From this, we easily extrapolate to the case of other normal human adults. Hard questions arise when our normal behavioral expectations, applicable to such an adult, cannot be met—when even the familiar images of deviance do not apply. We can distinguish at least three such situations: severely impaired humans; potential humans; and human-like nonhumans, such as higher animals, extra-terrestrials, or advanced robots. In each case, many would deny that an entity so different from ourselves, so incapable of assuming the full range of social functions of the normal person, is a person.

Yet to frame the question in this way makes personhood a matter of degree—a prospect that seems especially distasteful when we recall the constitutional compromise that counted a slave as three-fifths of a person.[7] Indeed, the logical role of personhood in our legal system seems to require us to deem it a nominal variable—to hold that one either is a person, hence equally endowed with fundamental rights, or one is not.

One way to do this would be to make the recognition of personhood dependent upon one's possession of a single nominal attribute, biological status as *Homo sapiens* being the most obvious candidate.[8] Such an approach, however, does justice to none of the hard cases posed above. It might exclude hypothetical nonhuman entities who could do virtually everything we can and shared most of our values, yet include some humans who could do virtually nothing and scarcely be said to possess values at all. Such results clearly would be both unjust to individuals and costly to society at large.

The claim that such results would be unjust draws much of its sense from the Kantian dichotomy of person and object.[9] A person is a sapient, autonomous, rational subject, capable of communicating and otherwise participating in our form of life. An object, in contrast, is not a coparticipant, but an instrument freely available for our use, without rights of its own. We can easily say that it is unjust to persons to treat them as mere objects, and it is also unjust to oblige persons to treat mere objects as if they too were persons. But this assumes that we already know what a person is; the task before us is to determine how that question is to be justly decided.

Rawls's theory of justice[10] seems to suggest that we put on a veil of ignorance and assess our candidate without regard to biology or belief system, so long as it manifests reason and moral sensibility. This view solves some of our problems, but surely not all of them. Once again, sapience, rationality, and communicative competence are matters of degree. Rawls leaves it unclear how cases of severe impairment, temporary or chronic, should be handled. The impaired can, at best, participate only vicariously in the deliberations of the "original position," where the social contract is formulated. To eliminate unjust, selfish biases Rawls deliberately uses an extremely thin, context-free conception of the person in the original position. But a just social contract must provide for the impaired, and Rawls does not acknowledge that, because their needs and capacities are fundamentally different, we cannot reason for them in exactly the same way as we reason for ourselves. For similar reasons, his treatment of obligations to future generations is open to serious criticism. At minimum, we must recognize that a vicarious claim to personhood presents problems that a direct claim does not.

A related problem is that Rawls's criteria for personhood seem one-sidedly ideational and linguistic. We may doubt whether an entity with the apparent competence to engage in moral deliberation and discussion, but not manifesting feelings, desires, and plans of its own, should qualify as a person. For example, a computer that passed Turing's famous test, by sending messages that could not be reliably distinguished from those of a real person, might perhaps be said to think; but the persons familiar to us are always more—and sometimes less—than thinking machines.[11]

Even if we limit ourselves to criteria of reason and moral sensibility, it is not entirely clear how Rawls determines who satisfies those criteria and who does not. On the one hand, some of his early formulations can be interpreted as recognizing families and corporations as persons; on the other, he once stated in a faculty seminar that his theory does not, in itself, establish that Negroes are persons. In his latest book, he defines personhood as possession, "to the requisite minimum degree," of two moral powers (a capacity for a sense of justice and for a conception of the good) and the powers of reason. On this basis, he treats the personhood of human slaves as self-evident; yet he repeats that his is a "normative" and "political," not a "scientific" or "metaphysical," conception of personhood.[12]

Most philosophers who have recently addressed the question seem agreed that it is impossible to specify a set of sufficient or even necessary conditions for personhood.[13] There is no universal, abstract form of life, in the sense of a daily routine or a set of social roles with which any person should feel comfortable. It is true that life and health, status and security are close to being universally valued; that most people live in groups and participate in patterned routines of production and reproduction. Yet, though apparent exceptions to these norms attract great interest, those involved may be viewed as heroes or saints rather than as deviants. In either case, it is not their personhood that is placed in question. What range of competencies, then, should be required?

Well, as Wittgenstein would say, a line must be drawn somewhere. In real life, lines are always drawn in the context of a range of concrete situations in which the person would predictably have to function. That is why Rawls's "veil of ignorance" approach seems so unsatisfactory.

Context-sensitive tests would have the advantage of recognizing the real differences in capacity that natural persons exhibit without undermining their claims to personhood. They would also provide flexibility in handling claims from entities not of our species. Yet it seems anomalous to define the core concept of personhood particularistically in a society ostensibly committed to universalistic norms. By creating different classes of legal persons, we would seriously undermine the notion that all persons are equally endowed with certain fundamental rights. We would also open the door for decisions influenced by the rankest sorts of prejudice.

Personal Identity

A related aspect of the issue of personhood-in-context is personal identity. Persons (and only persons) have duties as well as rights. The very qualities that constitute us as persons—ability to foresee consequences, to choose, to consent—are those that make it possible and appropriate to assign us rights and duties. Our rights and duties, in turn, are personal to ourselves and attach in consequence of our own personal histories, actions, and commitments. We share them with others only when we agree to do so. As philosophers have noted, these concepts quickly become unworkable if we have difficulty identifying an individual and cannot be sure what actions and commitments have been his/hers. While such difficulties are very rare, it is instructive to consider how the task of identification—including self-identification—is ordinarily accomplished.

As Parfit[14] argues, physical appearance is normally utilized; yet it clearly does not define identity—one can change in appearance and still be the same person. Even more striking, one can lose memory or even consciousness and still be the same person. What is it, Parfit asks, that persists? And what justifies holding *me* responsible for acts performed long ago by one who looked, felt, and thought quite differently from the way I do today? Of course, this might be answered by reference to a concept such as the 'soul'; but that is clearly not an acceptable answer for our secular government, nor for many nonreligious individuals.

Parfit's view is that *nothing* persists. If personal identity is no illusion, it must rest on the relative subjective connectedness of one's experience over a lifetime. The identity of Mr. Jones at time T1 with Mr. Jones at time T2 is thus a matter of degree; but so is the identity of Mr. Jones with Mrs. Jones. While this surprising position does deprive personal rights and duties of their normal deontological grounding, Parfit holds that most of our everyday moral practices can be sustained on utilitarian grounds.

Special difficulties arise, however, in making decisions with reference to the unborn—in particular, decisions that will foreseeably have an impact not just on how people live, but on which people live or how many. It is one thing to assess my own interests, or those of an existing person with whom I can consult, or about whom I know a great deal, or with whose situation I can easily empathize. It is another to assess the interests of unspecified or statistical persons, and especially to wonder whether they would choose to come into existence—a decision none of us actually makes for ourselves.

Standard utilitarian approaches, if they can address such questions at all, tend to generate repugnant answers—to prescribe a very large population of people living at the borderline of subsistence. This is clearly not what Bentham meant by "the greatest good of the greatest number." But again, if our conception of the person is to include some notion of excellence or flourishing toward which the person strives, we are faced with agonizing choices. We cannot facilitate such flourishing for unknown others without making specific assumptions about what this concept entails for them. We can scarcely avoid doing so on behalf of our offspring; but government cannot do so for all of us without imposing on society a specific conception of the good life—an imposition that our liberal, tolerant, individualist tradition regards as the essence of tyranny.

Yet again, for government to abstain may condemn posterity to living with the consequences of widespread unreflective (or arbitrary and irrational) private action.

Personhood in American Law

In traditional Jewish law, children, deaf-mutes, and the insane formed one special legal class, while slaves and women formed a second.[15] Still more extreme, in traditional Japan, a caste composed of executioners and other taboo occupations was officially designated "nonhumans."[16]

We may smile at such classifications, but our history provides its own examples of arbitrariness. In the *Dred Scott* case, Chief Justice Taney said that blacks in effect were property, not persons. The Founders clearly had not considered blacks to be part of the "People of the United States"; otherwise they would have felt bound to accord them equal rights. Since they were neither U.S. citizens nor subjects of a foreign state, they had "no rights which the white man was bound to respect," and, for constitutional purposes, stood simply as property of which their owner could not rightly be deprived. This conclusion was reached without offering any explicit definition of personhood, and without regard to the fact that the Constitution three times referred to slaves as "persons."[17]

In *Roe v. Wade*,[18] which upheld a woman's right to an abortion, the Supreme Court again sidestepped the definition of personhood, instead approaching the issue in an essentially positivistic manner. The Court observed that the law has not traditionally treated the fetus as a person, but its effort to provide grounding for this tradition proceeded largely from the situation of the pregnant woman, rather than from that of the fetus itself. Yet the woman's right to privacy, concededly not absolute, would not take priority over the fetus's right to life if it had such a right. Moreover, the woman's right to control her own body is not logically sufficient to entail that the fetus is not a person, at least in the case of a fetus viable outside her body or, for that matter, a frozen embryo stored in a laboratory. At any rate, as matters now stand, the woman's right of privacy apparently includes not just a right to expel the fetus from her body, but also a right to determine, until the moment of birth, whether an additional person shall be brought into being. While *Roe* and subsequent cases have held that the state may also have some legitimate interest in this matter, at least in the third trimester, the law seems clear that the father, mysteriously, has none at all. (See chapter 8 for further discussion).[19]

In marked contrast to its skeptical treatment of the slave and the fetus, the Court in 1886 summarily accepted the claim that corporations are legal persons.[20] Though they do not possess the full panoply of rights guaranteed to natural persons, their property rights have been generously protected over the years. The state, of course, is another judicially recognized "artificial person," endowed not only with a wide range of legal rights, but also with a degree of special "sovereign immunity" vis-à-vis the legal claims of ordinary citizens.

Who Decides?

These much-criticized decisions, which make more political than philosophical sense, draw attention to several concerns that go well beyond their specific merits. One is the appropriate role of various private and public agencies in making decisions respecting personhood. Another is the interaction between moral-political and scientific-technological forces in shaping our attitudes on these questions.

Possible judges of personhood may be found in the public sector—including legislatures, executives, courts, and the people acting through constitutional amendment, and in the private sector—including immediate family (where the candidate is human), business organizations (where the candidate is artificial), and scientific experts. Each may have claims to participate based on relevant knowledge, stake in the outcome, and associated or analogous responsibilities.

We are accustomed to the phenomena of elected officials recognizing foreign states and fixing requirements for immigration and naturalization of aliens. In these matters—each resembling recognition of personhood, insofar as personhood fundamentally pertains to membership in the community—we recognize the need for uniform policy. By the same token it seems clear, especially in the aftermath of *Dred Scott*, that personhood must be nationally rather than locally defined; one should not lose one's personhood by crossing state lines. Indeed, the law necessarily defines what constitutes life and death, as well as personhood itself.

Now, the law usually regards decisions on state recognition and on immigration policy as purely "political," and not implicating personal rights that courts can protect. The rationale for this position has already been questioned in chapters 1, 3, and 4. Neither the general law/politics distinction nor the specific dichotomy between matters of state and matters of personal rights holds up well under close scrutiny; even less clear in law and in principle are the outer limits of the government's role in determining the makeup of the community when questions of international relations are *not* involved.

As things stand today, hard decisions on family planning and treatment of the gravely handicapped or ill are generally left to the family; yet the law may intervene where fundamental rights are judged to be at stake. Government today can also use tax and welfare incentives to influence private decisions on family planning or allocation of medical care. It can regulate the availability of new biotechnology through patents or FDA licensing. Scientific discoveries and other developments continually give rise to pressures for new forms of regulation. Shall we leave the introduction and use of new technologies entirely to private choice, or ban them entirely, or have the government impose a policy? Each option has troublesome features.

Consider, for example, the likelihood that science will soon make it possible for parents to control with high reliability the gender of their offspring. Many individuals, for reasons ranging from frivolous to medically urgent, might be eager to avail themselves of such a choice. Yet, if the typical preference for boy babies over girls were allowed free reign, the sex ratio of our and other societies would become greatly skewed, with profound consequences for future generations. At the same time, the prospect of government rationing of access to such technology would alarm many citizens of a free society.

What we must bear in mind is that the question of what is a person cannot be separated as a practical matter (though it can as a logical matter) from questions about the size and composition of our community or about the particular rights that all persons shall possess. Our decisions on the former point will inevitably have a major impact on what we can say or will want to say about the latter; and the way we define the person is likely to be driven to a large extent precisely by the impact we expect our definition to have. Thus, Chief Justice Taney's argument against the citizenship of free blacks relied heavily on the political consequences that would flow from granting them constitutional rights.

It is difficult to argue that such consequentialist reasoning is wrong in principle. Dworkin has indeed argued powerfully that utilitarian concerns are not admissible to justify a violation of someone's rights, because rights, by definition, are "trumps" that take priority over concerns about the costs of respecting them.[21] Yet to make the same claim about the role of utilitarian concerns in the decision to *grant* rights would involve us in an infinite regress: we would have to posit something like a right to have rights. In other words, if possessing rights is a logical consequence of personhood, it is difficult to see how there could be a right to become a person.

Nevertheless, *Dred Scott* seems a classic example of a wrongful denial of personhood, because it relied entirely on white attitudes and interests, adducing no relevant facts about blacks themselves to justify the conclusion that they could have no rights. Neither their sufferings, their desires, nor their potential contributions as citizens were taken into account. By resorting to a vulgar positivism (a person is whoever we say the Founders said it is), the Court avoided entirely the point that any nonracial test of personhood (in terms of competencies, and so on) that excluded all blacks would also exclude most if not all whites.

Roe v. Wade,[22] for all its vagaries, can at least rely upon the obvious empirical differences between the fetus and the normal person, and upon the inescapable need to establish the times when personhood begins and ends. And if the moment of birth is a somewhat arbitrary choice from the fetal standpoint, from that of the mother it is extremely salient.

The personhood of corporations is admittedly a fiction: they are not persons, but things—properties, in fact, created and used by persons for their own ends. Yet, while they cannot vote, the First

Amendment has been interpreted to permit them to spend money freely in pursuit of political influence.[23] Moreover, in our law the "life" of a corporation is in a sense more secure than that of an ordinary person—let alone a slave: corporate charters are not revoked to punish egregious company misconduct.[24] Thus do the principles of moral philosophy sometimes bow to the conveniences of business.

As for the state, we have seen that it is not just a legal person but a superperson: as "representative" of "the People," it is empowered to override our personal rights in the pursuit of what it deems "compelling governmental interests," and the courts are generally loath to question either its good faith or its sound judgment in so doing. Nor are courts invariably scrupulous, objective, and neutral in "balancing" the claims of the entire nation against those of the often selfish, even deviant or wicked, opposing litigant.

For all the criticism to which the courts are subject for their handling of issues like these, it surely does not follow that such issues should be left entirely to the elected branches of government. If anything, the "political" branches are even more likely to attend only to the interests of the established and the powerful, ignoring those who cannot vote or even, sometimes, speak for themselves. Private entrepreneurs, meanwhile, can be expected to behave in ways that are often selfish and prejudiced—and always, by definition, unaccountable to the community for their impact on others, until laws are made to hold them so accountable.

Critiques of Liberal Personhood

There are those who argue that, no matter how purely and consistently liberal we may be, the problems of personhood cannot be satisfactorily resolved within the liberal framework. Perhaps, then, the questions raised so far in this chapter are fundamentally misconceived.

One critique is the conservative or republican version, voiced by thinkers such as Burke and MacIntyre.[25] It emphasizes the need to balance freedom with authority, individualism with community, rights with responsibilities, progress with tradition. It suggests that many of the personal and social problems prevalent today can be attributed to our failure to maintain such a balance. And it rebukes liberalism for placing the free, isolated individual at the center of the moral-political universe, thus not only depriving him/her of the resources and supports needed to survive and flourish, but ignoring the obvious fact that persons are not and cannot be self-created. Persons come to exist, and to be the specific persons they are, by virtue of the nature and the activities of the social system in which they grow up—their families, schools, churches, even governments. There is no such thing as a person in the abstract, but only specific persons, each situated in a specific social world.

Therefore, society cannot truly be neutral about the values and choices of its members; nor should government, in general, strive to be so. Instead, it should strive for the maintenance and propagation, over time and perhaps even throughout the world, of its cherished way of life. Diversity should be tolerated, but only within limits. We should focus not on our rights as persons against each other, but on our duties as citizens toward the People to which we belong. Perhaps we have too many rights—too much "personhood"—already!

It is entirely appropriate to point out the costs of recognizing a given right, the abuses to which the exercise of rights (as well as powers) is subject, and the vital role of society (if not of government) in the constitution of personhood. All this, I believe, goes to the questions of what kinds of personal flourishing we should strive to encourage and support, and what kinds of rights are essential for such flourishing. It does not place in question the axiom that personal flourishing is the polity's central goal. In the contemplation of *this* Constitution, the people can flourish only insofar as persons do.

Another sort of critique rejects the liberal conception of personhood root and branch. Here, neither Kant's rational individual nor Burke's national community is a unique moral agent. Rather, both person and nation are by-products of underlying material forces. The individual is essentially a replaceable unit in a world economy whose decisive agents are either classes (in the leftist version) or firms (in the rightist version). For the left, the key to liberation is abolishing private property—or, in another version, labor itself as we know it[26]—and ending unjust, unnecessary domination through any means necessary. Postrevolutionary society will see the end of exploitation and the birth of a fundamentally new, genuinely free person. For the right, the only value is more and more efficient production—never mind by whom or for what. Neither of these materialisms can take liberal constitutional thought, and especially personal rights, very seriously. If constitutionalism matters, it is only as a lubricant of the wheels of commerce.

I shall not elaborate here on the many debates about law and rights to which these critical discourses have given rise.[27] While the questions they raise deserve careful consideration, I find their *reduction* of history and law to economic forces and/or class relations both empirically unpersuasive and morally repugnant. While it may be that most or all of us are mistaken about many things and even misled by hegemonic ideologies about vital things, it is clear that constitutional discourse—if it is to continue at all—must be engaged in by persons, more or less as we find them, who are deemed capable of holding and authentically acting on moral and political beliefs and preferences. Let us choose to so continue.

A third type of critique accepts as valid the liberal project of individual liberation, but argues that the traditional liberal program cannot attain that end. By conceptualizing freedom as "freedom from" rather than "freedom to," by mistakenly equating tyranny with *governmental* oppression, and by misconceiving the rights of privacy and private property, the Founders not only failed to abolish but actually reinforced the domination of the rich over the poor, men over women, whites over blacks, and so forth. In effect, they guaranteed personhood for the privileged few.

Some versions of this critique, upheld, for example, by Michelman and Radin,[28] would save liberalism by rethinking the relationship between political rights and property rights, giving government the power and the duty to intervene in the "private" sphere against social and economic domination and exploitation. They would expand personal rights, guaranteeing to every person the health, education, and welfare resources that are essential to convert nominal constitutional freedoms into actual, meaningful options for a personally satisfying and socially useful life. This sort of critique I find far more cogent and promising than the communitarian or economist versions (see chapter 8 for further discussion).

Conclusion

At present, we are far from attaining the degree of principled consensus that would make either a politically or a judicially imposed definition of personhood truly satisfactory. Consider, for example, a proposed "Human Life Statute" which defines "person" to include not just the zygote, but also "governments, government agencies, political subdivisions, partnerships, associations, corporations, legal representatives, mutual companies, joint-stock companies, trusts, unincorporated organizations, trustees, trustees in bankruptcy, or receivers."[29]

In this list, personal dignity seems at war with administrative convenience for recognition as the core American value. I can think of no creditable argument for convenience as a *principle* (let alone the most fundamental principle), as opposed to a means toward some other valuable end.

A principled approach to personhood, I submit, would regard all humans as persons, beginning at birth and surviving even a finding of legal incompetence. Nonhumans, in contrast, would be required (and permitted) to demonstrate their social and moral competence. In deciding what counts as competence, we should engage in ongoing dialogue, in which both private and public speakers participate. Because history shows how dramatically things can change and how serious is the risk of unjust exclusion, we must strive to proceed with a flexible and generous spirit.

The problems afflicting contemporary liberalism can be analyzed on many levels, including phenomena of political, social, economic, and legal structure as well as culture. One major factor in liberalism's disarray is its failure to offer our polity a compelling vision of our current situation and our aspirations for the future. A sufficient answer will not be found through abstract theoretical endeavor alone, especially of the metaphysical sort. Yet it seems safe to say that, for this diverse and individualistic polity, a more principled and at the same time more realistic conception of the person and her flourishing is well worth pursuing.[30]

❖ Chapter 7 ❖

What Makes a
Right Fundamental

But . . . that's just perfectly idiotic!

—Albert Sachs

*T*he topic of this chapter is the methodology of rights discourse. Investigation of specific substantive problems with contemporary rights discourse is reserved for chapter 8.

Modern theories of the judicial function begin with the premise that ours is a democratic form of government in which basic decisions are to be made by majority vote. Yet it is also a constitutional form of government in which the powers of the majority are subject to definite limits. According to the doctrine adumbrated in the famous *Carolene Products* footnote,[1] those limits are breached when the majority seeks to violate fundamental rights, or to harm persons whom the political process cannot be relied upon to protect, or to impair the self-corrective processes designed into the political system.

That decision did not identify which rights are fundamental, beyond suggesting that the economic rights implicated in "ordinary commercial transactions" are not among them. Within a few years,

---

An earlier version of this chapter was published in 49 *Review of Politics* 515 (1987).

though, the Court had indicated that First Amendment rights were special, because of their central role in the self-corrective processes alluded to above:

> When we balance the Constitutional right of owners of property against those of the people to enjoy freedom of press and religion . . . we remain mindful of the fact that the latter occupy a preferred position. . . . [T]he First Amendment "lies at the foundation of free government by free men . . . ."[2]

It is worth noting that this can be interpreted as essentially a utilitarian argument for the primacy of First Amendment rights: their preservation is defended more as a long-term benefit for the society and the political system than as a need, desire, or desert of the individual currently asserting the right.

Thus Justice Frankfurter, citing Holmes, explained the rationale for the "preferred position" of free speech by arguing that the "progress of civilization" depends on maintaining the capacity for "displacement of error."[3] Yet, as he was keenly aware, the justices of an earlier generation had been equally convinced that the progress of civilization depends on keeping free-market enterprise largely immune to governmental regulation. It is not easy to show why the former belief is more scientific, less dogmatic than the latter; noneconomic theories of progress are equally subject to controversy and displacement.

Frankfurter's own response to this dilemma was to espouse judicial restraint in dealing with First Amendment claims as well as claims of economic rights. Courts, he held, were no more warranted in imposing their political than their economic predilections upon the elected agents of the people. Yet the denial that some rights are more fundamental than others has also appealed to certain judicial activists, who see the courts' reluctance since 1937 to enforce property rights as an unprincipled surrender to political pressures, no longer warranted if it ever was.

It is this perspective, as well as discomfort with categorical methodology, that seems to motivate such diverse pronouncements as Justice Stewart's insistence that property rights are personal rights,[4] Justice Stevens's attack on the multitiered approach to equal protection analysis,[5] and the Court's recent revival of ordinary scrutiny "with teeth" in striking down as "irrational" statutes not identified as impairing a "fundamental right" or using a "suspect classification."[6]

If the methodology and substance of "preferred freedoms" analysis remain controversial, the Court has been equally unsystematic and divided in the "incorporation" debate. Which of the Bill of Rights guarantees pertaining to criminal procedure, for example, are sufficiently fundamental to be deemed incorporated in the due process clause of the Fourteenth Amendment? Here the prevailing approach has been to appeal to a concept of 'ordered liberty,'[7] or the "notions of justice of English-speaking peoples"[8] (a category surely both over- and underinclusive!) in order to identify the protections that are fundamental. Activist and restraint-oriented justices have often disagreed on results; yet all have looked freely and without rigorous empirical support to historic pronouncements, ostensible current public opinion, and their own instincts to determine what "shocks the conscience"[9] or is repugnant to the "traditions and conscience of our people."[10] The methodology is so indistinct that one is apt to conclude that a right simply is fundamental when a majority of the Court says it is.

Conceptions of Persons and of Rights

An alternative and more promising approach to identifying fundamental rights would engage the axiom that constitutional rights are personal rights[11] by seeking to derive a theory of rights from a relevant conception of the person. The first obstacle confronting such a project is that our jurisprudence, and especially our judiciary, has tended to shy away from exploring the concept of personhood. As chapter 6 showed, little legal material is available and still less is helpful to the present effort. The philosophical literature, however, suggests several ways to conceptualize the relationship between personhood and rights, corresponding to several ways to conceptualize personhood itself.[12]

One approach deserving mention is the legal-positivist. On this view a person is simply what the law says it is, including, in our society, ships and corporations, but not necessarily all members of our biological species (for example, slaves or the unborn). Here personhood is nothing more than a convenience, giving the entity access to the courts. It implies nothing of empirical or moral significance about the entity itself. Thus, it can tell us nothing about what specific rights the entity ought to have.

A related but more substantial approach is the political-positivist. On this view, to be a person is to be recognized as a member of society. Whoever is so recognized is a person; whoever is not, is not. Just as admission to citizenship in a specific political community is a matter of grace, not a matter of right, so too with membership in the broader human community.

On this view, again, recognition will be a precondition for possessing rights, but the nature of the decision to recognize will not itself determine what rights it entails, because the decision is purely discretionary and need not depend on any particular facts about the applicant. Indeed, on the positivist approach, the relationship may be just the opposite: the fact that all persons are accorded certain rights will determine the costs and benefits to society of admitting a given applicant, and personhood may be recognized or denied on that utilitarian ground alone.

Positivism of the legal and/or political stripe is reflected, though never expressly endorsed and argued for, in the record of Supreme Court decisions on slavery, corporate personhood, and abortion. In each case, as noted in chapter 6, the Court avoided any definition or principled analysis of personhood, simply appealing instead to the way the law, the society, and/or the political branches of government purportedly had traditionally regarded the entity in question. In striking contrast, some of the same justices felt free to appeal to untraditional principles, derived from higher law or social science, when the time came to identify and enforce the fundamental rights attaching to personhood, including, in particular, property rights.

Logically, a positivist approach to personhood suggests, if it does not absolutely require, a positivist approach to rights. On that approach, a person's rights are simply what the law giver says they are, and those rights are fundamental which the law giver has identified as such. This approach requires no further rationale for deeming a right fundamental.

Another possible approach is the scientific-empirical. On this view the question is not whether society has in fact accepted one as a member, but whether one actually possesses empirical characteristics that entitle one to be so recognized. Those characteristics might be biological, psychological, sociological, or what have you, so long as they are objectively demonstrable. Unlike the Kantian and related approaches (see below), the scientific approach allows that personhood could be a matter of degree. Unlike the positivist approach, the scientific approach to personhood entails a theory of human nature. The characteristics we identify as definitive of a person will have much to say about the basic needs and desires of persons.

Thus, this approach should be far more fruitful than the positivist one for a theory of rights—provided, of course, that the requisite facts can be established. Empirical approaches to personhood aspire to placing rights on a scientific basis instead of an inherently controversial moral one. Thus, they appeal to generalizations about biological need and/or psychological desire, taking it as axiomatic that universal needs and desires are entitled to respect. In light of human diversity, though, science is unlikely to justify the *equality* of fundamental rights that has been a basic premise of Western moral thought.

The question of personhood has been approached in an empiricist spirit by thinkers as diverse as Aristotle, Locke, Hume, and Marx. All sought to derive propositions about how we should or must live from propositions about how we actually are, deriving the latter from empirical (though not always rigorously scientific) observation.

In recent years this approach has been somewhat discredited, partly by the severe difficulties experienced in establishing consensus about the scientific facts, partly by the argument that normative consequences would not flow from the facts, even if they could be established, and partly by revulsion against the kinds of inegalitarian policy inferences drawn by observers of human nature from Plato and Aristotle to Friedrich Nietzsche and Herbert Spencer.

Indeed, the argument that such theories as Spencer's Social Darwinism have no place in our jurisprudence was a major element in the Legal Realists' assault, led by Holmes, on the view that property rights enjoy a preferred status in constitutional law.[13] Modern social science, at any rate, has so far failed to supply legal and philosophical thinkers with persuasive accounts either of what unites us or of what divides us.

In the absence of such scientific accounts, we steer between (to mangle a metaphor) the silly of dogma and the abyss of radical skepticism. We must contend with the ambiguities and contestedness inherent in our conventional beliefs, yet we must identify and protect fundamental rights. The more we rely upon the sheer fact of widely shared assumptions (conventionalism), the more we risk losing critical distance from our prejudices.

Nor do alternatives such as "moral realism," with its tempting promise of escape from conventionalism and positivism, offer a satisfying closure. We are surely no nearer to truth (or even consensus) on moral questions than we are on basic issues in social science. In the real world of American politics, a "realist" who professed to know the whole moral truth would play, for the unconverted, the role of intolerant oppressor.

Those more sophisticated realists, such as Barber,[14] who enjoin us to maintain a healthy skepticism about our own current grasp of moral truth, and even about the possibility of ever fully knowing it, do not threaten to oppress us. Yet, by admitting uncertainty as to what the truth is, they undermine the "objectivity" of any critique they may offer of our conventional understandings and forfeit any clear authority for their tentative answers to our urgent questions. To announce that moral truth exists may save us from positivistic nihilism, but it does not in itself tell us how to decide specific cases. That is why Brian Bix[15] can suggest that metaphysical realism does not truly guide legal reasoning but only decorates it.

Where does this leave us? As Sandel[16] points out, liberalism needs a conception of the person that (1) is rich and realistic enough to have significant consequences—one that respects the real differences between individuals and the hard choices that our specific form of life requires. In this sense the conception needs to be political, not merely metaphysical. At the same time, liberalism needs a conception that (2) is neutral as between different political factions and different private conceptions of the good—one that upholds the equal dignity of all and does not merely reflect or institutionalize some set of historically contingent and morally arbitrary biases. In this sense, it needs to be nonpolitical.

Meeting these criteria simultaneously clearly will be difficult. Insofar as our conception of the person confines itself to what is demonstrably universal, it threatens to fall short of the first *desideratum*. Insofar as it regards the facts of human diversity and of our specific form of life, it threatens to fall short of the second.

Despite these imposing difficulties, there seems no decent and promising alternative to the enterprise of political philosophy. The person-centered approach traces back to Plato and took its modern form with Enlightenment thinkers such as Kant and Hegel. Today it is exemplified by neo-Kantian thinkers such as Nozick, Rawls, Dworkin, and Ackerman (see below).

Their central concern with the dignity and rights of persons is (not coincidentally) highly congruent with the logical structure and normative emphasis of liberal constitutionalism. Unfortunately, the courts have shunned all such theories. Instead, the judicial positivist approach is implicitly utilitarian. Now, utilitarianism is emphatically not a person-centered theory, insofar as its primary concern is for collective satisfaction rather than for individual rights—a flaw often evident in the results of judicial balancing.

The philosophical approach or family of approaches usually points to certain specific attributes of persons—their self-consciousness, rationality, autonomy, and so forth—as grounding their inclusion in the human community and their entitlement to certain rights. Philosophical approaches to personhood (or at least those of interest here) are typically linked to deontological theories of rights. That is, such theories identify a right as fundamental by linking it to claims about what the person basically is. (This strategy need not suppose that all individuals in all societies have shared the identical attributes.)

These theories may at the same time, without contradiction, be consequentialist, resting the justification for rights upon a conception of what the specified sort of person's flourishing would require. (Rawls's "reflective equilibrium" approach is a relevant example.) Different thinkers have emphasized biological need, psychological desire, or moral desert as the wellspring of fundamental rights. Theories that ground a person's rights in the actions he or she has voluntarily performed, such as one's labor or one's contracts, are desert based. So, in a different sense, are theories focusing on the potentialities for moral agency, rationality, and pursuit of projects as basic to personhood.

A historical forbear of these philosophical approaches was the theological one equating personhood with possession of a soul. Ensoulment or rationality would seem to be a fact about the person that has important consequences for the theory of rights. Yet these "factual" concepts, both in their classical and in their modern forms, have proven conspicuously resistant to clear definition, let alone scientific measurement. By default, sometimes mere membership in the human species is taken as a necessary and sufficient condition for personhood, with little attention paid to the issues posed by borderline cases such as immaturity or severe impairment.

More important, as Sandel[17] points out, on close inspection it appears that the attributes of personhood emphasized are not always independent of and prior to the rights and duties that are claimed to flow from personhood. Rather, typically the attributes are deliberately selected and defined so as to justify the particular normative consequences desired. This strategy is openly embraced in Rawls's method of "reflective equilibrium." Facts that get in the way are thus declared incidental, and not constitutive of the person. The "facts" that count are moral ones—those that determine what we deserve.

The difficulty, once again, pertains to the elusive norm of neutrality. Rawls's[18] persons in the original position are disembodied, declassed, and bereft of any particular character. Reason may suggest that, *ceteris paribus*, they would rather have more income than have less; but, in the absence of more specific needs or desires, it turns out that their only "rational" goal is to avoid an unspecified worst possible outcome. A real person who calculated in this way would strike us as paranoid-schizophrenic, not rational. At the opposite extreme, Nozick's[19] parties to the social contract have a much *too specific* character: they seem possessed by a desire for unlimited acquisition of property. It is unclear why anyone not so possessed—and surely many people are not—would agree to a contract designed to further that goal above all others.

Conceptions of Neutrality

Modern political and legal philosophers have in large part forsworn the old search for an objective theory of the good, accepting instead the mandate of fairness or neutrality. They recognize that we will continue to differ in our visions of the good and that a theory of rights cannot be expected to unify, stabilize, or energize a society insofar as that theory prefers the needs, desires, and contributions of some to those of others.

The literature offers varied approaches to realizing neutrality. Nozick, for instance, attains it by blinding himself to the realities of groups and their power. All interactions in his world are between freely contracting, essentially equal individuals. More precisely, any inequality will be a manifestation of differences in talent or motivation that are not morally neutral but rather deserve reward or punishment.

The only restriction on interactions is that coercion, narrowly defined as the direct use of force, is not permitted. Otherwise, all are entitled to take what they desire and to keep what they have, even if others perish as a result. Your right to life may be explicitly subordinated to my property rights. For Nozick, this choice is neutral: it leaves all survivors free to pursue their desires according to their talents.

Rawls shares Nozick's awareness of the challenges that group power poses for a theory of individual rights, and he too resorts to a sort of blindness. Yet Rawls's subtler approach does not lead so quickly to abhorrent results. He allows us to remember that group power exists and can threaten us, but he asks us to forget where we personally stand in the power structure. Our rational calculations will consider not how to provide for our particular needs and desires, but rather how to design a framework within which we might most safely pursue those needs and desires, whatever they might be.

Rawls does not attribute moral significance to accidents of nature that distribute talents unequally, or even to free choices that result in differential contributions to the aggregate social wealth. Thus his approach, unlike Nozick's, does not directly legitimize pervasive inequalities. However, "justice as fairness" does not guard against exploitation as effectively as it might. It is designed to solve an indefinite array of hypothetical problems, instead of the specific ones that any real society must face in the light of its particular history and composition. Rules that seem neutral out of context may seem less so when push comes to shove.

In his latest book,[20] therefore, Rawls acknowledges the need for a historically situated theory of rights, designed to meet a specific society's needs. His new approach, nevertheless, remains highly abstract and disembodied. A society dedicated *only* to rationality, reasonableness, fairness, and tolerance may be one that few would passionately oppose; but it is also one that few would passionately join. For all the danger that passions can bring to public life, it does not follow that their presence is an unqualified evil—or that a life governed solely by reason is even conceivable.

Ackerman's theory of neutrality predates his latest work in constitutional politics.[21] His approach, like Rawls's, is process oriented. Ackerman asks us not to forget what we know, but to disregard any claim that presupposes that one person or vision of the good has greater moral worth than another. For him, the central right is to a neutral justification for any exercise of power, public or private. Each individual is entitled to enter the marketplaces of discourse and of action with "a liberal education and a fair share of economic power" to back him up. Within this basic structure of "undominated equality," fair exchange of ideas and goods can occur.

Like Rawls (and Dworkin), Ackerman has difficulty in spelling out the meaning of an "equal start in life" in a context of major differences in individual physical and mental endowments. He too simplifies his task by assuming such differences away. He too pursues his inquiry in a basically atomistic context, abstracted from the groups and institutions that are pervasive in our lives. Yet it is precisely these individual differences and group relationships that give rise to the need for theories of fundamental rights in the first place!

Dworkin[22] agrees that the state must be neutral between competing notions of the good, but he holds, unlike Rawls, that equality is a principle prior to neutrality. Rawls (and Ackerman) seem to assume that these two criteria are equally fundamental and mutually consistent. Dworkin points out that this need not be the case, and he argues that of the two, equality is the more fundamental. The difficulty with this is that without a concept like neutrality, the meaning of equality is left radically unclear.

Dworkin advocates "sovereignty over a range of personal possessions essential to dignity" as a fundamental right, thus translating the norm of "equal concern" for all persons to one of "equal resources." Yet, like Nozick and Rawls, Dworkin seems to have discarded information without which rational decisions cannot be made. Treating persons as equals should not mean blinding ourselves to morally relevant differences between them, and it is the concept of 'neutrality' that specifies which differences are morally relevant. By defining equality before we define neutrality, we risk interpreting "equal resources" to mean that all persons, regardless of age, size, or health, must have equal food rations. At the same time, we encounter serious difficulty in explaining why a democratic government should support projects needed or desired only by a minority.[23]

The questions remain: how can neutrality itself be defined in a politically neutral manner, without disregarding the morally significant differences among individuals? Indeed, is it valid to attribute morally significant qualities—or even existence—to persons, abstracted from and prior to their entry into specific social arrangements or political and legal institutions? Failure to deal satisfactorily with this issue is the core of the charge that liberalism, by its very axioms, is precluded from solving the problems it wishes to solve.

Much of the effort of the Critical Legal Studies (CLS) movement has been devoted to showing that the formal categories of classical legal thought are inherently politically biased, self-contradictory, or both. Tushnet,[24] for example, has explored the dilemmas faced by antebellum Southern judges in dealing with rights and duties of slaves, whose status stood uneasily astride the person/property dichotomy. Horwitz[25] has shown how an ostensibly neutral and well-settled law of property could be radically overhauled to accommodate the needs of emergent industrial capitalism.

Even the very individualism of liberal thought has not escaped a radical criticism. Unger[26] has shown, among other things, how an individualistic analysis of society tends to obscure both the phenomena of group power and exploitation, and the extent to which human identity and self-realization are unthinkable outside the context of community life.

Granting the incisiveness of much of this CLS criticism, the difficulty is in determining what it means for a theory of fundamental rights. Indeed, scholars of this persuasion are often reluctant to grant the possibility or the value of any such positive theory.

The fate of past efforts to develop a new, more egalitarian theory of property rights[27] indicates that such a theoretical project must indeed face political and intellectual obstacles. Not surprisingly, an innovation that seems *more* politically and morally neutral to reformists is apt to seem *less* so to others. The "new property" theory, after some initial successes, was dropped by the Supreme Court long before the advent of Reagan's and Bush's appointees;[28] its implications were seen, with some justification, as potentially revolutionary.

If only neutral theories of rights are acceptable but there can be no such theory, what are we to put in its place? The CLS critics sometimes suggest that a passionate, authentic moral commitment is the answer. Yet a neutral theory of fundamental rights was supposed to command support by general consensus—indeed, on the social contract approach, by a unanimous agreement. Such a theory could make the passionate *private* pursuit of nonshared values possible and tolerable.

Partisan commitments, on the other hand, cannot do the unifying and pacifying work that a Constitution is supposed to do—unless all other parties are liquidated by persuasion or armed struggle. Few if any of our law professors are dedicated to armed struggle. They must not only grant tolerance to those not yet persuaded, but themselves call for tolerance from a sometimes irate mainstream majority. In so doing, they seem to rely upon the very liberal theories whose coherence and fairness they have denied. To follow this course on sheer pragmatic grounds is to acquiesce in the cynical positivism of the status quo. Moreover, it leaves those who are open to persuasion in doubt about the very thing they most wish to know—what would *you* do if in power?

Having chided liberal thinkers for insufficient passion and radicals for too much or too divisive passion, Rawls for a too thin conception of personhood and Nozick for one too thick, where am I to turn? Surely not to the Framers' intent as expounded by Bork, Berger, Berns, or McDowell![29] Their differing versions of that intent are as passionate, divisive, and unscientific as the CLS critiques from the Left—without any of the latters' contemporary relevance, compassion, and promise. We cannot recover the polity envisioned by Madison, Jefferson, Hamilton, or Wilson, nor should we want to.

The only possible answer brings us back to the heart of constitutional politics: the search for a principled, unifying consensus. Insofar as we fail to keep or gain one, we fail to have a living, working Constitution.

The Politics of Fundamental Rights

To call the search for fundamental rights a political project is to restate the obvious: before there can be positive law, there must be politics. If the argument seems shocking, this reflects (1) the unsavory connotations the word *politics* bears today and (2) failure to keep in mind the distinction between ordinary and constitutional politics, as well as, perhaps, (3) residues of belief in "natural law" that is discovered, not made.

Critics of constitutionalism attack a straw man in trying to show that the conceptual structure of constitutional thought is marred by incoherence or contradictions, and jumping thence to the conclusion that constititionalism is not viable and should be abandoned in favor of another approach. What these critics overlook is the near certainty that similar havoc can be wrought with any conceptual system that undertakes to deal with fundamental, essentially contested moral, legal, and political questions.

But so what? When Gödel proved that Hilbert's project for the perfection of mathematics could not be realized, most mathematicians managed to carry on with their researches, and properly so. If we cannot have a system meeting certain criteria of logical perfection, still we can accomplish many other worthwhile things: "Even if it is 'turtles all the way down,' some turtles are less slippery than others."[30]

A fairer test of constitutional thought might look to the relative quality of political life in societies where its concepts and procedures are used to shape and moderate conflict and to formulate collective goals, as compared to societies in which other sorts of language games are played. A political system is just insofar as it deals with the demands of all participants in ways that are generally accepted as legitimate—provided, of course, that no one is wrongly excluded from participation, and that participants' acceptance is not invalidated by discernable coercion, manipulation, or the like. Granting that the definitions of these terms are highly contestable, we can and must attend closely to the nature of such contests and the fate of the contestants.

In our constitutional system, the contests are politics of a specific form. First, there are two procedural criteria for establishing a right as fundamental: that the right has been recognized as such through a process accepted as valid, and that the fundamental character of the right is supported by persuasive, principled arguments. These criteria are not mutually independent. What makes the process valid is that it strives to hear and weigh impartially all relevant arguments. What makes arguments seem persuasive and principled is, in part, the impartial character of the forum and the integrity of the advocates who offer and the judges who accept the arguments.

Litigation, remember, is only one form of constitutional politics.[31] It has the tempting advantage of low decision-making costs compared to electoral struggle, constitutional amendment, or civil war. It has the corresponding disadvantages that victories are narrow in scope and that the defeated party is not so likely to be persuaded and won over as might be the case with Ackerman's populist sort of constitutional politics.

As Learned Hand famously warned us, judicial enforcement of rights cannot guarantee public understanding and support for those rights.[32] Rights may be eroded by public indifference, organized resistance, transformative court appointments, and so forth. Even worse, years of litigation sometimes yield only adverse or equivocal decisions.

But the integrity of forums, advocates, and judges cannot be a sufficient condition for establishing rights. Because any meaningful notion of integrity will not be entirely politically neutral, to demand only this would leave open the possibility that rights are *simply* a reflection of power relationships, and that recognition or nonrecognition of a right can be criticized only on the ground that power relations have been misperceived.

That vulgar positivist view fails to describe historical realities, because it misconceives the practice of rights discourse as a language game in our society. There is indeed a "politics" involved in establishing, securing, expanding, or attacking a right.[33] But this politics is distinctive in its normative logic, as well as in the specialized forums and personnel who tend to dominate its activities.

The norms of neutrality and universalism are especially important for the continuing legitimacy of the system of rights. For all the logical weaknesses of these norms, they do serve to keep the process as open to all persons and all ideas as we presently know how to make it. Moreover, they go beyond "mere" procedural regularity.

Neutrality and universality are imperfect in that claims cannot be recognized until they have been submitted through proper channels, the use of which requires a modicum of resources and motivation. Moreover, the odds of success may indeed tend to improve as the political and economic resources of claimants increase. Some biases, indeed, are traceable to the constitutional text itself.

Nevertheless, a norm against overt status discrimination does constrain both the form and the content of acceptable claims. The logic of *Carolene Products*[34] attempts to redress systemic imbalances by a sort of jurisprudential affirmative action. And if there is still arguable bias in decision making, we have several established ways to pursue reform, even to the point of fundamental amendment of the system.

The historical record, I have argued, reflects a secular trend toward greater openness and equality. Rights perhaps initially sought with very limited, selfish ends in view have come to be formulated, justified, and applied in significantly broader terms. The class of ultimate beneficiaries far exceeds the original advocates of the right, coming to include some who once were not part of the system at all. Some of the initial victors have had to accept significant sacrifices so that others could share in enjoyment of the newly established rights.

The workings of this trend can be discerned in domains as diverse as voting rights, freedoms of speech and of religion, the right to counsel and other safeguards in criminal cases, and the extension to tenants of property rights once enjoyed only by owners of real estate.

In short, even if the original demand for a right and its governmental recognition could be explained by a simple calculus of power relations, the later impact of its recognition would not be predictable from those original power relations. Even if the actual application over time of a nominally universal right is mediated by changing power relations, this mediation is governed by a special logic: the long-range logic of legitimation, not the short-run logic of gains and losses distributed according to the current political balance.

A positivism that looks only to the power of force, money, and numbers cannot provide an adequate account of why we have the rights we have today. Nor is a positivist dismissal of the question of what rights we *should* have a plausible move. That is a question we have long been in the habit of asking. We go on asking it, and it is difficult to see what, if we ceased to ask it, we might do instead.

From the personhood perspective, our constitutionalism possesses a viable system of fundamental rights insofar as it can protect the conditions for the flourishing of individual persons against competing claims that may enjoy majority support and may also plausibly be said to rest on recognized public rights (that is, governmental powers). As Dworkin puts it, fundamental rights must be effective "trumps."[35]

It is obvious that the decisions in such cases must be supported by principled argument and not merely by fiat or by appeal to expediency. Ultimately, however, the success of such arguments depends on empirical measures as well as on conceptual analysis:

directly or indirectly, we must consult the participants as to how well their needs, wants, and moral sentiments are being satisfied, and as to what would need to change in order to enhance their satisfaction. Though the number or the social status of advocates must not determine the result, the personal urgency of the demand for a right is indeed relevant to its priority.

That answers will be contingent on circumstances—that changing situations may call for recognition of new fundamental rights or redefinition of old ones—is not inconsistent with the concept of 'rights,' but flows directly from a correct grasp of what rights are about. That courts may not be the best qualified judges of the empirical issues should make us grateful that constitutional politics is not reserved for them alone.

To speak of "fundamental" rights is to suggest that certain rights deserve to be, and normally will be, supported by the broadest and deepest consensus. Normally they will be the slowest to change, and in particular they will not be diminished or infringed without the most compelling justification—which, by definition, could only be the recognition that some other value is even more fundamental.

Conceptually, whether a given right is fundamental or how fundamental it is should depend on a weighing of one or more of these questions:

1. Is the right specifically identified as fundamental by a controlling text or authority, or logically entailed by a right so recognized?
2. Is the right empirically necessary to the realization of a recognized fundamental right?
3. Is possession of the right entailed by what it means to be a person, so that no person devoted to human dignity could reasonably prefer to live in a society in which the right was not recognized?

Accordingly, advocates of an unrecognized fundamental right may assert that in fact the right already exists, but that its scope and application have not yet been properly conceptualized or that its logical significance within the whole system of rights has not yet been properly recognized. This argument, highly textual in nature, is the easiest for a court to accept.

Alternatively, they may assert that changed conditions, new empirical knowledge, or current conceptions of human dignity make out a case for recognizing a new right or upgrading an existing one, in order better to attain already established rights. This argument smacks more of "policy making," but, as the school desegregation cases[36] show, courts will sometimes be receptive to it.

Arguments against recognizing or upgrading a right will likely deny the claimants' assertions. They may also stress the social costs of recognizing the new right. The latter argument would be entirely irrelevant if the right were already recognized as a "trump" over such utilitarian concerns. Prior to that stage, it must be carefully but skeptically weighed.

Arguments for downgrading an existing right would have to point to patent error in the prior recognition or to fundamental change in circumstances that bears not on social costs but on the conditions for personal flourishing. Such arguments should shoulder an extremely heavy burden of proof if we mean to take vested rights seriously.

Arguments proposing new rights or opposing existing ones may be motivated by the short-run goals of a specific interest group, but, if so formulated, they cannot be accepted as principled claims. A universalistic rhetoric, backed by meaningful accountability in implementation, is—if not "an unqualified human good"[37]—far more appealing and stabilizing than demands based on more particular wants or needs—let alone threats.

By conceptualizing fundamental rights in broad terms—a right to travel, not a right to visit the subtreasury—we assure that more people will be inclined to support the claim of right, that more people will actually benefit from its recognition, and, not least important, that the concrete implementation of right and remedy will have to be adapted to varying circumstances.

The rule of law is sustained by a perception of inclusiveness and timelessness as well as by a basis in current and widely appreciated fact. Even though a given right will not be of great value or urgent practical importance to all persons at all times, the argument that almost any person might find it fundamentally important at some time is just the sort of argument that is needed.

And what, you may ask, has become of the dialectical tension between liberal and republican visions of the polity? Is liberal rights discourse to occupy the entire field? The answer is threefold. First, as indicated above, the politics of rights is clearly open, both in theory and in practice, to objections that claims for recognition of rights are unfounded or mistaken—either textually or empirically. Second, even once recognized, fundamental rights are subject to limitation in the name of "compelling public interests," as chapter 5 made clear. The contest between those rights and interests is central to our current way of resolving the liberal/republican tension.

The third and most crucial point is that republican thought is not indiscriminately hostile to rights. Historically, it has defended specific theories of liberty and property rights. Chapter 8 will argue that new conceptions are needed today.

✣ Chapter 8 ✣

Rights We Need Today

But surely, Mr. Hoffman: no one *of substance* has ever
suggested such a thing!

—Charles Fried

*I*n chapters 6 and 7, I explored some weaknesses of formal theories of fundamental rights and advocated an approach more responsive to the threats to personal dignity, integrity, and
flourishing that are most prominent in our society today. In this
chapter I elaborate on some of those threats and the rights for
which they call. I shall not specify the rights in the manner of a
legal brief; my aim here is to indicate in a general way their focus,
their interrelationships, and their importance for personal flourishing.

I schematize the major lacunae in our jurisprudence of fundamental rights under these headings: (1) the right to life; (2) the
right of privacy; (3) political rights; (4) socioeconomic rights.

This schema has the virtues of being *both* textually grounded ("no
person shall be deprived of *life, liberty, or property* without due
process of law") *and* responsive to the historical evolution of unenumerated rights. Its sequencing points to an ordering of constitutional
values that seems textually, historically, and politically appropriate.[1]
Finally, the schema is comprehensive: it seems to allow for discussion
of all the personal rights issues that are now controversial or apt to

195

be so (though I concentrate on those of most interest to me).

Some may question the justification for focusing on the due process clause, and for attributing to it substantive as well as procedural force. The justification is, in short, that we must make the best of the materials available. Most of our substantive rights jurisprudence, past and present, is already engaged with that clause. In addition to its intrinsic meaning, it has been held to incorporate most if not all of the Bill of Rights. A purely procedural reading of the clause has not recommended itself, for this would (1) render it unable to incorporate the substantive Bill of Rights guarantees and (2) permit a horrendous parade of possible abuses both by federal and by state governments, if only they are duly enacted by the "political branches." Finally, the ensemble of the concepts of 'life,' 'liberty,' and 'property' promises to be broad enough, yet specific enough, for the task at hand. Available textual alternatives (the privileges and immunities clause and the Ninth Amendment) offer less in the way of intrinsic content and historical gloss.

Life

The issues concerning the right to life are fateful and complex—too complex for exhaustive treatment in this space. Even once we are satisfied that the right not to be "deprived of life . . . without due process of law" has substantive as well as procedural content, urgent questions about the parameters of this right remain. They include, in particular, questions about when the state has power, or the citizen a right, deliberately to take life, as well as about when life begins and ends.

A person-centered approach makes it clear that the right to life must be the most fundamental of our rights, since life is prerequisite to the pursuit and enjoyment of all other rights. Yet to make even this right absolute and inalienable would set the stage for intolerable contradictions.

Note, with regard to inalienability, that if powers can usually be delegated by their holders (who are only trustees), it is even clearer that rights can be waived by their "true owners." A "right" I am *obliged* to exercise is in fact a duty, not a right. The notion of an "inalienable right" that I am not free to waive, but that can still be taken from me at the behest of others, is even more offensive to the logic of rights.[2] Yet this is the status of our most precious right if we hold that (1) capital punishment is permitted, but that (2) there is no "right to die with dignity." The second claim belies the first. The law today presents an anomalous situation in which capital punishment is allowed while mercy killing is punished. Analogously, abortion of a nonviable fetus or nontreatment of a defective neonate is lawful, but "wrongful birth" suits are not.

Situations occur where we might consider that to prolong an individual's life would actually do her wrong. Moreover, cases occur where loss of life cannot be avoided and we must choose (or refuse to choose) which life to save, which to sacrifice. Even more often we must decide how much to spend on efforts to reduce somewhat a given mortality rate. Clearly, such gains have finite value and can be traded off against other benefits.

If we cannot consistently place an absolute value on every individual life, we can still hold that, just as legal personhood is not a question of fact or a matter of degree but rather essentially a normative, either/or decision, so too the definition of life should not depend on changing scientific discoveries and technological capabilities, and all lives should be, by definition, equally valuable. The notion of an exceptional life not worth preserving would then be incoherent.

It is equally logical to hold that personhood is in essence an ensemble of measurable behavioral attributes, and thus basically a matter of degree, with the threshold for legal recognition set in a prudent and revisable way. On this view the beginning and end of life would likewise be only provisionally defined. Moreover, some lives would be more valuable than others, because they are richer in the attributes of personhood; some might even be so lacking in value as to be not worth having or saving.

It is evident that few today are comfortable with either of these views in its pure form: the first seems too rigid, the second, too flexible. Our jurisprudence, meanwhile, equivocates. On the classical, Lockean view, the state had some duty to respect and preserve lives, but it was up to individuals to define and secure the quality of life they desired. Whether a particular life was worth living was not the state's concern. Moreover, the law against suicide barred persons from acting on such judgments even in their own case. The dignity of life was thus radically abstracted from its specific quality.

Scientific progress has led to rising expectations and to elevated ideas of what makes life worth living. Meanwhile, the heightened role of government in economic and social affairs has expressed and reinforced our sympathy for the ideas that government should guarantee a minimal quality of life, should recognize a right of individuals to recourse when such quality cannot be secured, and even (for some) that government should condone paternalistic action by others to end subminimal lives when individuals are incapable of acting for themselves.

Advocates tend to see this trend as enhancing personal dignity and autonomy, while opponents tend to denounce it as having the opposite effect. What they ought to agree on is that social conditions have changed, and what it means to be a secure, autonomous person has changed as well.

Contest over the meaning of the right to life itself arises, fortunately, only *in extremis*. Yet the broad support for capital punishment indicates that many of us see our own lives as qualitatively more valuable than those of others. For too many of those others, extreme circumstances have become the ineluctable status quo. The poor quality of their lives results partly from our own studied indifference, inscribed in laws that promote "free" competition and perpetuate the resulting inequalities but impartially forbid the rich and the poor alike to loiter, to steal, to lash out. Of course, the law then holds the worst wrongdoers *exclusively* responsible for the foolish, desperate actions by which their right to life is forfeited.

Capital punishment is cruel, unusual across the civilized world, and, moreover, ineffective as a deterrent. Its contribution to the flourishing of law-abiding citizens is overwhelmingly negative. If deprivation of life is pointless and barbaric, it is without "due process of law." The legislatures or the people would do well to abolish it. Even if the Framers did not regard capital punishment as "cruel and unusual," it was that broad concept, not their specific conception of it, that they placed in the Eighth Amendment. The Court has repeatedly declined to hold the death penalty unconstitutional.[3] It might be imprudent but would not be an abuse of power for the Court to revisit the question.

Capital punishment, at any rate, is not the only possible meaning for the expression *deprived of life*. Contest is incessant over what government may, should, or must do to help "normal" persons flourish in the conditions of modern life—that is, to enjoy a life worth living. Debating our options is the stuff of ordinary politics; constitutional politics, in contrast, aims at *commitments*. Some of these are negative commitments, to refrain from acting. Others may be affirmative.

Privacy

For many, the largest part of the answer to the previous question is that government should take care to avoid doing too much to help persons flourish, lest its own size and activity interfere unduly with individual autonomy and dignity (not to mention economic productivity). Indeed, the Constitution has recently been held to include a fundamental right of privacy, designed to protect us against just such eventualities.[4] Because the Constitution does not mention privacy as such, this decision has occasioned a great debate on approaches to constitutional interpretation, with special reference to the uses and abuses of "substantive due process" in its varied historical manifestations.[5]

It is neither possible nor necessary to explore here all the technical ramifications of this debate. The starting point should be obvious, however. Both proponents and critics of our constitutionalism seem to agree that basic to its conceptual structure is a wall of separation between public and private spheres, with the state forbidden to intervene in the latter. If this is correct, then the claim that our Constitution contains no right of privacy as against government is a contradiction in terms.

The right to have a life of one's own—to define and pursue one's own vision of the good—is implicit in the right to life itself, and not (in general, at least) contradictory to it. Privacy must be fundamental, insofar as the entire system of constitutional rights is based upon it. In this sense, privacy is not an afterthought—a "penumbra"—of the Bill of Rights; indeed, the exact opposite is true. On the approach favored here, the necessary and proper question then becomes: Where does personal integrity, as conceived today, require the line of separation to be drawn?

In theory, one could assess under the privacy heading such questions as the proper scope of regulation of economic activity. One could argue that, while overregulation clearly invades a vital dimension of the personal privacy right, underregulation is also subject to critique in that unchecked capitalism threatens to impoverish, culturally as well as fiscally, both the public and the private spheres, to the detriment of the general welfare and personal flourishing. This line of argument offers to address both liberal and republican concerns. The issues it raises, however, have historically been dealt with under the heading of "property rights."

One aspect of privacy of major concern today is the right to prevent government from gathering, transmitting, and using certain kinds of information about one. While limits are placed by the Fourth and Fifth Amendments on certain intrusive techniques of surveillance, the Court unfortunately has refused to take seriously the claim that the mere knowledge that one's activities are observed and recorded can have a chilling effect on the exercise of constitutionally protected rights.[6]

This passing reference to the criminal justice system draws attention to a set of problems that I cannot explore in detail. Instead I shall confine myself to two very general observations. First, to place criminal justice under the "privacy" heading in my schema of rights may strike the reader as strange. Yet it should be recalled that the birth of the constitutional right of privacy was intimately linked with questions of criminal law enforcement, from wiretapping[7] through envisioned searches of bedrooms in hot pursuit of illegal use of condoms.

Justice Douglas in his *Griswold* opinion[8] included the Fourth and Fifth Amendments in his list of those whose "penumbras" implied a right of privacy. Insofar as privacy refers to a right to be let alone, this surely includes being seized and invasively treated by officers of the law. While criminal justice issues are usually placed under the "liberty" heading, I am reserving that category for positive, political rights. Regulation of private behavior is a deprivation, in the first instance, of negative freedom.

My second observation pertains to the political significance of the "law and order" issues that play such a huge role in contemporary politics. The conventional account opposes conservative, typically Republican stands on this issue to liberal, typically Democratic ones (although recently Democrats have flocked more and more to the "conservative" bandwagon). It is worth emphasizing, however, that the now ascendant "conservative" stand has very little to do with classical republican thought. Where the republican tradition presumed the citizen innocent and warned him to distrust his government, the current Court presumes the government innocent and encourages it to distrust its citizens.

This statist perspective encompasses a vision of the person not as autonomous and self-reliant but as weak and dependent on governmental surveillance, manipulation, and regulation for his/her very survival. Whatever empirical support this view might have, it is not the view of what it means to be a citizen on which our Constitution was founded. It is compatible with neither republican nor liberal theories, at their best, of the rights most precious to us.

The main point here is that racially tinged law-and-order campaigns reflect the contemptuous, sometimes hysterical view of *outsiders* that has indeed formed a conspicuous, unhappy strand in republican thought. Liberals, for their part, need not abandon the principle of personal responsibility in order to insist that, for criminal-Americans(!) as much as for any other minority group, fairness and (re-)integration—not condign punishment—is the primary constitutional mandate.

The limits of privacy are, of course, most urgently debated in connection with the question, formerly governed by criminal laws, of abortion. Now, it seems clear that, at a minimum, if we take personal integrity seriously we must grant the existence of a fundamental, though not necessarily absolute, right to control the processes internal to one's body. This does not dispose of the entire abortion controversy, but it does establish a proper context for appreciating the delicacy of the question of fetal personhood discussed in chapter 6.

The privacy issue focuses attention on the woman's situation. Ideally, pregnancy, with the potentials for fulfillment and responsibility it brings, is an occasion for enhancing her personhood. Unwanted pregnancy is another matter, but it can have some aspect of personal value if accompanied by choice. Where choice is foreclosed by law, however, the woman's personhood is drastically diminished: she is reduced to a sort of breeding machine.

Some have seen the *Roe v. Wade*[9] decision as centering not on control of one's body as such but on control of family planning decisions. The precedents relied on by the Court and retrospectively labeled "right of privacy" decisions were indeed focused on the question of familial control over procreation and childrearing, and it can well be argued that such decisions ought to be private in a free society. However, this argument has two difficulties of its own. First, we can more readily identify a public interest in regulating some of these practices, for, whether or not the fetus is a person, reproductive and childrearing decisions often have major consequences for the welfare of others.

Second, while the right of privacy in the bodily sense belongs exclusively to the pregnant woman, when it comes to family planning it is not so obvious why the prospective father, especially if he is married to the woman, can have no rights in the matter. This question the Court has summarily dismissed,[10] suggesting that in its view the physical indignity of unwanted pregnancy is the critical fact. If so, a right to evict the fetus, not a right to destroy it, is implied. Such a conclusion could potentially (given the availability of artificial wombs, for example) reconcile the woman's right to privacy with a fetal right to life.[11]

Moving beyond the abortion issue, we might attempt to reconcile the tension between individual privacy and family privacy by identifying the enjoyment of intimate relationships as the fundamental personal interest at stake. On this view, the constitutional freedom of association pertains not just to political and civic activities, but it also includes the right of consenting adults to pursue sexual gratification as they see fit. Just as freedom of speech is not reserved for speech that is explicitly political but applies also to commercial or purely expressive speech, so too, freedom of association should apply to any voluntary social activities not harmful to others.[12] It follows, I think, that sexual privacy should not be confined to those who are married, nor should the right to marry be confined to those of whose sexual orientation the majority approves.[13]

This argument draws strong support from the philosophy of Mill[14] and from currents in modern psychology, but it runs up against the traditional view—indebted, I think, to the Puritan strand of our heritage—that laws enforcing conventional sexual morality are *ipso facto* proper exercises of the police power. The tenacity of the latter view is logically anomalous, if politically comprehensible, in an increasingly pluralistic society which both prohibits any establishment of religion and recognizes the functional equivalence of personal moral codes with traditional religious beliefs.[15]

Liberty

Relying on the right of privacy to limit the scope of governmental power is one way to safeguard personal liberties. While the right of privacy is in essence a right to be let alone by government, to lead a dignified, autonomous life, we turn now to a complementary concept—a right to participate in government, to pursue a meaningful communal life alongside the private one. Political rights, then, secure liberty in the positive sense, while privacy secures it in the negative sense. Despite some unclear boundary areas, it seems useful to highlight separately these two vital issue domains.[16]

The starting point for a jurisprudence of affirmative political rights is the concept of 'effective access' for all citizens to the political process, that is, meaningful representation. As John Hart Ely has argued,[17] the government, and the courts in particular, have some responsibility for the situation of those who, for structural reasons, lack effective access. While the right of privacy surely includes a right not to participate in politics, to deem most of today's nonparticipation freely chosen is to put form over substance.

In many ways, the argument goes, our education and communication systems discourage the development of political interest and competence on the part of all but a relatively small segment of the population. Interest-group activity thus comes to be dominated by a self-perpetuating elite. Whatever may be said for an "iron law" of political sociology that holds elitism to be inevitable, it does appear that certain specific and malleable features of our legal and political structures serve to exacerbate these inequalities. Moreover, there is a textual basis for arguing that those features violate a fundamental constitutional right to effective political access.

Proceeding from the account of representation developed in chapter 2, we now explore how the person-centered approach developed in this part can augment our understanding of political rights. It does so by directing us to attend to the political flourishing (the "liberty") of individual citizens, and not just to the unity, tranquility, and efficiency of the system as a whole.

Consider the position of an individual citizen, musing about where she fits into our system of representation. Suppose she is a disgruntled resident of, say, North Carolina who does not feel much in common with the average citizen of that state, and does not feel that its elected representatives are "her" representatives in any meaningful sense. Now, first of all, there is a close connection between the concepts of 'membership' and of 'representation,' even though the concepts are at different levels and are logically independent. (Not only is it possible to be a member of a polity without being represented save in a fictional sense—for example, disenfranchisement of women before the Nineteenth Amendment—it is also possible for nonmembers—for example, aliens—to be effectively represented in various ways, *de jure* or *de facto*.)

The point, however, is that at some level, an experience of persistent, inadequate representation is apt to generate a feeling that one either is not or does not want to be a member of the polity. When our disgruntled citizen comes to reflect on the status of her membership in the people of her state (or her country), the following postures are available to her:

1. Deny that such a people even exists or, alternatively, that she belongs to it; exit, physically or spiritually. (In the spirit of secession, she denies the legitimacy of the polity—the Union—itself.)
2. Admit she belongs, but charge the rules of the politics/representation game and/or the conduct of the people with improperly impeding her engagement in political discourse; try to change the game, or exit. (She denies the legitimacy of the "regime": the rules of the game.)
3. Accept the legitimacy of the game; tolerate the outcomes or work for better ones. (She may deny the legitimacy of the current leadership or simply reject some of its policies.)

Again, this posited connection between membership and representation is contingent on certain assumptions about political rights inherent in citizenship. A connection between representation and the very concept of personhood (see chapter 6) can be traced back as far as Hobbes, who defined the "representative"/sovereign as an artificial person. For Hobbes, that person enjoyed unique and plenary rights vis-à-vis the natural persons who were his subjects, while owing them no enforceable duties.[18]

Today, in contrast, by and large we proceed from the assumption that adult citizens (natural persons) have an affirmative right to be represented, and that this right is realized through the electoral process and by communicating with those who win elections. Voting is commonly seen as the crucial mode of public participation in our politics, and it is certainly true that access to the ballot is a *necessary* condition for full political empowerment.

The Constitution does not expressly guarantee a "right to be represented," nor does it state that all citizens have a right to vote. Yet it does create an array of elective offices endowed with formidable powers, and it prohibits denial of the franchise based on racial, gender, or age categories. Moreover, the rights to speak, to assemble, and to petition for redress of grievances are explicitly guaranteed; the right to organize ("freedom of association") has also been held implicit in this First Amendment scheme.

These (largely though not exclusively) political rights cannot be based directly on a conception of personhood: to hold that all persons have a fundamental right to vote would arouse seemingly unanswerable objections, especially with regard to aliens and to children.

For aliens, the best reply available seems to be that they should indeed have the right to vote *somewhere*. The plight of the stateless is beyond the scope of this work; see chapters 3 and 4 for some reflections on the impact of the nation-state system upon human rights. For children, the appropriate concept is a right to be prepared for effective citizenship—a right to education (see below for further discussion). As for convicts and disabled persons, in my view they should indeed be allowed to vote if desirous and capable of doing so.[19] For competent adult citizens, the right to vote is indeed fundamental, and probably best regarded (*pace* the Supreme Court) as a "privilege . . . of citizenship."

Even granting the latter claim, to regard the right to vote as *sufficient* for political empowerment is to adopt a fiction that may bear little relation to reality, for example, where "discrete and insular minorities"[20] are concerned. We have already seen that universal suffrage, even with court-ordered reapportionment of legislative districts and high vote turnouts, is compatible with gross inequalities in the distribution of power.

The basic reason is that other forms of participation besides voting are essential to the effective exercise of power, and these often require resources that are not evenly distributed and whose distribution is not, under present law, in any sense a matter of governmental responsibility. These resources include, conspicuously, wealth, social status, knowledge, and motivation. Whether or not personhood is a matter of degree, political power certainly is. To declare all persons equal in dignity might conceivably make them so. To declare them equal in power only mocks the fact of inequality. This is why strict governmental "neutrality" sometimes can be utterly unfair and "affirmative action" permissible.

The arguments of Beitz and Guinier, reviewed in chapter 2, show convincingly that a norm of formal equality such as "one person, one vote" is inadequate to the constitutional goal of effective access for minority groups and viewpoints. Even if no specific approach to representation is mandated, a set of rules that systematically excludes or underrepresents identifiable interests is constitutionally suspect. How much representation, and of what kind, is enough? No one-dimensional standard will produce fair results in all cases, yet several points can be made with some confidence.

It is obvious that the First and the Fourteenth Amendments are the primary textual resources available for a constitutional jurisprudence of positive political rights and that these resources go only so far. While the First Amendment may confer a right to be politically active, it cannot be read to confer a right to be successful. One could develop arguments that to enjoy freedom of speech entails rights to an adequate education, access to the media of mass communication, and so forth; but, even if I am supplied all these things, the audience will still have the right (and very likely the inclination) to switch to a more entertaining channel. Thus effective access in the sense of obtaining the results desired clearly cannot be guaranteed.

The right to an education will be further considered under the "property" heading. Regulation of the media is often litigated under the "free speech" heading, but the constitutional right is that of the media owner—not that of the citizen who may wish to gain effective (or any) access as a speaker. The day when any citizen was effectively free to set up his own competitive channel is, of course, long gone. By declining to revise First Amendment doctrine accordingly, the Court has alchemically transmogrified political speech from a personal right of all citizens into a property right for those who can afford it.

Freedom of association, a right long held implicit in the First Amendment,[21] was a concept developed to protect fragile, nonmainstream organizations beleaguered by a hostile state. Its logic, however, is just as useful to the already powerful when they seek to pool resources and organize for maximum political influence. "Neutrality" blinds the law to this distinction, so that the right comes—contrary to the initial intention—to exacerbate inequalities of power.

Three rather easy, if narrow, arguments could help to rectify some of these problems. First, vested interests have no constitutional right to remain so. Thus, our political rights should be taken to include a ban on laws that hinder independents and third parties from competing in elections or that prevent write-in voting.[22] Where public funds are made available to defray campaign expenses, they must be distributed to all competitors, even those with no record of past success. Contrary decisions[23] are insensitive to interests in recognition and access to agenda setting that transcend a group's or a candidate's prospects for immediate electoral success.

Second, access to the mass media is essential for publicizing one's ideas as well as garnering votes. The cost of access today places it beyond reach for too many who might otherwise make important contributions. Recent judicial interpretations of the First Amendment have bolstered the significance of ability to pay by granting free speech rights to corporations[24] and by holding that print media cannot be compelled to cover more than one side of a story.[25] In addition, Congress has repeatedly condoned election-year suspension of the FCC's equal-time rule.

These decisions would make more sense if the marketplace of "free trade in ideas"[26] were literally *free*. Having recognized that access to the courts and to the polls cannot be lawfully denied on ground of inability to pay,[27] the courts should extend this principle to the rest of the political process—including those parts of it that are not formally part of the governmental structure.[28] They should also recognize that the political rights of artificial "persons" need not and should not be coextensive with those of citizens.

Third, the freedom to speak and the right to vote are meaningless if one does not know what is going on. While government cannot guarantee that citizens will actually acquire knowledge about its activities, it can and should refrain from hindering them from so doing. More specifically, the First Amendment should be held to guarantee a right to know about governmental activities. Government cannot *own* information. It processes information as the people's agent; an agent who withholds information from his principal wrongs his principal.

Bureaucrats will always argue that secrecy is necessary to prevent private interest groups from seeking to influence governmental decisions, because such influence attempts "could interfere seriously with the objective, dispassionate atmosphere in which these issues are analyzed and presented" by themselves to elected officials.[29] This perspective betrays a shocking contempt for the modern conception of a republican form of government. It ought to be unlawful to act upon it. (For discussion of the much-abused national security rationale for governmental secrecy, see chapter 4.)

This nearly concludes my very brief look at First Amendment doctrine. The religion clauses, inspired by the search for political peace after the religious wars of the seventeenth century, are couched in terms of negative rather than positive liberty. Thus the only point I wish to make here about the jurisprudence of the religion clauses is that it too has recently taken on an increasingly intolerant trend.

As one who was annually compelled to participate in alien religious ceremonies held in a public school, I can think of few better illustrations of establishment insensitivity to minority viewpoints than Chief Justice Burger's confident declaration that Christmas is a secular, not a religious holiday.[30] The person-centered perspective teaches that whether an individual's sense of equal dignity has been invaded is emphatically *not* a judgment that others should make for her, either by majority vote or by judicial fiat.

I leave aside the Second and Ninth Amendments, for opposite reasons. The Second is obsolete for purposes of political empowerment, since, even though the right to bear arms was reserved in part to guard the people against the threat of governmental tyranny, it will never be read to guarantee us what that would take: arms equivalent to the government's best.

The Ninth Amendment, for its part, despite some interesting scholarly work and a few passing judicial references, has not yet been born as a real force in constitutional discourse—perhaps because, like the privileges and immunities clause, the courts are intimidated at the thought of where such a jurisprudence might lead them. For some reason, judicial expansion of personal rights, unlike judicial expansion of governmental powers, is seen as a mortal threat to the integrity of the "political" process.[31]

As for the Fourteenth Amendment, it is unfortunate that the privileges and immunities clause has scarcely survived the disastrous *Slaughterhouse Cases*[32] decision, for its phrasing is obviously more hospitable to substantive rights than is that of the due process and equal protection clauses. *Privileges of citizens*, in particular, are quite naturally understood to include affirmative political rights. How else, after all, are citizens to be legally distinguished from other persons?

As noted in chapter 3, the Bill of Rights refers to "the people" in the special context of political rights. The broader, "civil" rights[33] to life, liberty, and property (and also freedom of speech and religion) are not so confined; the due process clause, in particular, appears to grant an immunity (negative liberty) to all persons. And, while the equal protection clause indubitably announces a principle of equal treatment by government of all persons *subject to* the law, its application to political *agency* is more problematic, both historically and conceptually. How any political rights this clause creates could be extended to "persons" who are not citizens is just one difficulty.

The Court's application of the equal protection clause to political rights has, until quite recently, focused largely on practices specifically aimed at preventing "discrete and insular minorities" from participating on the same terms as the majority. In these cases the equal protection clause does not create a substantive political right; it merely regulates the *extension* of a right created elsewhere.

Courts have embroiled themselves in greater conceptual and political difficulties by tentatively accepting a broader responsibility for the integrity of the "marketplace of ideas" that is the political process. This role and, in particular, the periodic review of legislative districting plans requires a sensitive confrontation of the tensions between liberal and republican conceptions of representation.

The "marketplace" metaphor reflects the assumptions of liberal pluralist thought, in which politics consists of exchange and accommodation among discrete interest groups. The concern for integrity or purification of the marketplace, however, has a distinctly republican complexion: it envisions a politics aimed at truth and/or the common good, opened to all viewpoints by judicial enforcement of the First Amendment, equal protection rules, and so forth.

Now, a norm of openness to ideas does not exactly correspond to one of openness to individual voices. Often, indeed, our politics seems richer in voices than in ideas. Lennertz[34] usefully distinguishes between a (liberal) "politics of noise," in which group representatives stake out and bargain over their self-interested claims, and a (republican) "politics of speech," in which civic-minded representatives of the whole people engage in open-minded inquiry and persuasive discourse aimed at the best available conception of the common good. He then explores the possibilities for reading the Constitution in ways that support a politics that is good both in liberal and in republican senses.

Lennertz rejects the formalistic one person, one vote standard on the ground that it expresses a purely liberal conception of representation. Instead, "[t]he legitimate realm of the 'good gerrymander' must be established to extricate the court from its slide down the slippery slope to proportional representation."[35]

Admittedly, distinguishing good from bad gerrymanders requires judicial consideration of substantive, as opposed to merely formal, theories of justice. That courts must balance competing republican and liberal visions of justice in order to do so should be no surprise. That courts may be relatively unsuited or partly powerless to resolve some kinds of political problems does not make the whole issue of fair representation an *a priori* nonjusticiable political question.

While contemporary politics may seem far closer to the "noise" than to the "speech" paradigm, it is clear that the electoral system is indeed structured, to a significant extent, according to the dictates of the latter. For example, the winner-take-all system generally used in House and electoral college voting seems fair *if*, on the one hand, we assume that the winners carried the day by making better arguments that persuaded open-minded voters. They can then plausibly claim to represent even those who mistakenly voted against them.

If, on the other hand, voting were simply a head count of fixed interest groups with fixed preferences, a proportional representation system would seem infinitely fairer, and even essential to provide meaningful representation for minority groups. Only on republican principles, in other words, is it easy to make sense of the following claim:

> An individual or a group of individuals who votes for a losing candidate is usually deemed to be adequately represented by the winning candidate and to have as much opportunity to influence that candidate as other voters in the district. We cannot presume in such a situation, without actual proof to the contrary, that the candidate elected will entirely ignore the interests of those voters.[36]

Passing over for now the large distinctions between being "not entirely ignored," being "adequately represented," and being "equally represented," this statement by Justice White reminds us that the republican view of representation is indeed still firmly entrenched in the Constitution. While Lennertz, Levinson,[37] and many others have seen proportional representation as the logical culmination of liberal-democratic approaches to equal voting rights, the Supreme Court has repeatedly stated that the Constitution requires no such thing.

Not that proportional representation is a panacea. Even if one were to hold that some form of PR *were* constitutionally required, this would by no means guarantee an equal distribution of overall political influence. After all, no matter how the voting system is structured, the ostensibly inclusive (democratic) "marketplace" will retain its familiar distortions: insofar as effective access to this "free" marketplace in fact depends on wealth and education, access is equal neither for persons nor for ideas. Indeed, insofar as access is very often exercised through meetings with unelected bureaucrats, it does not even depend directly on the right to vote, much less on the number of votes one's organization can deliver.

However it is channeled, it is safe to say that the discourse will often favor the interests of affluent factions more than the common good. Of course there are many ways to obscure this, for example by claims that "what's good for General Motors is good for the country."[38] An ironist might suggest that "marketplace of ideas" is an oxymoron.

A small start was made toward putting political inequality (beyond the brute practice of outright disfranchisement) on the judicial agenda when, after long hesitation, federal courts began entertaining claims that districts were malapportioned in their population size.[39] This soon produced the one person, one vote standard for districting,[40] but the Court did not stop there. Eventually, it announced in *Davis v. Bandemer* that a constitutional right was violated when district boundaries were "gerrymandered"—that is, that even if the populations of the districts within a state were equal in size, its districting scheme could still be found to unfairly dilute the weight of a petitioner's vote if the lines were so drawn as to impair petitioner's chances of electing her candidate of choice.[41]

Lowenstein[42] attempts to minimize *Bandemer*'s impact by arguing that only historically victimized political minorities (and not the major parties, whose overall access to the system is secure) can invoke the equal protection clause to challenge gerrymandered districting. His rather forced reading of the case, aimed at keeping courts out of the partisan "political thicket," has not gained general scholarly assent. Grofman, for example, maintains (quoting Justice White's opinion) that the *Bandemer* holding is that "each group in a state should have the same chance to elect representatives of its choice as any other political group."[43] Yet the courts have done little in the aftermath of *Bandemer* to clarify or to enforce any such norm.

Which electoral systems would satisfy Justice White's principle? As the discussion in chapter 2 showed, his words are subject to several, very different interpretations. Is the right actually vested in persons, or in groups? Is each group to have "the same chance" regardless of its size and of its agenda? Or, just the opposite, a chance proportionate to its numerical strength? Or is there merely a right not to have government knowingly stack the deck against us? No answer is free from difficulty.

A number of scholars argue (see chapter 2) that a *Bandemer* claim is more logically and realistically analyzed as a *group* claim: a right of the group—typically a racial or ethnic minority—to remain or to become powerfully joined together within electoral districts, and not dispersed in a sea of strangers.

The First Amendment freedom of association can be adequately grasped and "neutrally" enforced as a simple right of individuals to make their private associative choices without state interference. Districting, in contrast, always involves deliberate state action directly affecting the political prospects of all politicians and all citizens in ways that depend completely on group political alignments and residential patterns. Thus, in a gerrymandering case a complaining voter is not asking to be left alone, but to be placed with enough of her like-minded peers to make victory possible. In the context of winner-take-all elections, it is difficult to see how *all* citizens could actually simultaneously enjoy such a right. So it is tempting to formulate the claim as a right of electoral association belonging to particular groups.

If there is such a right, however, we will have to grapple with the question, which groups possess it? The answer certainly cannot be *all* groups, for we can neither list them all nor assign all voters to one and only one group for districting purposes. At any rate, the Court in *United Jewish Organizations of Williamsburgh v. Carey*[44] declined to recognize any such general group right.

With only one dissent, it disposed of the case on more traditional grounds: black voters have individual rights under the Fourteenth and Fifteenth Amendments, and the Voting Rights Act justified the state legislature in developing a racially conscious districting plan to support those rights. Meanwhile, the complaint of the Hasidic Jewish community that was split in two by the same plan could only be grasped—and therefore easily dismissed—as one of discrimination against whites!

District lines have always been drawn with favored partisan and social interests in mind, and lawmakers will not ignore those interests in their districting decisions unless somehow compelled to do so. A requirement of political blindness or methodological randomness in districting would be a shocking departure, responsive in an exaggerated way to liberal-individualist ideas but wholly overlooking the republican tradition, in which factors such as community history and culture are also relevant. It would also, of course, be inconsistent with the Voting Rights Act, which mandates special solicitude for the impact of districting upon particular minorities that historically have had "less opportunity than other members of the electorate to participate in the political process and to elect representatives of their choice."[45]

In *Thornburg v. Gingles*,[46] the Supreme Court held that the vote dilution barred by the Act can occur only where (1) the minority group is sufficiently large and compact to constitute a majority of a single-member district, (2) the minority is politically cohesive, and (3) the white majority votes sufficiently as a bloc to enable it usually to defeat the minority's preferred candidate. Extended debate and litigation over the meaning and application of these standards was to be expected.

In four recent decisions,[47] the Court further muddied the waters by recognizing a new, constitutional cause of action distinct from vote dilution. These 5-4 decisions held that certain black-majority congressional districts in North Carolina, Georgia, and Texas, drawn after Justice Department rejection of earlier districting plans, ran afoul of a constitutional principle that makes suspect all racially motivated districting, including the "ameliorative" variety the Justice Department had encouraged. Section 5 of the Voting Rights Act, the Court held, was designed only to prevent states from subverting existing minority voting strength; Congress did not have the constitutionally suspect intention of authorizing a racially segregated districting system or of granting affirmative preference to minorities in the redistricting process.

Since the majority's color blindness compels them to insist that race does not affect a member's ability adequately to represent her constituents, the harm that they think racially motivated districting causes to the complaining parties is most obscure. Nevertheless, districting is now valid only if the state can prove either (1) that it acted primarily on traditional, racially neutral grounds such as compactness, contiguity, respect for political subdivisions or communities defined by actual shared interests, or incumbent seat protection (ah, neutrality!), or else (2) that the use of racial criteria was justified by a compelling public interest such as eradicating the effects of past discrimination.

While the overall impact of these scarcely coherent decisions remains to be determined in case-by-case litigation, there is reason to believe that the new doctrine will have serious impact on the number of minority faces in public office. These voting rights cases share a core "principle" with other recent decisions that apply "strict scrutiny" to affirmative action programs and cut back on available remedies for school segregation. As some justices would have it, the colorblind Constitution permits no distinction between policies that oppress vulnerable minorities and policies designed to protect them.

The unequal distribution of power thus threatens to become again invisible and/or immune to governmental remedy, as overt racial discrimination was in the *Plessy* era. The traditional biases of the electoral system and the advantages they confer upon the powerful are privileged as "neutral," and the Constitution—including, ironically, the equal protection clause—serves as an effective barrier to progressive reform. If the political aspects of racial inequality cannot be addressed despite the Civil War amendments, the same is true *a fortiori* of socioeconomic inequities less directly linked to "state action." Here, I think, we see a reactionary version of "neutrality" running rampant, unchecked by the realistic, person-centered perspective.[48]

Reversing these trends and addressing the realities of contemporary politics in a more balanced way would oblige the Court to go well beyond "one person, one vote" in developing its constitutional theory of fair representation. The Court has barely begun to do so. However, it is widely held that *Davis v. Bandemer*,[49] the leading case on partisan gerrymandering, extends to partisan minorities the same political rights that the Voting Rights Act grants to certain ethnic and linguistic minorities.[50] This precedent could *potentially* apply not simply to the second-strongest political party in a region, but to other politically disadvantaged parties, groups, and movements. One could even attempt to expound the *Bandemer* right as a right of all voters. Thus, the law might develop in very different directions.

First, the Court could prudently abstain from developing a general theory of representation and announce that the Constitution no more imposes such a theory than it does a theory of political economy.[51] It could, in other words, abandon the notion of unconstitutional gerrymandering and decline to go beyond "one person, one vote." This would leave the "political branches" relatively free to identify and respond to specific political practices they deem unfair.

It must be noted, however, that incumbents, by definition, are the beneficiaries as a class of whatever unfair practices may now exist, so that their incentives for intervening will always be ambivalent at best. Moreover, insofar as effective access to the political process for all citizens is both a fundamental personal right and a compelling public interest, an approach that disabled courts from *guaranteeing* such access, even in the face of governmental inaction, would be profoundly self-defeating.

Second, a quantitative standard of proportional representation for each interest or group addresses the issue of effective access, but poses severe problems of enumeration and attendant risks of exclusion. Each of us can be seen as belonging to many interest groups of different kinds—some by birth, some by choice, some politically organized, some not. There is no way of counting all these groups and no reason to insist that all need or deserve the same kind or amount of political representation. PR has the weakness of overemphasizing the power of numbers and ignoring the coherence of the group, the intensity of its preferences, and, of course, the merit of its ideas—all of which seem relevant to what representation it deserves.

Yet, for government to determine the eligible groups would, in the absence of a neutral method, create certain "special favorites of the law." Elected officials' choices predictably tend to favor vested interests. The record does not show convincingly that courts would do much better. In today's judicial climate, for example, it appears that, despite the Fifteenth Amendment and the Voting Rights Act, racial minorities would be uniquely ineligible to benefit from a PR approach.

A system such as "cumulative voting," suggested by Guinier,[52] alleviates some of these difficulties, for it is geographical districting that most grievously embroils government in allocating political influence among different groups. Still, PR in any form is too unconventional to recommend itself, at least as a judicially imposed innovation.

Moreover, if "equal protection of the laws" requires equal influence in making the laws, we will need to produce precise measures of influence that not only are unavailable but are probably inconceivable, influence being the elusive, multidimensional concept that it is. Perhaps this is why Justice White in *Bandemer* offered the less exacting "adequate representation" as the appropriate norm, that is, "for a level of parity between votes and representation sufficient to ensure that significant minority voices are heard and that majorities are not consigned to minority status."[53]

Third, the logic of the "free marketplace of ideas" can be taken merely to prohibit intentional governmental discrimination against particular persons or groups, so that all are equal before the law. It can be construed, as Justice White's just-quoted statement suggests, to imply a more generous, affirmative-action requirement that all ideas or voices be ensured a chance to be adequately heard in electoral competition and/or in governmental deliberations. A still more radical interpretation would call for the political analogue of antitrust policy: a concerted governmental attack on "unfair" concentrations of private political power, with a view to reducing disparities in effective access.

The nondiscrimination standard is valid so far as it goes, yet it clearly does not guarantee effective access for all. Moreover, it ignores the fact that any redistricting proposal will predictably affect the electoral prospects of various groups. Only a purely random plan could escape the charge of knowingly aiding some causes and harming others.

The affirmative action standard has its own major weaknesses. No workable and principled way of identifying all the eligible, "significant" ideas or voices is apparent. Either this standard would produce an unwieldy, fragmented field for candidate debates and policy deliberations, or, more likely, it would be so applied as to heavily favor the best established and/or most popular voices.

Moreover, this standard may require only that each voice enjoy one moment on the air or one solitary representative—that it not be, in Justice White's words, "entirely ignored" by the political process. That is, a court might deem such token representation "adequate" even though it scarcely amounts to effective access.

The third, "antitrust" alternative runs afoul of the First Amendment insofar as that Amendment is conventionally understood to protect fundamental rights to associate, to organize, and to raise and spend money for political purposes. Absent these rights, our system of political parties and organized interest groups could not exist in its present form. Yet the exercise of those rights predictably leads to the establishment of potentially oppressive vested interests. Lowi[54] argues that our current system of parties and interests is so inimical to the rule of law that it is, effectively, unconstitutional. For courts to undertake its wholesale reconstruction, however, would be truly revolutionary. If Ackerman is correct, we ourselves have made this system and must take the lead in remaking it.

The Court's specific political rights doctrines can, however, be criticized along lines I have suggested and reformulated to take better account of the perspectives and needs of political outsiders and underdogs. Courts have no occasion or warrant for devising and imposing an entire election system. They need only determine, case by case, whether specific rules or practices violate the complaining party's fundamental rights. That party must first explain the sense in which she does not enjoy the same chance as anyone else for electoral success. She must demonstrate that her diminished chances result in some sense from governmental action or inaction that is within a court's power to redress.

This norm does not assign a hitherto unknown fundamental right to particular groups or to groups in general. We can instead grasp it as a right of each voter to be free, regardless of her social background or political preferences, from arbitrary or invidious governmental interference with her effective access to the political process. The definition of "arbitrary," "invidious," and "effective," if it is not to be done in purely formalistic terms, will entail a careful examination of the local "totality of circumstances," inevitably including the distribution of political preferences and of the political groups who hold them. This approach offers little support for the recent racial districting decisions.

The quest for abstract neutrality will of course be futile, as illustrated by Cain's proposal for "the political system, not the Courts"(!) to adopt reforms guaranteeing that "both parties" will have meaningful input in redistricting plans, and even that supermajorities will be needed for their adoption.[55] Cain seems to assume, without argument, that by granting fair access to the two major parties, we guarantee that all citizens' interests are adequately represented. The difficulties with this assumption should already be very clear. Note, moreover, that if the First and the Fourteenth Amendments address only disabilities imposed by state action, other disabilities will persist whatever courts, and perhaps even legislatures, may do.

The indicated arguments for expansion of political rights hardly entail a revolution in the allocation of political influence. Their acceptance would leave untouched the basic structure of socioeconomic inequality, which is for many citizens personally as well as politically disabling. Natural persons would continue to live in a world heavily controlled by artificial corporate persons which, though chartered by the state and shielded by its laws, are "private" entities and hence not responsible to the electorate or bound to respect others' constitutional rights.[56] Thus, it bears asking whether our constitutional understanding of economic rights is not in need of revision. Along with life and liberty, we must also be concerned with property.

Property

While many issues are hotly contested, a few points ought to be clear to all sides. First, property is for persons; it is not a value in itself. Property rights, in Justice Stewart's words, are personal rights; as Chief Justice Warren put it, "legislators represent people, not trees or acres."[57] Second, the point of recognizing property rights is that a modicum of economic security is essential to the flourishing of persons, both in the private realm, for defense against the compulsion of others (negative liberty), and in the public, for the ability effectively to pursue one's political interests, whatever they may be (positive liberty).

Third, it follows that a perspective that identifies "efficiency," defined as the maximizing of aggregate wealth without regard to distribution, as the primary value is inconsistent with one that identifies respect for persons as the primary value. In this sense there is nothing "neutral" about the quest for efficiency.

Since our Constitution does identify respect for persons as the primary value, it is an exaggeration to claim that the Constitution does not incorporate any economic theory. Because of poverty's dehumanizing effects, governmental indifference to the plight of the poor is an attitude inconsistent with an oath to support the Constitution. Whatever conflict we may have about the meaning of "the general welfare," our primary commitment must be to the welfare of persons, not to that of an abstract aggregate. To take rights seriously is to decline to sacrifice the rights of one for the aggregate benefit of others. This axiom, however, does not determine what specific rights we possess. On that question, consensus is hard to come by.

I believe that the proponents of the "new property," who argue for a fundamental right not to be deprived arbitrarily of personal security, are correct: the commitment to the flourishing of personhood, in the conditions of our society, entails a case for minimal welfare rights.[58] In contrast, the current move to replace federal welfare "entitlement" programs with discretionary block grants to the states is a step in the wrong direction. This move would empower local governmental agencies, ostensibly in the hope that power will then "trickle down" to persons receiving discretionary aid.

The scheme is empirically misguided for two reasons. First, in many cases the result will be that no aid or drastically insufficient aid is given. Second, to receive minimal assistance at another's discretion is even less conducive to one's dignity and empowerment than to receive it as a matter of right. It is true that existing entitlement programs have often failed to accomplish these lofty goals. The proper response is reform, not abolition.

Under current judicial doctrine, either approach is constitutional. For fear of imposing on government an affirmative duty to redistribute wealth, the Court has denied that there is a fundamental right to an education—let alone to such other prerequisites of a secure and dignified life as health care, decent housing, a minimum income, or a job. It does not scrutinize strictly policies that mete out formally equal but actually disparate treatment to rich and poor. It trusts the "political branches" to handle these matters fairly, even though (1) it knows that wealth is very unevenly distributed and (2) it has held that the use of wealth to pursue political influence is a potent, constitutionally protected right.

Accordingly, in *San Antonio Independent School District v. Rodriguez*,[59] the Court declined to order an equalization of per-pupil spending between the wealthier and poorer Texas public schools. The Court's misgivings may have been politically and fiscally realistic, but they are difficult to square with the equally realistic requirements for effective participation in society today. Moreover, the fact that four justices disagreed shows that the contrary position is not beyond the pale of our constitutional traditions—or was not in 1973, at least. Indeed, a number of state courts have since assumed the responsibility declined by the Supreme Court in *Rodriguez*.

As long ago as 1923, the Supreme Court said that constitutional liberty includes

> the right of the individual to contract, to engage in any of the common occupations of life, to acquire useful knowledge, to marry, establish a home and bring up children, to worship God according to the dictates of his own conscience, and generally to enjoy those privileges long recognized at common law as essential to the orderly pursuit of happiness by free men.[60]

This list may well have originated as a straightforward description of the rights that slaves did *not* have. Yet, whether or not the common law has recognized the fact, few of these goals can be pursued meaningfully, much less realized, by a "free man" who is uneducated and economically destitute.

That the recognized "privileges and immunities of citizens" should pass over the essentials of personal security in favor of a "right to visit the sub-treasury"[61] cannot bespeak a defensible conception of "ordered liberty" unless the polity consists exclusively of bankers and would-be bankers. Though Spencer's Social Darwinism (or a vulgar materialist distortion thereof) has lost its erstwhile status of constitutional orthodoxy, apparently a more compelling vision has yet to take its place.

As Sunstein points out in his critique of status-quo neutrality, parts of our constitutional discourse go on as if nothing had changed.[62] Yet, in place of Everyman, the proud, self-governing citizen of classic republican thought, we have Noman. For *"homo economicus"* today is confronted with an impersonal, corporate world in which his liberty, his equality, and his very personhood often seem mere formalities. He has distinct rights within the private and public realms, but those realms are only formally separate, and he often lacks the resources needed to enjoy his rights fully. Noman may all-too-rationally resolve, in this situation, not to "be what he can be" but to get what he can get. The system does not adequately support personal flourishing.

As suggested in regard to political rights, the equal protection clause must at least be read to *permit*—even if we dare not read it to *require*—government action designed to alleviate the injuries and disabilities associated with socioeconomic inequality. *Carolene Products*[63] held that strict judicial scrutiny is warranted by measures that injure politically weak, unpopular minorities. For exactly the same reasons, measures like the typical affirmative action plan, which altruistically aim to remedy past injuries and assist those same minorities, present an extraordinarily compelling claim for judicial deference. To subject such measures to strict scrutiny, as the Court has recently begun to do,[64] is to advance an exclusionary partisan agenda under the guise of "neutrality."

On the person-centered approach, an inquiry into property rights must begin with the question of how the set of personal relations ordered by property fits into human lives. Property is first of all a precondition for survival, for the realization of other needs. It can also be argued, as some philosophers and some psychologists have, that control and manipulation of property is basic to the development of a sense of personal identity and competence.[65] Pursuit of material satisfactions and production of material goods do consume a great deal of most persons' time and energy, and the choice of "what to do for a living"—which goods to produce and to consume—seem very central to self-definition and social status for most people in societies like our own. ("And what do you want to be when you grow up?")

Historic defenses of property have focused on its relationship both to negative and to positive political freedom. On the one hand, arbitrary taxation or confiscations by government are the essence of tyranny; on the other, possession of property is not just a private need but a requisite for enlightened, responsible political participation, including voting and holding office. Those without property, so the argument goes, are defenseless against oppression, vulnerable to corruption, and unlikely to have the education or the stake in the public welfare on which political virtue generally depends. In that sense, liberty and property are inseparably linked.

The core concept of personhood, in the context of liberal individualism, directs our attention to the boundary between self and other as constitutive of the person. The historic theory of property rights asserts that property is essential to the establishment, maintenance, and extension of that personal boundary. It also asserts that exchange of property is central to the ways that individuals transcend the personal boundary and come into fruitful relationship with each other.

While it recognizes that the phenomenon of property has both private and public, personal and political aspects, the classical theory does not necessarily conclude from this that property rights must also have both private and public components. In mainstream thought at least, the focus has been on private property rights. Indeed, the power of government to hold, acquire, and operate property in the name of the public, as well as its power to regulate the acquisition and use of property by private owners, have been deemed problematic.

This may perhaps be dismissively explained in terms of the selfish interests of dominant, wealthy classes who made the laws and trained the philosophers. Can it be justified, though, by resort to the axioms that rights are personal, that social arrangements must be conducive to the interests of individuals, and that the way to achieve this result is to allow maximum leeway for individual choice?

This empirical argument succeeds only if a key proposition can be sustained: that individual choice is maximized by a regime of relatively unrestricted private property rights. This proposition seems plausible only on unrealistic assumptions of relative equality of holdings or ample abundance of unowned or newly created property—unless, that is, we are prepared to calculate maximum liberty on an aggregate basis, disregarding its distribution.

Concerns over the just distribution of property are by all accounts among the chronic issues in political life, if not the central issue around which all of politics revolves. Economic growth is another major factor in politics. No doubt it may be importantly affected by the incentives that property rights can provide; the rate of growth, in turn, has vital implications for aggregate welfare.

Personal rights, however, are trumps. Rawls[66] is surely correct in specifying maximum *equal* liberty, for a theory that drops this constraint cannot be deemed person-centered. Consistently, Rawls approaches property through its most egalitarian aspect—access to "primary goods," those crucial to satisfaction of basic personal needs and thus to pursuit of whatever further desires one may have. His "difference principle" draws great intuitive force from the assumption that, if a scheme of property rights is detrimental to personal dignity, this effect will be most evident in the lives of the materially worst-off members of society.

Such an assumption surely is not absolutely neutral, even if we hold that a dollar has more marginal utility to the poor person than to the rich. For example, it tacitly rejects two views once widely professed: that wealth is an obstacle to spiritual salvation, or, on the contrary, that poverty is a punishment for sin or a sign of failure to receive salvation through grace. Yet Rawls holds neither wealth nor poverty to be morally blameable. Thus his approach is entirely consistent with the constitutional separation of church and state. In our secular polity neither rich nor poor have a favored spiritual status. The question is how the special needs of the poor are to weigh against the special contributions of the rich to wealth creation.

Madison held that the chief task of constitutional design was to contain and moderate the perennial struggle between the propertied and the unpropertied—the most important political conflict in any society.[67] Majority rule tended to elevate the "rights of persons" at the expense of the "rights of property," hence the need for auxiliary precautions to safeguard the latter.[68] As *The Federalist* made clear, judicial review was one of the main precautions so devised.[69] But this implicitly class-based view of a dichotomy between "personal" and "property" rights runs afoul of the modern axiom that all constitutional rights are personal rights.

Though the Constitution seems to have been viewed by some as a bulwark for property against the "excesses of democracy,"[70] in political terms it could not have been ratified on that basis. It and its amendments were drafted and defended in broader, nobler terms: as granting not privileges to one class against another, but rights to all citizens against their government. Among those rights, of course, were life, liberty, and property—in that order.

There is not much "legislative history" connected with this phrase, but I think its meaning appeared quite straightforward in light of the minimal role of the state at that time. Given the nature of the "deprivations" that citizens then had to fear, the due process clause was addressed primarily, if not solely, to the criminal justice system. (That is not to say, of course, that we must read it so narrowly today.)

When the state moves against a man to punish him, it typically does one or more of three things: it can take his life, lock him up, or seize his property. It seems fair to say that these penalties are listed in order of decreasing gravity. Loss of life automatically forfeits liberty and property. Loss of liberty makes the acquisition, protection, and enjoyment of one's property exceedingly difficult, while loss of property (at least in the monetary sense) can generally be repaired if one remains alive and free.

Whether it follows that the "due process" to which one is entitled would be different in each case is perhaps unclear, but certainly, the Fifth and Fourteenth Amendments do not provide obvious support for the proposition that property rights are of primary or even special importance relative to other kinds of rights. Yet that proposition is arguably found in Locke[71] and also in much of the Supreme Court's jurisprudence prior to 1937. How was it, how could it have been, supported? Unfortunately, explicit judicial discussion and defense of the proposition are not to be found.

What we find instead is the habit of mind ably set forth by Nedelsky[72]—a tendency to see major issues as revolving around property rights, and to dismiss as insubstantial any claims that cannot be so formulated. Judges and lawyers had in fact made their careers by concentrating on property issues, and felt most comfortable in dealing with them. In addition, cases and arguments couched in terms of property rights were relatively secure against the charge that courts cannot and should not involve themselves in partisan or political questions.

Thus, for example, *Marbury v. Madison*[73] in the Court's view involved not a challenge to the president's exercise of political discretion, but a straightforward property question of when title to office vests in an appointee. *Fletcher v. Peck*[74] involved not an inquiry into the motives of state legislators, but a straightforward question of contract law affecting private parties' title to a piece of real estate.

More spectacularly, the *Dred Scott*[75] decision did not give the Court's judgment on the justice of slavery or on the claim of blacks to be recognized as persons; those matters had been conclusively determined by the People who made the Constitution. The Court's duty was simply to enforce the property rights of slaveowners, which Congress was powerless to abridge. Even the dissenters were unable to escape this frame of reference: one justice defended the outlawing of slavery in certain territories not by appealing to the personal rights of blacks, but by arguing that slavery tended to depress real estate values, and that Congress had power to protect those values!

The focus on certain kinds of rights appears to have facilitated a bias in favor of certain kinds of claimants, namely, those who held the most property. To be sure, the correlation between type of claim and type of claimant was imperfect and the judicial preference for property claims was not absolute. When the Cherokees were dispossessed of their lands by the State of Georgia, their suit was rejected, in part because it was too "political" to be justiciable;[76] but when a white preacher was jailed for his activities among the Cherokees, his plea for liberty impelled the Court to rule that the state's entire course of proceedings toward the tribe had been beyond its constitutional authority.[77]

Still, most of the constitutional issues brought before federal courts until this century were couched in terms of property rights (or the allocation of governmental powers to regulate property), even when something different was arguably at stake underneath. Property rights were usually expansively construed and aggressively defended, while provisions of the Constitution designed to safeguard personal and political rights were largely ignored or narrowly construed. In particular, the Fourteenth Amendment, intended primarily to benefit those freed from slavery, was transformed into an engine of corporate power.[78] It took a long time before an effective challenge to these developments was mounted.

Today, the law lets little if anything turn on whether a particular right is designated a "property" right or not.[79] Yet the questions are still worth asking: Is it possible to draw a clear line between persons and property, or between personal rights and property rights? Is it necessary, or even useful?

The blurring of the line between "person" and "property" seems to have profoundly illiberal consequences. This is true both of the institution of slavery, which could not have existed were blacks fully recognized as persons, and of the legal personhood of corporations, which, by extending certain valuable, ostensibly personal rights to groups that have pooled their resources to do business and whose members already have personal rights, in effect permits double counting.

In both of these cases, liberals have argued that the person/property distinction is clear and that the entity in question has been misclassified. The positivist claim that "attribution of legal personality to institutions . . . should . . . require no special justification"[80] is as repugnant to the liberal perspective as was the claim that denial of legal personality to human beings required no justification.

The abortion controversy admittedly confuses the issue, since from one perspective the "right to life" position appears analogous to the abolitionist one. Though the denial of personhood to a fetus or to a frozen embryo, making it in effect disposable property, could be seen as illiberal, contemporary liberals have stressed the disastrous implications for a woman's personhood of interfering with her procreative autonomy. To say the least, this argument is far stronger than one defending a right to own slaves as essential to personal flourishing. On the other hand, the conventional anchoring of the woman's right in her ownership of her body obscures the discrete personal interest in the fate of her "posterity" (as the Preamble puts it)—an interest also held by the potential father. Ironically, a similar confounding of place with person has led the Court to uphold protective barriers around abortion *clinics* while denying them to abortion *patients*.[81]

The value for republicans of the personal rights/property rights dichotomy was apparent in the thought of Madison; its value for liberals became evident in the modern doctrine of preferred freedoms. Yet today, both establishment conservatives and Critical Legal Studies radicals tend to deny that the distinction makes sense. Thus, the political thrust of this distinction is heavily dependent on context.

It is safe to say that the extension to all of nominally equal property rights can have the effect of maintaining or even of enhancing extremely unequal distributions of property. Many of those rights will be of great interest and value to a few and inconsequential or harmful to the rest. But can other, more "personal" kinds of property rights be distinguished on the ground that they are of more equal practical value to all?

Both the desire to exercise a right and the need or opportunity to do so obviously vary with the person and the situation. Situations tend to vary according to social class, but, both for classes and for individuals, they also change over time. Thus a right initially demanded and written into law by one relatively elite group—such as the right to counsel in criminal cases—may turn out to offer equal or greater benefits to those less privileged. This could be true even of property rights if they were refocused on urgent personal needs.

The Framers esteemed property as a crucial safeguard of political freedom as well as an engine of economic progress. They may have differed on the relative merits of agriculture and commerce or of free and slave labor, but not on the value of property as such.[82] While recognizing that the unequal distribution of property was a primary cause of factional conflict, they were optimistic that their constitutional design would enable such conflict to be contained.[83] They conceptualized property largely as the rights to own land and to make enforceable contracts. Only later, as the limitations of these rights became evident with the closing of the frontier and the rise of industrial capitalism, would progressive forces see property's privileged place in the law as a barrier to personal flourishing.

The growing influence of the concept of 'equality' in our jurisprudence has been a crucial secular trend, manifested not just in applications of the equal protection clause but also in reinterpretations of other fundamental rights and even of governmental powers. Yet this chapter has no separate section on equality because, in my view, equality in the abstract is not a useful concept. Until we specify the substantive good or right with whose equal distribution we are concerned, and the real-world context as well, nothing useful can be said about what a commitment to equality entails. Expressions such as *equal dignity* and *equal respect* are only slightly more revealing.

When we consider specific political or property rights the issues become more pointed, but that is a mixed blessing. What unites jurisprudents of many stripes today is the Realist view that a specific conception of property cannot be politically neutral. Therefore, to assign a special place, more or less favored, to property rights relative to other rights cannot be justified on a neutral basis; courts have no business singling out property rights for special treatment.

Yet a concept of 'property' focused on primary subsistence needs is resistant to a neutrality-based critique insofar as it is rooted in fundamental characteristics common to all persons. Here the generality appropriate to formulations of fundamental rights is highly relevant: while it is not true that everyone needs food stamps, it is true that everyone needs food. This fact entails, I argue, a public duty to aid those who cannot feed (or house, heal, educate, or occupy, that is, securely situate) themselves.

The closeness of primary needs to everyday experience also goes far toward avoiding the conceptual difficulties presented by some of the more abstract, intangible forms of modern property. Some critics have argued that no coherent definition of property can encompass all and only the diverse phenomena that the law has recognized as such.[84] This problem does not seem severe with regard to fundamental, primary needs.

My approach to the concept of property resembles that of Margaret Jane Radin[85] in that we both take the concept of 'personhood' as the starting point for analysis of legal rights. I am also in agreement with her view that neither a simple legal positivism nor an ahistorical natural rights theory (such as, for example, moral realism) can provide a satisfactory basis for exposition and critique of our system of rights. Positivism makes critique logically impossible, while realism is both philosophically troublesome and, in the real world of politics, potentially intolerant.

Radin labels her alternative approach "pragmatism." This term seems to me potentially misleading in that many view pragmatic approaches as inherently unprincipled. Thus they view pragmatism as characteristic of "ordinary politics" and not appropriate for judicial reasoning. Radin appears, however, to share my view that it is possible to be both realistic and principled. Rights discourse is responsive to changing social conditions—including changing moral beliefs.

Radin develops a specific conception of personhood that draws for inspiration on Hegel's theory of property. Her intention is not to claim (falsely) for Hegel a large role in the history of Anglo-American jurisprudence, but to show how a defensible conception of property can be grounded in the requirements for human flourishing. This entails, in her view, embracing and developing a distinction, not clearly and consistently expressed in our law, between personal and fungible forms of property. Personal property is property with which someone's identity has become (and continues to be) *justifiably* bound up. The term *justifiably* tells us that the distinction between the two forms of property is determined not by the mere will of the "owner" but also by generally accepted, if fluid, social norms.

Radin makes many interesting observations about patterns and trends in the law that I shall not go into here. Instead, I shall concentrate on a few points of special interest or difficulty.

First, in what may be a clever piece of political indirection, Radin cheerfully grants the epithet of *liberal* to the republican/libertarian conservatives of today—shunning it for herself, ignoring the rich potential that liberal thought has always offered for egalitarian reform, and overlooking the positive aspects of New Deal liberal practice.[86] Liberals, she holds, see government as "them," while republicans see it as "us."[87] This move may be rhetorically prudent in light of the current unpopularity of the term *liberal*, but theoretically it is confusing. One might with equal justice claim that republicans see ordinary people as "them," while for liberals they are "us."

Radin formulates the political problem as a need to confront the challenge of the "Hobbesian" view of politics, in which government is depicted not as the presumptively faithful seeker of the public interest but as a presumptively selfish, corrupt, exploitative "rent-seeker."

Passing the question whether this is in fact Hobbes's view of government, Radin fails to observe that the "Hobbesian" view cannot justify a *selective* presumption of governmental untrustworthiness or a *selective* application of strict scrutiny. Thus, the practice (of crucial concern for Radin) of judges such as Scalia and Bork is not "Hobbesian." They *purport* to hold all rights equally fundamental, yet in fact they tend to defer to "majority rule" when rights *other than* property rights are in question, while applying far stricter scrutiny in defense of property rights.

Hobbes, in any case, was an absolute monarchist, not a democrat. Hobbesian monarchism may still, as chapter 4 argued, be part of our problem—but so is a very different phenomenon: modern capitalism. Radin has yet to develop an adequate exposition and defense of democratic theory, though it seems necessary to her qualified reliance on community norms—that is, on *justified* community norms—as her basis for a theory of personal flourishing.

Second, Radin's call for an objective test of whether a given property is "personal" is justified by two concerns: first, the imperative, if we are to dichotomize property, to rule out as morally wrong the "compleat capitalist's" obsession with amassing an empire of property holdings, seen as a good in itself (a personal surrender, one might say, to "commodity fetishism"); and second, a reluctance to privilege any more idiosyncratic, psychopathologic property fetishisms.

Both of these concerns are valid; the first, at least, is crucial to Radin's project. Nevertheless, by opting for an "objective" test, she makes a huge sacrifice: the viability of a nonconformist's lifestyle cannot be maintained by invoking (personal property) rights as a trump. Those whose claims are too aberrant, it seems, only show us thereby that they "have a screw loose." The community can reasonably declare their preferences and (subjectively) vital needs "unjustified," and therefore no bar to takings of their property.

There may be strong pragmatic arguments for this approach, but I am loath to embrace it as truly person-centered. It seems to tilt the scales drastically in a majoritarian direction, or worse. For example, Hobbesians might argue—though Radin does not—that our nonconformists have a "personal right" to therapeutic treatment. This right, in turn, could even become inalienable: in effect, a liability to compulsory treatment.

A third serious issue pertains to Radin's discomfort with "welfare rights," which are distinguishable from privileged rights to "personal property" in that the latter depend on a preexisting personal investment in a particular object such as a residence or a

wedding ring, her two most frequent examples. Part of her discomfort arises from the pragmatic reality that the Supreme Court
has already spurned the case for welfare rights. A larger factor is
Radin's sense that, for example, a long-time occupant of rental
housing has a personal stake in remaining *there* that is qualitatively different from a homeless person's stake in obtaining housing *somewhere*.[88]

Radin argues that the welfare-rights approach does not provide
adequate justification for imposing the costs of providing adequate
housing on the landlord rather than on the taxpayer.[89] She thinks
that, in contrast, the concrete personal stake of incumbent tenants
in *their* dwelling justifies imposing rent control on the landlord, if
his action in raising rent would otherwise force the tenant to move.
This apparently entails a judgment that the landlord is morally to
blame for exercising his legal rights by raising the rent when this
will force someone involuntarily to move—but that the owner of a
new building is not equally to blame for pricing his apartments so
expensively that those most in need of housing cannot afford to
move in.

Since the landlord's interest is presumptively equally fungible in
both cases, it is not evident why he has greater moral duties to the
tenant (whom he may never have met) than to the would-be tenant.
Moreover, I would argue that, from a person-centered point of view,
the first social imperative is to house the homeless. Deciding who
shall pay is a less urgent problem. Perhaps landlords should simply
be told that those who prefer to deal with the homeless through the
police rather than through social service agencies should accept the
necessary takings as a noncompensable exercise of the "police
power."

The distinction between the stake of a resident and that of a non-
resident in a given piece of property is real, but it runs the risk of
placing higher priority on people's sentimental attachments than
on their very survival. Moreover, by embracing the commonsense
attachment of ordinary persons to (some of) their ordinary things,
Radin inadvertently legitimizes the reification of "property" on
which the regnant ideology may implicitly depend. Given the mystique of equal, neutral rights, *all* (legal) persons—corporations included—are today equally endowed with rights to *all* (lawful)
property. Control of fungible property may be a less fundamental
right, but it is still a right.

The focus on property, in other words, obscures our grasp of the
realities of *power*.[90] Despite the vagaries of the concept of 'power,'
Morris Cohen's older distinction between "property for use" and

"property for power" may offer a more promising avenue for critique, because it makes more visible the *political* aspect of the tension between property rights and personal rights.[91] When critics argue that property rights are as precious as other rights, the best response, I think, is to reply that fundamental rights, by definition, are personal. Corporations, not being persons, can have no such rights, and persons' rights to fungible property (or "property for power," if you will) are not fundamental either.

Radin is conscious of the dehumanizing tendencies of a logic (such as that of the Law and Economics school) that would subsume all values under a uniform, commodified metric. Here no right is fundamental; all are either for sale or up for grabs. Posner, for example, argues that the logic of "efficiency" requires that legal rights be assigned to those who would pay most to purchase them on a hypothetical market—and that those rights should be granted free of charge![92]

In response, Radin hopes to establish a clear line between rules of property that our society can recognize as good for persons and other rules whose goodness is deeply contested or contestable. She needs to refute, for example, Epstein's bizarre theory that virtually all regulations of the use of property are "takings" for which owners must be compensated.[93] Her approach of course begins with the identification of "responsible subcategories" of property.[94] Her distinction between wedding rings and parking lots is useful in analyzing the opposing interests in contests over regulations that are sometimes essential to the personhood of one side without materially harming that of the other.

A purely rights-centered approach is inadequate, however, to distinguish between different types of governmental action. A categorical theory of governmental powers apparently lies behind Justice Scalia's claim that redistributive regulations and redistributive taxes are equally suspect under the takings clause. Confusingly, Radin attributes to Scalia a "Hobbesian" reason why regulations are suspect: "We should expect that governmental entities will always be trying to achieve wealth transfers for favored groups without going through *the democratically mandated long cut of openly debating and weighing them in the taxing and spending process*" [emphasis added].[95]

No coherent theory of democracy is discernable here. Radin does not pause to explain on what ground Scalia might deem taxation more "democratic" than regulation, how it would follow that the two are *equally* suspect, or how democratic debate could in any case justify by itself the violation of a fundamental personal right.

If we take the term *democratic* here in a purely procedural sense, it would seem that any duly legislated (or delegated) act of wealth redistribution is equally democratic. On the other hand, if democracy is taken to entail a substantive principle regarding equal sharing per capita of the costs and/or benefits of government, the method by which redistribution is attempted is still irrelevant. By this standard even the graduated income tax would be unconstitutional, despite the Sixteenth Amendment.

Whatever Justice Scalia's logic may be, if he wants to insist that *any* law imposing *any* burden unequally upon the citizenry requires strict scrutiny, then he will be obliged to subject *every* law to strict scrutiny. This would be not only silly but, by his own standards, the very opposite of judicial respect for democracy.

Radin's approach to the takings problem is far superior in political realism to Scalia's formalistic one. Her decisive move is to dispense with "neutrality": first, personal property deserves stronger protection than fungible property; second, "we must consider the relative political strength of various groups of claimants in weighing the decision to label government rearrangement of property rights a taking."[96]

Property rights have an important place in the system of rights insofar as property is essential for personal security. By the same token, as Radin argues, a personal right to harm or coerce others by withholding essentials from them cannot easily be justified as fundamental, assuming that the same goods are not also essential to oneself. It surely cannot be justified by an "efficiency" argument that is ruled out in principle by the axiom that all persons have certain fundamental rights.

A governmental power to punish or coerce people by withholding essentials would, for similar reasons, be justifiable only by reference to a compelling public interest. If there is a fundamental right to a minimal level of welfare, therefore, efficiency concerns are insufficient to override it. Governmental actions aimed at honoring that right will, by definition, not be "takings."

If we take the question to be whether such rights ought to be recognized in the first place, efficiency issues cannot be dismissed out of hand. Nevertheless, the primary concern should be which persons would be benefited and harmed in their personal flourishing, and in what ways, by each alternative. The distinction between principle and mere expediency remains vital.

The system of rights is a language game, and the meaning of a right, like that of a sentence, is its use. It is from this perspective that we should consider the claim that property rights are a distinct class of rights and the competing claim that all rights are equally fundamental. Within the grammar of our system of rights, the "new property" (property for persons) serves persons better than the old (property for power).

Conclusion

I have argued that our jurisprudence is deficient in failing to recognize as fundamental rights certain prerequisites for personal flourishing. Those include minimal subsistence needs, education, and effective access to the economic and political processes that make for self-respect, social integration, and representation in the public sphere.

I have also argued that purely utilitarian, efficiency-oriented arguments are insufficient to justify denial of such rights. *A fortiori*, prejudice and monetary self-interest are insufficient—indeed unworthy—considerations.

While much remains to be done, it seems necessary to respond at once to one possible criticism: that my account of constitutional rights is severely skewed to the liberal side and unresponsive to republican concerns. My reply must be twofold, addressing both the rights I have argued for and some issues I have passed over.

First, the arguments both for political rights and for subsistence rights are not just consistent with but vital for the republican vision, because citizens deprived of those rights cannot participate in self-government. Republicans cannot easily argue against such rights without arguing, repulsively, for exclusion from the polity of those who need them.

Second, while "excesses of liberalism" are certainly conceivable in theory, the notion that our Constitution prescribes such excesses seems downright hysterical.

Our problems of anomie, crime, welfare dependency, budget deficits, and inflated bureaucracy are not plausibly blamed on the unbridled exercise of "liberal" constitutional rights. An adequate account would pay far more attention to environmental pressures and poor private and public choices. Neither balancing the budget nor returning prayer to schools by constitutional reform—to mention two current "republican" proposals—is a promising response to such problems. Rather, our best hope lies in an ordinary politics elevated by improved political education and communications. Therefore, everyone should embrace the rights advocated here.

Afterword

*A*merican constitutional thought is a fascinating, perplexing enterprise. At its best, it grapples with many of the most important issues of human life and tries to resolve them in ways that accord with our most noble principles. At its worst, it inflicts or sanctions cruel and brutal actions or inactions, in the name of "facts" that are not real and "principles" that are not consistently and sincerely followed.

Many responses to this state of affairs are available. For some, the system approaches the limit of the humanly possible. Though imperfect, they say, it is far better than Bosnia. Still, the possibility of reparable defects seems worth considering. Is it only "human nature" or an "iron law of oligarchy" we are up against? Could not the distribution of wealth and power be improved upon? Could not new, badly needed rights be recognized in principle and worked for in practice? Is the government endowed with all the powers, limitations, and structural advantages needed to accomplish our ends? Do our ends themselves need rethinking?

Clearly, no one person could answer such questions as these: only "the people" can answer them. The pertinent discourse is already in being; but, to borrow Ackerman's terms without his optimism, it is seldom conducted with the needed "depth, breadth, and decisiveness."

For all the flaws of our constitutional system, there are good grounds for resisting despair. It is important to remember the extent to which the rule of law is evident in the parts of the Constitution that have worked automatically, without controversy. In particular, the absence of coups d'état and succession crises in our

233

history is taken for granted. Such successes support the turn to the Constitution in harder cases, and that resort too has often brought general satisfaction.

Many of the system's flaws, in fact, are less in the Constitution than in ourselves. As a people, we may enjoy a Constitution better than we deserve. We often behave as if we could not care less, for the Constitution or for each other. We worship presidential idols, revel in political apathy and ignorance, glamorize those who disdain the rule of law, and treat fear and hatred of the weak as political virtues.

Our political culture, along with the Constitution's silences and paradoxes, makes it difficult for us to agree upon the rudiments of a positive national agenda. Vast amounts of wealth and effort are diverted to illusory collective security needs, both foreign and domestic, with dire costs, in lost opportunity and direct repression, for personal rights. The enjoyment of the rights we have is vastly unequal, while some rights we need are not recognized even on paper. When rights or claims of right conflict, we sometimes "let the courts handle it," sometimes engage in cynical partisan struggle, and sometimes attempt to do both at once.

There are many flaws in our Constitution and the ways we use it, but, modest reform proposals aside, no one seems able to muster support for a significantly different system. Until this changes, we must strive to make the best of what we have. Before we kill all the lawyers, we had better be clear about who or what shall replace them.

The law and the courts are not above or outside politics, but they are capable, if their distinctiveness is respected, of complementing and improving the workings of our other political domains and processes. The Warren Court exemplifies—indeed, almost uniquely so—what is best about the judicial form of constitutional politics.

That is not the only or the ultimate form. We need not and must not concede to any court the final say about what the Constitution means; but we do need to remain open to judicial voices that, at their worst, show us where we need to work for change and, at their best, remind us of our most outstanding achievements and our deepest commitments as a people.

Notes

Introduction

1. *See* Daniel Boorstin, *The Genius of American Politics* (Chicago: University of Chicago Press, 1953), at 170; *compare* Michael Foley, *The Silence of Constitutions* (New York: Routledge, 1989).

2. *Compare* Alasdair MacIntyre, *After Virtue: A Study in Moral Theory* (Notre Dame: University of Notre Dame Press, 1981), at 1–2.

3. *See, e.g.*, Herbert McClosky and Alida Brill, *Dimensions of Tolerance* (New York: Russell Sage Foundation, 1983).

4. *See, e.g., United States v. O'Brien*, 391 U.S. 367 (1968); *Tinker v. Des Moines Independent School District*, 393 U.S. 503 (1969) (dissent).

5. *Powell v. McCormack*, 395 U.S. 486 (1969).

6. Alexander Hamilton, James Madison, and John Jay, *The Federalist Papers* (C. Rossiter, ed.) (New York: New American Library, 1961), no. 37.

7. *See* Jeffrey Segal and Harold Spaeth, *The Supreme Court and the Attitudinal Model,* (New York: Cambridge University Press, 1993), at 353–55, and works therein cited; Thomas Marshall, *Public Opinion and the Supreme Court* (Boston: Unwin Hyman, 1989).

8. *Compare* Richard Bernstein, *Amending America* (New York: Times Books, 1993), at 268, 276, arguing for the superior subtlety of non-Article V methods and warning against "politicization" of the Constitution through excessive resort to Article V, *with* Stephen Griffin, *Constitutionalism in the United States: From Theory to Politics*, in Sanford Levinson, ed., *Responding to Imperfection: The Theory and Practice of Constitutional Amendment* (Princeton: Princeton University Press, 1995), arguing that the heavy—but

probably unavoidable—reliance on non-Article V methods of constitutional adaptation undermines constitutionalism itself. *See also* Stephen Griffin, *American Constitutionalism: From Theory to Politics* (Princeton: Princeton University Press, 1996), and David Kyvig, *Explicit and Authentic Acts: Amending the U.S. Constitution, 1776–1995* (Lawrence: University Press of Kansas, 1996), both received too late for comment. For more on the law/politics dichotomy, *see* chapter 1.

9. Quoted in Jürgen Habermas, *Between Facts and Norms* (Cambridge: MIT Press, 1996), at 444.

10. *See* notes 3 and 7 above.

11. *See* Bernstein, note 8 above, ch. 12, for a review of recent proposals.

12. *The Federalist Papers*, note 6 above, no. 37.

13. Bernstein, note 8 above, at 240 (footnote omitted).

14. A number of these will be discussed at some length in this text. Others will receive less attention because, though their work is important and provocative, their approach or focus is so different that extensive comment would lead me too far afield. I have in mind such works as Sanford Levinson, *Constitutional Faith* (Princeton: Princeton University Press, 1988); Sotirios Barber, *On What the Constitution Means* (Baltimore: Johns Hopkins University Press, 1984); John Brigham, *The Cult of the Court* (Philadelphia: Temple University Press, 1987); William Harris, *The Interpretable Constitution* (Baltimore: Johns Hopkins University Press, 1993); Paul Kahn, *Legitimacy and History: Self-Government in American Constitutional Theory* (New Haven: Yale University Press, 1992); Louis Seidman and Mark Tushnet, *Remnants of Belief: Contemporary Constitutional Issues* (New York: Oxford University Press, 1996).

Part I. Law and Politics

1. Richard Bernstein, *Amending America* (New York: Times Books, 1993).

2. Alexander Hamilton, James Madison, and John Jay, *The Federalist Papers* (C. Rossiter ed.) (New York: New American Library, 1961), no. 49; *see also* Bernstein, note 1 above, at 223.

3. *See* Bernstein, note 1 above, at 256.

4. *See* Bruce Ackerman, *We, the People: Foundations* (Cambridge: Belknap Press, 1991), at 320–21.

5. Donald Lutz, *Toward a Theory of Constitutional Amendment*, 88 Amer. Pol. Sci. Rev. 355 (1994).

6. *See* note 4 above.

7. For recent critical discussion of the judicial role, *see* John Brigham, *The Cult of the Court* (Philadelphia: Temple University Press, 1987); Susan Burgess, *Contest for Constitutional Authority: The Abortion and War Powers Debates* (Lawrence: University Press of Kansas, 1992). On the theoretical incoherence of the separation of powers doctrine, *see* Alan Hunt, *Explorations in Law and Society: Toward a Constitutive Theory of Law* (New York: Routledge, 1993); Paul Kahn, *Legitimacy and History: Self-Government in American Constitutional Theory* (New Haven: Yale University Press, 1992).

8. Note 2 above, no. 47.

9. On the role of this doctrine in constitutional law, *see* Howard Gillman, *The Constitution Besieged: The Rise and Demise of Lochner Era Police Powers Jurisprudence* (Durham: Duke University Press, 1993).

10. *E.g.*, Donald Horowitz, *The Courts and Social Policy* (Washington: Brookings Institution, 1977).

Chapter 1. The Myth of the Political Question

1. E. P. Thompson, *Whigs and Hunters: The Origin of the Black Act* (New York: Pantheon Books, 1975), at 263.

2. *Id.* at 265.

3. *Id.* at 266.

4. For criticism, *see* Alan Hunt, *Explorations in Law and Society: Toward a Constitutive Theory of Law* (New York: Routledge, 1993).

5. Jennifer Nedelsky, *Private Property and the Limits of American Constitutionalism: The Madisonian Framework and Its Legacy* (Chicago: University of Chicago Press, 1990), at 189.

6. *Id.* at 190.

7. *See* note 34 below and accompanying text; *see also* chapter 4, at note 11 and accompanying text.

8. Nedelsky, note 5 above, at 193.

9. *See generally* M. J. C. Vile, *Constitutionalism and the Separation of Powers* (Oxford: Clarendon Press, 1967).

10. Nedelsky, note 5 above, at 197.

11. *Id.* at 209.

12. *Id.* at 269.

13. *Id.* at 270.

14. *Id.* at 272–76.

15. *See* Roberto Unger, *False Necessity: Anti-Necessitarian Social Theory in the Service of Radical Democracy* (New York: Cambridge University Press, 1987), ch. 5. For further discussion of the role of judicial review in a discourse-centered constitutional theory, *see* Paul Kahn, *Legitimacy and History: Self-Government in American Constitutional Theory* (New Haven: Yale University Press, 1992).

16. Frank Michelman, *Law's Republic*, 97 Yale L. J. 1493 (1988). *See also* work cited in note 18 below.

17. Cass Sunstein, *Beyond the Republican Revival*, 97 Yale L. J. 1539 (1988); Cass Sunstein, *The Partial Constitution* (Cambridge: Harvard University Press, 1993).

18. Frank Michelman, *Conceptions of Democracy in American Constitutional Argument: Voting Rights*, 41 Florida L. Rev. 443, 450, 456 (1989).

19. For useful criticisms, *see* Don Herzog, *Some Questions for Republicans*, 14 Political Theory 473 (1986).

20. Michelman, note 16 above, at 1513.

21. Sunstein, *The Partial Constitution*, note 17 above.

22. Bruce Ackerman, *We, the People: Foundations* (Cambridge: Belknap Press, 1991) is volume 1 of a promised trilogy.

23. *Id.* at 6, 263.

24. *Id.* at 272f.

25. *Id.* at 278.

26. *Id.* at 283–84.

27. The classic treatments include V. O. Key, Jr., *Politics, Parties, and Pressure Groups* (5th ed.) (New York: Crowell, 1964); Walter Dean Burnham, *Critical Elections and the Mainsprings of American Politics* (New York: W. W. Norton, 1970).

28. Ludwig Wittgenstein, *Philosophical Investigations* (New York: Macmillan, 1958), at 223. On the intermittent existence of the people, *compare* Michelman, note 16 above, at 1518–23.

29. *Brown v. Board of Education of Topeka*, 347 U.S. 483 (1954) (school desegregation).

30. *Griswold v. Connecticut*, 381 U.S. 479 (1965) (right of privacy in contraceptive use).

31. Sanford Levinson also notes that Ackerman needs to work out more fully the distinction between amendments and interpretations of the Constitution. *See* Sanford Levinson, ed., *Responding to Imperfection: The Theory and Practice of Constitutional Amendment* (Princeton: Princeton University Press, 1995), at 34 n. 66.

32. Some have argued that the Constitution rests so essentially on certain substantive principles that any purported amendments violating these would be unconstitutional. The debate is fully ventilated in Sanford Levinson, ed., note 31 above, chs. 5–10.

33. *See* Jeffrey Segal and Harold Spaeth, *The Supreme Court and the Attitudinal Model*, at 353–55 (New York: Cambridge University Press, 1993), and works therein cited.

34. 5 U.S. (1 Cranch) 137 (1803).

35. Alexander Hamilton, James Madison, and John Jay, *The Federalist Papers* (C. Rossiter ed.) (New York: New American Library, 1961), no. 49.

36. *New York Times Co. v. United States*, 403 U.S. 713, 729 (1971) (concurrence).

37. 5 U.S. (1 Cranch) 137 (1803).

38. *Id.* at 166.

39. 418 U.S. 683 (1974).

40. *E.g.*, Philippa Strum, *The Supreme Court and "Political Questions": A Study in Judicial Evasion* (University, Ala.: University of Alabama Press, 1974).

41. Hunt, note 4 above, at 292–93.

42. 17 U.S. (4 Wheat.) 316 (1819).

43. 6 U.S. (2 Cranch) 170 (1804).

44. *United States v. Smith*, 27 Fed. Cas. 1192 (No. 16,342) (C.C.D. N.Y. 1806). A similar assessment seems warranted regarding John Marshall's handling of the Aaron Burr trial, in which, after issuing a subpoena to the president, Marshall acquitted Burr without contesting Jefferson's partial defiance of the subpoena. *See United States v. Burr*, 25 Fed. Cas. 30, 55, 187 (Nos. 14692d, 14693, 14694) (C.C.D. Va. 1807).

45. *Martin v. Mott*, 25 U.S. (12 Wheat.) 19 (1827).

46. *Cherokee Nation v. Georgia*, 30 U.S. (5 Pet.) 1 (1831).

47. *Worcester v. Georgia*, 31 U.S. (6 Pet.) 515 (1832).

48. *Cohens v. Virginia*, 19 U.S. (6 Wheat.) 264 (1821).

49. 48 U.S. (7 How.) 1 (1849).

50. Daniel Rodgers, *Contested Truths* (New York: Basic Books, 1987); George Dennison, *The Dorr War: Republicanism on Trial, 1831–1861* (Lexington: University Press of Kentucky, 1976).

51. *Dred Scott v. Sandford*, 60 U.S. (19 How.) 393 (1857).

52. *See* Don Fehrenbacher, *The Dred Scott Case: Its Significance in American Law and Politics* (New York: Oxford University Press, 1978).

53. *E.g.*, *The Prize Cases*, 67 U.S. (2 Black) 635 (1863).

54. Dennison, note 50 above, at 205.

55. Theodore Lowi, *The End of Liberalism* (New York: W. W. Norton, 1979).

56. *Mississippi v. Johnson*, 71 U.S. (4 Wall.) 475 (1867); *Georgia v. Stanton*, 73 U.S. (6 Wall.) 50 (1867); *Texas v. White*, 74 U.S. (7 Wall.) 700 (1869).

57. *Pacific States Telephone Co. v. Oregon*, 223 U.S. 118 (1912); *Ohio ex rel. Davis v. Hildebrandt*, 241 U.S. 565 (1916).

58. *Minor v. Happersett*, 88 U.S. (21 Wall.) 162 (1874).

59. *Compare* Strum, note 40 above, *with* Fritz Scharpf, *Judicial Review and the Political Question: A Functional Analysis*, 75 Yale L. J. 517 (1966).

60. *Baker v. Carr*, 369 U.S. 186, 217 (1962).

61. *Id.* at 267.

62. *See* Morton Horwitz, *The Transformation of American Law, 1870–1960* (New York: Oxford University Press, 1992).

63. *See Coleman v. Miller*, 307 U.S. 433 (1939).

64. Article I, section 5.

65. *Powell v. McCormack*, 395 U.S. 486 (1969).

66. *See* Strum, note 40 above, ch. 4.

67. 444 U.S. 996 (1979).

68. Alexander Bickel, *The Least Dangerous Branch: The Supreme Court at the Bar of Politics* (Indianapolis; Bobbs-Merrill, 1962).

69. John Brigham, *The Cult of the Court* (Philadelphia: Temple University Press, 1987); Susan Burgess, *Contest for Constitutional Authority: The*

Abortion and War Powers Debates (Lawrence: University Press of Kansas, 1992); and Sotirios Barber, *On What the Constitution Means* (Baltimore: Johns Hopkins University Press, 1984); Sanford Levinson, *Constitutional Faith* (Princeton: Princeton University Press, 1988).

70. Thompson, note 1 above, at 266; Hunt, note 4 above, at 236 n. 9.

Chapter 2. Representation and Constitutional Politics

1. Hanna Pitkin, *The Concept of Representation* (Berkeley: University of California Press, 1967).

2. *Id*. at 116.

3. *Id*. at 135f.

4. Charles Beitz, *Political Equality* (Princeton: Princeton University Press, 1989).

5. *Id*. at 86.

6. *Id*. at 90.

7. *Id*. at 95.

8. *Id*. at 40.

9. *Id*. at 92.

10. *Id*. at 57.

11. *Id*. at 61–62.

12. *Id*. at 73–74.

13. *See* Introduction, note 9, and accompanying text.

14. Beitz, note 4 above, at 110.

15. *Ibid*.

16. *Id*. at 114.

17. *Id*. at 144.

18. *Id*. at 148–49.

19. *Id*. at 150.

20. *Id*. at 153.

21. *Ibid*.

22. *Id.* at 157.

23. *Id.* at 176.

24. *Id.* at 180.

25. *Id.* at 186.

26. *Id.* at 190.

27. *Id.* at 196.

28. *Id.* at 228.

29. Robert Grady, *Restoring Real Representation* (Urbana: University of Illinois Press, 1993).

30. Lani Guinier, *The Tyranny of the Majority: Fundamental Fairness in Representative Democracy* (New York: Free Press, 1994).

31. Peter Schuck, *Partisan Gerrymandering: A Political Problem without Judicial Solution*, in Bernard Grofman, ed., *Political Gerrymandering and the Courts* (New York: Agathon Press, 1990).

32. *See* his opinions in *Shaw v. Reno*, 509 U.S. 630 (1993) and *Bush v. Vera*, ___ U.S. ___ , 116 S.Ct. 1941, 135 L. Ed. 2d 248 (1996).

33. Schuck, note 31 above, at 245.

34. Beitz, note 4 above, at 126.

35. *Id.* at 130.

36. For a critique of functional representation and defense of the party system, *see* David Ryden, *Representation in Crisis: The Constitution, Interest Groups, and Political Parties* (Albany: State University of New York Press, 1996). This work reached me too late for comment.

37. Guinier, note 30 above, at 150f.

38. *Ibid.* However, a district court is reported to have adopted cumulative voting as a remedy in an order of April 5, 1994, in a case arising in Worcester County, Maryland. Caucus for a New Political Science Newsletter, Fall 1994, at 5.

39. *See* Benjamin Barber, *Strong Democracy* (Berkeley: University of California Press, 1984); Jane Mansbridge, *Beyond Adversary Democracy* (New York: Basic Books, 1980).

40. For an overview, *see* Paul Abramson, *Political Attitudes in America* (San Francisco: Freeman, 1986); Seymour Lipset and William Schneider, *The Confidence Gap* (Baltimore: Johns Hopkins University Press, 1987).

41. *See generally* Robert Erikson, Norman Lutbeg, and Kent Tedin, *American Public Opinion: Its Origins, Content, and Impact* (4th ed.) (New York: Macmillan, 1991); W. Russell Neuman, *The Paradox of Mass Politics: Knowledge and Opinion in the American Electorate* (Cambridge: Harvard University Press, 1986); and works cited in note 40 above.

42. Article I, section 5.

43. *See* Charles Beard, *An Economic Interpretation of the Constitution of the United States*, excerpted in Leonard Levy, *Essays on the Making of the Constitution* (New York: Oxford University Press, 1987), at 27–28.

44. Jennifer Nedelsky, *Private Property and the Limits of American Constitutionalism: The Madisonian Framework and Its Legacy* (Chicago: University of Chicago Press, 1990), at 47, 56.

45. Alexander Hamilton, James Madison, and John Jay, *The Federalist Papers* (C. Rossiter, ed.) (New York: New American Library, 1961), no. 35; *but compare* Pitkin, note 1 above, at 191.

46. *The Federalist Papers*, note 45 above, no. 10.

47. Note 1 above, at 191.

48. *See* note 45 above.

49. Calhoun's "concurrent majority" proposal also emphasized the representation of interests, as opposed to persons. *See* John Calhoun, *A Disquisition on Government, and Selections from the Discourses* (Indianapolis: Bobbs-Merrill, 1953).

50. *Reynolds v. Sims*, 377 U.S. 533, 562 (1964).

51. 369 U.S. 186 (1962).

52. Note, *A "Frightful Political Dragon" Indeed: Why Constitutional Challenges Cannot Subdue the Gerrymander*, 13 Harvard J. Law and Pub. Policy 949 (1990).

53. 478 U.S. 109 (1986).

54. *See* note 51 above.

55. Moore, note 52 above, at 975; *compare* Schuck, note 31 above, at 244.

56. Moore, note 52 above, at 984.

57. *Davis v. Bandemer*, note 53 above, at 144 (Burger, C. J., concurring).

58. *The Federalist Papers*, note 45 above, nos. 51, 78.

59. Moore, note 52 above, at 994.

60. *Riggs v. Palmer*, 115 N.Y. 506, 22 N.E. 188 (1889).

61. John Hart Ely, *Democracy and Distrust: A Theory of Judicial Review* (Cambridge: Harvard University Press, 1980).

62. Lawrence Tribe, *The Puzzling Persistence of Process-Based Theories of Constitutional Law*, 89 Yale L. J. 1063 (1980).

63. 48 U.S. (7 How.) 1 (1849).

64. Bruce Ackerman, *We, the People: Foundations* (Cambridge: Belknap Press, 1991); Alexander Bickel, *The Least Dangerous Branch: The Supreme Court at the Bar of Politics* (Indianapolis: Bobbs-Merrill, 1962).

65. Samuel Bowles and Herbert Gintis, *Democracy and Capitalism* (New York: Basic Books, 1986).

66. *Compare* Stuart Scheingold, *The Politics of Rights: Lawyers, Public Policy, and Political Change* (New Haven: Yale University Press, 1974).

67. Frederick Douglass, *The Constitution and Slavery*, in Bertell Ollman and Jonathan Birnbaum, eds., *The United States Constitution* (New York: New York University press, 1990); *Is the United States Constitution for or against Slavery*, in Philip Foner, ed., *The Life and Writings of Frederick Douglass*, vol. 5 (New York: International Publishers, 1975).

68. Stanley Fish, *There's No Such Thing as Free Speech . . . and It's a Good Thing, Too* (New York: Oxford University Press, 1994).

69. James Lennertz, *Republicanism and Representation: Districting for Civic Discourse*, presented at 1992 meeting of the American Political Science Association.

70. *The Federalist Papers*, note 45 above, no. 52.

71. *Id.*, no. 60.

72. *Powell v. McCormack*, 395 U.S. 486 (1969).

73. *The Federalist Papers*, note 45 above, no. 35.

74. *Id.*, no. 54.

75. *Id.*, nos. 55, 56.

Part II. The Many (Against Nationalism)

1. *See* chapter 5.

2. *See* Don Herzog, *Happy Slaves: A Critique of Consent Theory* (Chicago: University of Chicago Press, 1989).

3. *See* Louis Hartz, *The Liberal Tradition in America: An Interpretation of American Political Thought since the Revolution* (New York: Harcourt Brace 1955).

4. *See* part III for more on these questions.

5. Adam Smith, *The Wealth of Nations* (New York: Viking Penguin, 1986).

6. Louis Hartz, note 3 above; J. G. A. Pocock, *The Machiavellian Moment: Florentine Political Thought and the Atlantic Republican Tradition* (Princeton: Princeton University Press, 1975); Joyce Appleby, *Liberalism and Republicanism in the Historical Imagination* (Cambridge: Harvard University Press, 1992); Michael Sandel, *Democracy's Discontent: America in Search of a Public Philosophy* (Cambridge: Harvard University Press, 1996); Gordon Wood, *The Radicalism of the American Revolution* (New York: Alfred A. Knopf, 1992); Bernard Bailyn, *Ideological Origins of the American Revolution* (Cambridge: Belknap Press, 1967); Kenneth Peter, *Foundation of the Empire of Factions*, presented at 1989 Meeting of the American Political Science Association.

Chapter 3. Peoplehood and Nationalism

1. Jacques Derrida, *Declarations of Independence*, 8 New Political Science 7 (1986).

2. Daniel Rodgers, *Contested Truths* (New York: Basic Books, 1987). A very different treatment is Wayne Moore, *Constitutional Rights and Powers of the People* (Princeton: Princeton University Press, 1996), received too late for comment.

3. *Id.* at 83.

4. *Id.* at 96.

5. *Id.* at 84.

6. *Id.* at 89.

7. *Id.* at 102.

8. 60 U.S. (19 How.) 393 (1857).

9. Sanford Levinson, *Constitutional Faith* (Princeton: Princeton University Press, 1988).

10. Derek Parfit, *Reasons and Persons* (New York: Oxford University Press, 1984).

11. Hearings on S. 158 before the Subcommittee on Separation of Powers of the Senate Judiciary Committee, 97th Cong., 1st Sess., Serial #J-97-16, at 705.

12. Cass Sunstein, *The Partial Constitution* (Cambridge: Harvard University Press, 1993).

13. Samuel Bowles and Herbert Gintis, *Democracy and Capitalism* (New York: Basic Books, 1986).

14. Eric Hobsbawm, *Nations and Nationalism Since 1780: Programme, Myth, Reality* (New York: Cambridge University Press, 1992).

15. *Id.* at 22.

16. *Id.* at 39.

17. *Compare* Seymour M. Lipset, *Political Man: The Social Bases of Politics* (Baltimore: Johns Hopkins University Press, 1981).

18. Benedict Anderson, *Imagined Communities: Reflections on the Origin and Spread of Nationalism* (New York: Verso, 1991).

19. *Id.* at 81.

20. *Id.* at 145.

21. *Id.* at 144.

22. Liah Greenfield, *Nationalism: Five Roads to Modernity* (Cambridge: Harvard University Press, 1992).

23. *Id.* at 487.

24. *Id.* at 11.

25. *Id.* at 490.

26. *Id.* at 399.

27. *Id.* at 409–10.

28. *Id.* at 412.

29. *Id.* at 426.

30. *Id.* at 422–25.

31. *Id.* at 7.

32. *Id.* at 472.

33. *Id.* at 431.

34. *Id.* at 440.

35. *Id.* at 476–77.

36. *Ibid.*

37. *Id.* at 479.

38. *Id.* at 481.

39. Yael Tamir, *Liberal Nationalism* (Princeton: Princeton University Press, 1993).

40. *Id.* at 163.

41. Joyce Appleby, *Liberalism and Republicanism in the Historical Imagination* (Cambridge: Harvard University Press, 1992).

42. For Appleby's separate treatment of capitalism, *see* Joyce Appleby, *Capitalism and a New Social Order* (New York: New York University Press, 1984).

43. See, *e.g.*, Bowles and Gintis, note 13 above; Charles Lindblom, *Politics and Markets* (New York: Basic Books, 1977); Jennifer Nedelsky, *Private Property and the Limits of American Constitutionalism: The Madisonian Framework and Its Legacy* (Chicago: University of Chicago Press, 1990).

Chapter 4. The Myth of Presidential Prerogative

1. For the early history, *see* Daniel Hoffman, *Governmental Secrecy and the Founding Fathers: A Study in Constitutional Controls* (Westport, Ct.: Greenwood Press, 1981). *See also* David Gray Adler, *Foreign Policy and the Separation of Powers: The Influence of the Judiciary*, in Michael McCann and Gerald Houseman, eds., *Judging the Constitution: Critical Essays on Judicial Lawmaking* (Glenview, Il.: Scott, Foresman and Co., 1989); Arthur Schlesinger, Jr., *The Imperial Presidency* (Boston: Houghton Mifflin, 1973).

2. *Dred Scott v. Sandford*, 60 U.S. (19 How.) 393 (1857).

3. *See* sources cited in note 1 above.

4. *Address of the General Assembly to the People of the Commonwealth of Virginia*, in *IV Letters and Other Writings of James Madison* (Philadelphia: J. P. Lipincott, 1865), at 510–11.

5. *McCulloch v. Maryland*, 17 U.S. (4 Wheat.) 316 (1819).

6. *Ibid.*

7. Article II, section 3.

8. 25 U.S. (12 Wheat.) 19 (1827).

9. 67 U.S. (2 Black) 635 (1863).

10. *Baker v. Carr*, 369 U.S. 186 (1962).

11. 5 U.S. (1 Cranch) 137, 166 (1803).

12. *E.g., Kleindienst v. Mandel,* 408 U.S. 753 (1972); *Snepp v. United States,* 444 U.S. 507 (1980).

13. *E.g., Ex parte Endo,* 323 U.S. 283 (1944); *Cole v. Young,* 351 U.S. 536 (1956); *Kent v. Dulles,* 357 U.S. 116 (1958).

14. 403 U.S. 713 (1971).

15. Erwin Griswold, *Secrets Not Worth Keeping,* Washington Post, Feb. 15, 1989, at 25A.

16. Article II, sections 2, 3.

17. 135 U.S. 1 (1890).

18. 158 U.S. 564 (1895).

19. *See* Hoffman, note 1 above.

20. 301 U.S. 324 (1937).

21. 315 U.S. 203 (1942).

22. Alexander Hamilton, James Madison, and John Jay, *The Federalist Papers* (C. Rossiter, ed.) (New York: New American Library, 1961), no. 69. *See also* Joseph Story, *Commentaries on the Constitution of the United States* (New York: Da Capo, 1970), sec. 1492.

23. *Fleming v. Page,* 50 U.S. 603, 615, 618 (1850).

24. Theodore Roosevelt, *An Autobiography* (New York: Scribner, 1958), at 479.

25. *See generally* Edward Corwin, *The President: Office and Powers, 1787–1957* (4th rev. ed.) (New York: New York University Press, 1957), at 227–62.

26. 453 U.S. 280 (1981).

27. *Greene v. McElroy,* 360 U.S. 474 (1959). *But see Department of the Navy v. Egan,* 484 U.S. 518 (1988), discussed below. Hard lawyers make bad cases.

28. *Ex parte Milligan,* 71 U.S. (4 Wall.) 2 (1866); *Duncan v. Kahanamoku,* 327 U.S. 304 (1946); *Raymond v. Thomas,* 91 U.S. 712 (1876); *Fleming v. Page,* note 23 above; *United States v. United States District Court,* 407 U.S. 297 (1972).

29. Article I, section 8.

30. *Ex parte Garland,* 71 U.S. 333 (1867); *United States v. Klein,* 80 U.S. 128 (1871); *Knote v. United States,* 95 U.S. 149 (1877).

31. *Myers v. United States*, 272 U.S. 52 (1926); *Humphrey's Executor v. United States*, 295 U.S. 602 (1935).

32. *Immigration and Naturalization Service v. Chadha*, 462 U.S. 919 (1983); *Bowsher v. Synar*, 478 U.S. 714 (1986).

33. Note 32 above.

34. *Peters v. Hobby*, 349 U.S. 331 (1955); *Cole v. Young*, 351 U.S. 536 (1956); *Service v. Dulles*, 354 U.S. 363 (1957); *Greene v. McElroy*, note 27 above.

35. 6 U.S. (2 Cranch) 170 (1804).

36. 175 U.S. 423 (1899).

37. *Mahler v. Eby*, 264 U.S. 32 (1924).

38. 333 U.S. 103 (1948).

39. 338 U.S. 537 (1950).

40. 484 U.S. 518 (1988).

41. 343 U.S. 579 (1952).

42. *Id.* at 635–38.

43. 299 U.S. 304 (1936).

44. On delegation of the war powers, *see also Yakus v. United States*, 321 U.S. 414 (1944); *Lichter v. United States*, 334 U.S. 742 (1948).

45. 343 U.S. 579, at n. 2 (1952).

46. *See* Adler, note 1 above.

47. *See, e.g., Prize Cases*, note 9 above; *United States v. Midwest Oil Co.*, 236 U.S. 459 (1915); *Swayne and Hoyt v. United States*, 300 U.S. 297 (1937); *Zemel v. Rusk*, 381 U.S. 1 (1965). Lower federal courts applied similar doctrines in cases involving the Vietnam War. *See generally* Leon Friedman and Bert Neuborne, *Unquestioning Obedience to the President: The ACLU Case against the Legality of the War in Vietnam* (New York: W. W. Norton, 1972).

48. *Raymond v. Thomas*, note 28 above.

49. Note 13 above.

50. Note 28 above.

51. Note 13 above.

52. Note 13 above.

53. Note 12 above.

54. Note 26 above.

55. 453 U.S. 654 (1981).

56. 468 U.S. 222 (1984).

57. Note 27 above.

58. Note 10 above.

59. 27 U.S. 253 (1859); *but see Japan Whaling Association v. American Cetacean Society*, 478 U.S. 221 (1986), discussed below.

60. 246 U.S. 297 (1918).

61. Corwin, note 25 above, at 177. *See also* Louis Henkin, *Is There a "Political Question" Doctrine?* 85 Yale L. J. 597 (1976).

62. 444 U.S. 996 (1979).

63. Note 59 above.

64. *Martin v. Mott*, note 8 above.

65. *Dakota Central Telephone Co. v. South Dakota ex rel. Payne*, 250 U.S. 163 (1919).

66. *United States v. Chemical Foundation*, 272 U.S. 1 (1926).

67. *Knauff v. Shaughnessy*, note 39 above.

68. Note 38 above.

69. *Id.* at 111.

70. "Though *Waterman* has not been over-ruled by the Supreme Court, its apparently sweeping contours have been eroded by recent circuit court opinions." *Pan American World Airlines v. CAB*, 392 F.2d 483, 492 (D.C. Cir. 1968).

71. *Fong Yue Ting v. United States*, 149 U.S. 698 (1893); *Knauff v. Shaughnessy*, note 39 above; *Harisiades v. Shaughnessy*, 342 U.S. 580 (1952).

72. Note 12 above.

73. *Miller v. United States*, 78 U.S. 268 (1871); *Ex parte Quirin*, 317 U.S. 1 (1942); *Hirota v. MacArthur*, 338 U.S. 197 (1948).

74. 457 U.S. 202 (1982).

75. *Hamilton v. Kentucky Distilleries and Warehouse Co.*, 251 U.S. 146 (1919).

76. *Home Building and Loan Association v. Blaisdell*, 290 U.S. 398 (1934).

77. *See, e.g., Prize Cases*, note 9 above; *Hirabayashi v. United States*, 320 U.S. 81 (1943); *Korematsu v. United States*, 323 U.S. 214 (1944); *Cafeteria Workers v. McElroy*, 367 U.S. 886 (1961); and cases cited in notes 64–66 above.

78. *Ex parte Milligan* and *Duncan v. Kahanamoku*, note 28 above.

79. 372 U.S. 144 (1963).

80. 389 U.S. 258 (1967).

81. 381 U.S. 301 (1965).

82. 378 U.S. 500 (1964).

83. *United States v. Nixon*, 418 U.S. 683 (1974), President's Brief, n. 43.

84. *Cf. Kennedy v. Mendoza-Martinez*, 372 U.S. 144 (1963).

Chapter 5. Compelling Governmental Interests

1. *Immigration and Naturalization Service v. Chadha*, 462 U.S. 919 (1983).

2. ___ U.S. ___, 115 S.Ct. 1624, 131 L. Ed.2d 626 (1995). *See also Seminole Tribe of Florida v. Florida*, ___ U.S. ___, 116 S.Ct. 1114, 134 L. Ed. 2d 252 (1996).

3. 426 U.S. 833 (1976) (minimum wage law inapplicable to state government jobs), *overruled, Garcia v. San Antonio Metropolitan Transit Authority*, 469 U.S. 528 (1985).

4. 83 U.S. (16 Wall.) 36 (1873) ("privileges or immunities of citizens of the United States" given exceedingly narrow interpretation).

5. 109 U.S. 3 (1883) (section 5 of the Fourteenth Amendment does not empower Congress to regulate private—as opposed to state government—actions).

6. *Cf. Steward Machine Co. v. Davis*, 301 U.S. 548 (1937).

7. *Dred Scott v. Sandford*, 60 U.S. (19 How.) 393 (1857).

8. *Ex parte Merryman*, F. Cas. 9487, Taney's Reports 246 (1861).

9. *See, e.g., Prize Cases*, 67 U.S. (2 Black) 635 (1863).

10. *See, e.g.,* Howard Gillman, *The Constitution Besieged: The Rise and Demise of Lochner Era Police Powers Jurisprudence* (Durham: Duke Uni-

versity Press, 1993); Paul Kahn, *Legitimacy and History: Self-Government in American Constitutional Theory* (New Haven: Yale University Press, 1992); Bruce Ackerman, *We, the People: Foundations* (Cambridge: Belknap Press, 1991).

11. *Lochner v. New York*, 198 U.S. 45 (1905).

12. *See* note 10 above.

13. *United States v. Carolene Products Co.*, 304 U.S. 144, 152 n. 4 (1938); *see* Stephen Gottlieb, *Introduction: Overriding Public Values*, in Stephen Gottlieb, ed., *Public Values in Constitutional Law* (Ann Arbor: University of Michigan Press, 1993).

14. *Hirabayashi v. United States*, 320 U.S. 81 (1943); *Korematsu v. United States*, 323 U.S. 214 (1944). Cited in Owen Fiss, *Groups and the Equal Protection Clause*, 5 Philosophy and Public Affairs 107, 116 (1976).

15. *Categorization, Balancing, and Government Interests*, in Gottlieb, note 13 above.

16. *See Panama Refining Co. v. Ryan*, 293 U.S. 388 (1935); *Schechter Poultry Corp. v. United States*, 295 U.S. 495 (1935).

17. *Compare* Gillman, note 10 above.

18. Note 1 above.

19. Theodore Lowi, *The End of Liberalism* (2d ed.) (New York: W. W. Norton, 1979).

20. *Brandenburg v. Ohio*, 395 U.S. 444 (1971).

21. *See generally* Mark Graber, *Transforming Free Speech: The Ambiguous Legacy of Civil Libertarianism* (Berkeley: University of California Press, 1991).

22. *Hirabayashi v. United States* and *Korematsu v. United States*, note 14 above.

23. T. Alexander Aleinikoff, *Constitutional Law in the Age of Balancing*, 96 Yale L. J. 943 (1987).

24. *Id.* at 991.

25. *Ibid.*

26. *Id.* at 1001. *See also* Gottlieb, note 13 above.

27. Gottlieb, note 13 above. *See also* Stephen Gottlieb, *Compelling Governmental Interests: An Essential but Unanalyzed Term in Constitutional Adjudication*, 68 Boston U. L. Rev. 916 (1988).

28. Gottlieb, note 13 above, at 7.

29. *See* chapter 4 above. *See also* Gottlieb, note 27 above, at 933, 935, 958–60, 964.

30. *E.g., Reed v. Reed*, 404 U.S. 71 (1971); *Frontiero v. Richardson*, 411 U.S. 677 (1973); *see also* Gottlieb, note 27 above, at 932, 952–53, 962.

31. Gottlieb, note 27 above, at 974.

32. On the latter point, *see* Gottlieb, *Compelling Governmental Interests*, note 27 above, at 932, 934, 956–58.

33. 438 U.S. 265 (1978).

34. Gottlieb, note 27 above, at 942–44.

35. Gottlieb, note 13 above, at 1, 9.

36. Note 15 above, at 261 n. 3.

37. Gottlieb, note 27 above, at 969.

38. *Id.* at 970.

39. *Id.* at 968.

40. *Id.* at 974.

41. *See* the Introduction.

42. *Kennedy v. Mendoza-Martinez*, 372 U.S. 144 (1962).

43. Article I, section 9. Gottlieb overlooks this clause, and that cited just below, in asserting, "Nothing in the language of the Constitution directs the courts to suspend the operation of other guarantees in favor of any conception of national security or guides the courts in the determination of when such a preference would be proper." Note 27 above, at 958.

44. Amendment V.

45. *See* Sotirios Barber, *On What the Constitution Means* (Baltimore: Johns Hopkins University Press, 1984).

46. Among the works that significantly influenced this account, the following deserve special mention: Alexander Hamilton, James Madison, and John Jay, *The Federalist Papers* (C. Rossiter, ed.) (New York: New American Library, 1961); Charles Beard, *An Economic Interpretation of the Constitution of the United States* (New York: Free Press, 1986); Bruce Ackerman, *Social Justice in the Liberal State* (New Haven: Yale University Press, 1980); Bruce Ackerman, *We, the People: Foundations* (Cambridge: Belknap Press, 1991); Sotirios Barber, note 45 above; Ronald Dworkin, *Taking Rights Seriously* (Cambridge: Harvard University Press, 1977); Ronald Dworkin, *Law's Empire* (Cambridge: Belknap Press, 1986); John Hart Ely, *Democracy and Distrust: A Theory of Judicial Review* (Cam-

bridge: Harvard University Press, 1980); Jennifer Nedelsky, *Private Property and the Limits of American Constitutionalism: The Madisonian Framework and Its Legacy* (Chicago: University of Chicago Press, 1990).

47. *See* Leonard Levy, *Essays on the Making of the Constitution* (New York: Oxford University Press, 1969).

48. *See* chapter 1.

49. Thomas Jefferson, *First Inaugural Address*, in Janet Podell and Steven Anzovin, eds., *Speeches of the American Presidents* (New York: H. W. Wilson, 1988), at 39.

50. *Compare* Kahn, note 10 above.

51. Note 45 above.

52. Further discussion of some of the major alternatives, ranging from a legal positivism in which following established procedures is the *sole* criterion to a Rawlsian theory of justice as fairness, far richer in substantive implications, may be found in chapter 7.

53. Robert Nagel, *"Unfocused" Governmental Interests*, in Gottlieb, note 13 above.

54. Robert Nozick, *Anarchy, State and Utopia* (New York: Basic Books, 1974).

55. John Rawls, *A Theory of Justice* (Cambridge: Harvard University Press, 1971). *See also* John Rawls, *Political Liberalism* (New York: Columbia University Press, 1993).

56. Ronald Dworkin, *What Is Equality?* 10 Philosophy and Public Affairs 185, 283 (1981).

57. Christopher Stone, *Should Trees Have Standing?—Toward Legal Rights for Natural Objects*, 45 Southern Cal. L. Rev. 450 (1972).

58. *Cf.* Robert Cover, *Violence and the Word*, 95 Yale L. J. 1601 (1986).

59. Jacques Derrida, *Declarations of Independence*, 8 New Political Science 7 (1986).

60. Cass Sunstein, *The Partial Constitution* (Cambridge: Harvard University Press, 1993).

Part III. The One (Against Positivism)

1. Quoted in Albert Kocourek and John Wigmore, eds., *Formative Influence of Legal Development*, Evolution of Law Series, vol. 3 (Boston: Little Brown, 1918), at 440.

2. *Per* Charles Evans Hughes; *see* Ralph Rossum and G. Alan Tarr, eds., *American Constitutional Law: Cases and Interpretation* (3d ed.) (New York: St. Martin's Press, 1991), at 1.

3. Oliver Wendell Holmes, Jr., *The Path of the Law*, in *Collected Legal Papers* (New York: P. Smith, 1952), at 173.

4. *See* Austin Sarat and Thomas Kearns, *Identities, Politics, and Rights* (Ann Arbor: University of Michigan Press, 1995).

5. Stephen Macedo, *Liberal Virtues: Citizenship, Virtue, and Community in Liberal Constitutionalism* (New York: Clarendon Press, 1991); Jürgen Habermas, *Between Facts and Norms* (Cambridge: MIT Press, 1996).

Chapter 6. Personhood and Rights

1. Louis Hanke, *Aristotle and the American Indians* (Chicago: Henry Regnery, 1959), at 104; Orlando Patterson, *Slavery and Social Death: A Comparative Study* (Cambridge: Harvard University Press, 1982).

2. *See, e.g.*, Fei Hsiao-Tung, *Peasant Life in China* (Cambridge: Oxford University Press, 1946).

3. *E.g.*, R. F. Kelly, *Historical and Political Interpretations of Jurisprudence and the Social Action Perspective in Sociology*, 15 J. Hist. Behav. Sciences 47 (1979) (Roman law).

4. Marcel Mauss, *A Category of the Human Mind: The Notion of Person, the Notion of Self*, in Michael Carruthers, Steven Collins, and Steven Lukes, eds., *The Category of the Person* (New York: Cambridge University Press, 1985).

5. Thomas More and Edward Coke were famous advocates of (different versions of) this idea. *See generally* Edward Corwin, *The "Higher Law" Background of American Constitutional Law* (Ithaca: Great Seal Books, 1955).

6. Locke was especially influential; *see* Louis Hartz, *The Liberal Tradition in America: An Interpretation of American Political Thought since the Revolution* (New York: Harcourt Brace, 1955).

7. Article I, section 2.

8. *Cf.* Raziel Abelson, *Persons: A Study in Philosophical Psychology* (New York: St. Martin's Press, 1977).

9. The Kantian view is reflected in recent works such as John Rawls, *A Theory of Justice* (Cambridge: Harvard University Press, 1971), and Loren Lomasky, *Persons, Rights, and the Moral Community* (New York: Oxford University Press, 1987).

10. Rawls, note 9 above; *see also* John Rawls, *Political Liberalism* (New York: Columbia University Press, 1993).

11. *Compare* Michael Philips, *Between Universalism and Skepticism* (New York: Oxford University Press, 1994), at 52f.

12. *See A Theory of Justice*, note 9 above, at 146, 149–50; *compare Political Liberalism*, note 10 above, at 18–19, 122–25, 152 n. 16.

13. *See* works cited in notes 8–10 above; Amelie Rorty, ed., *The Identities of Persons* (Berkeley: University of California Press, 1976); Margery Shaw and A. E. Doudera, eds., *Defining Human Life: Medical, Legal, and Ethical Implications* (Ann Arbor: AUPHA Press, 1983); Eugene Schlossberger, *Moral Responsibility and Persons* (Philadelphia: Temple University Press, 1992); Abraham Melden, *Rights and Persons* (New York: Oxford University Press, 1977).

14. Derek Parfit, *Reasons and Persons* (Cambridge: Oxford University Press, 1984).

15. Ze'ev Falk, *Law and Religion* (Jerusalem: Mesharim Publishers, 1981).

16. Dan Henderson, *Conciliation and Japanese Law: Tokugawa and Modern* (Seattle: University of Washington Press, 1965).

17. *Dred Scott v. Sandford*, 60 U.S. (19 How.) 383 (1857). *Cf.* Article I, sections 2, 9; Article IV, section 2.

18. 410 U.S. 113 (1973).

19. *Planned Parenthood v. Danforth*, 428 U.S. 52 (1976).

20. *Santa Clara County v. Southern Pacific Railroad Co.*, 118 U.S. 394 (1886).

21. Ronald Dworkin, *Taking Rights Seriously* (Cambridge: Harvard University Press, 1977).

22. Note 18 above.

23. *E.g.*, *First National Bank of Boston v. Bellotti*, 435 U.S. 765 (1978).

24. *Compare Dartmouth College v. Woodward*, 17 U.S. (4 Wheat.) 518 (1819), *with Furman v. Georgia*, 408 U.S. 238 (1972).

25. On Burke, *see* Hanna Pitkin, *The Concept of Representation* (Berkeley: University of California Press, 1967), at 191–98, 205–06; Alasdair MacIntyre, *After Virtue* (Notre Dame: University of Notre Dame Press, 1981).

26. Moishe Postone, *Time, Labor, and Social Domination: A Reinterpretation of Marx's Critical Theory* (New York: Cambridge University Press, 1993).

27. On the leftist critique, *see* Alan Hunt, *Explorations in Law and Society: Toward a Constitutive Theory of Law* (New York: Routledge, 1993). On the Law and Economics school, *see* Richard Posner, *Economic Analysis of Law* (Boston: Little Brown, 1992).

28. Frank Michelman, *Welfare Rights in a Constitutional Democracy*, 1979 Washington U. L. Q. 659 (1979); Margaret Jane Radin, *Reinterpreting Property* (Chicago: University of Chicago Press, 1993). *See also* Samuel Bowles and Herbert Gintis, *Democracy and Capitalism* (New York: Basic Books, 1986).

29. Hearings before the Subcommittee on the Separation of Powers of the Senate Judiciary Committee, 97th Cong., 1st Sess., on S. 158, Serial #J-97-16, at 705.

30. For critiques of metaphysical approaches, *see* Don Herzog, *Without Foundations: Justification in Political Theory* (Ithaca: Cornell University Press, 1985), and John Rawls, *Political Liberalism*, note 10 above. For works recognizing personal flourishing as a crucial criterion for the determination of rights, *see* Michael Perry, *Morality, Politics, and Law: A Bicentennial Essay* (New York: Oxford University Press, 1988), and Margaret Jane Radin, *Reinterpreting Property* (Chicago: University of Chicago Press, 1993). Each of these works is rich in intellectual rigor, but none offers a comprehensive, detailed vision articulated with broad political appeal.

Chapter 7. What Makes a Right Fundamental

1. *United States v. Carolene Products Co.*, 304 U.S. 144 (1938).

2. *Marsh v. Alabama*, 326 U.S. 501 (1946).

3. *Kovacs v. Cooper*, 336 U.S. 77 (1949).

4. *Lynch v. Household Finance Corp.*, 405 U.S. 538 (1972).

5. *Craig v. Boren*, 429 U.S. 190 (1976).

6. *Cleburne v. Cleburne Living Center*, 473 U.S. 432 (1985); *Romer v. Evans*, ___ U.S. ___, 116 S.Ct. 1620, 134 L. Ed. 2d 855 (1996).

7. *Palko v. Connecticut*, 302 U.S. 319 (1937).

8. *Malinsky v. New York*, 324 U.S. 401 (1945).

9. *Rochin v. California*, 342 U.S. 165 (1952).

10. *Snyder v. Massachusetts*, 291 U.S. 97 (1934).

11. *Regents of the University of California v. Bakke*, 438 U.S. 265 (1978).

12. Abraham Melden, *Rights and Persons* (New York: Oxford University Press, 1977); Amelie Rorty, ed., *The Identities of Persons* (Berkeley: University of California Press, 1976); Derek Parfit, *Reasons and Persons* (New York: Oxford University Press, 1984).

13. *Lochner v. New York*, 198 U.S. 45 (1905) (dissent).

14. Sotirios Barber, *The Constitution of Judicial Power* (Baltimore: Johns Hopkins University Press, 1993).

15. Brian Bix, *Law, Language, and Legal Determinacy* (New York: Clarendon Press, 1993), at 157.

16. Michael Sandel, *Liberalism and the Limits of Justice* (New York: Cambridge University Press, 1982).

17. *Ibid. See also* Michael Philips, *Between Universalism and Skepticism* (New York: Oxford University Press, 1994).

18. John Rawls, *A Theory of Justice* (Cambridge: Harvard University Press, 1971); *Political Liberalism* (New York: Columbia University Press, 1993).

19. Robert Nozick, *Anarchy, State and Utopia* (New York: Basic Books, 1974).

20. *Political Liberalism*, note 18 above.

21. Bruce Ackerman, *Social Justice in the Liberal State* (New Haven: Yale University Press, 1980).

22. Ronald Dworkin, *What Is Equality?* 10 Philosophy and Public Affairs 185, 283 (1981).

23. *See* Ronald Dworkin, *A Matter of Principle* (Cambridge: Harvard University Press, 1985), ch. 11.

24. Mark Tushnet, *The American Law of Slavery* (Princeton: Princeton University Press, 1981).

25. Morton Horwitz, *The Transformation of American Law, 1780–1860* (Cambridge: Harvard University Press, 1977); *see also The Transformation of American Law, 1870–1960* (New York: Oxford University Press, 1992).

26. Roberto Unger, *Knowledge and Politics* (New York: Macmillan, 1975); *see also Social Theory: Its Situation and Its Task* (New York: Cambridge University Press, 1987).

27. Charles Reich, *The New Property*, 73 Yale L. J. 733 (1964).

28. *Board of Regents v. Roth*, 408 U.S. 564 (1972); *San Antonio Independent School District v. Rodriguez*, 441 U.S. 1 (1973); *Arnett v. Kennedy*, 416 U.S. 134 (1974).

29. *See, e.g.*, Robert Bork, *The Tempting of America: The Political Seduction of the Law* (New York: Free Press, 1990); Raoul Berger, *Government by Judiciary: The Transformation of the Fourteenth Amendment* (Cambridge: Harvard University Press, 1977); Walter Berns, *The First Amendment and the Future of American Democracy* (New York: Basic Books, 1976); Gary McDowell, *The Constitution and Contemporary Constitutional Theory* (Cumberland, Va.: Center for Judicial Studies, 1986).

30. Thomas Haskell, *The Curious Persistence of Rights Talk in the "Age of Interpretation,"* 74 J. Amer. Hist. 984, 1011 (1987); *see also* Don Herzog, *Without Foundations: Justification in Political Theory* (Ithaca: Cornell University Press, 1985).

31. *See* Stuart Scheingold, *The Politics of Rights: Lawyers, Public Policy, and Political Change* (New Haven: Yale University Press, 1974); Gerald Rosenberg, *The Hollow Hope* (Chicago: University of Chicago Press, 1991); John Brigham, *The Cult of the Court* (Philadelphia: Temple University Press, 1987); Susan Burgess, *Contest for Constitutional Authority: The Abortion and War Powers Debates* (Lawrence: University of Kansas Press, 1992); Samuel Bowles and Herbert Gintis, *Democracy and Capitalism* (New York: Basic Books, 1986); Alan Hunt, *Explorations in Law and Society* (New York: Routledge, 1993); Austin Sarat and Thomas Kearns, *Identities, Politics, and Rights* (Ann Arbor: University of Michigan Press, 1995).

32. Learned Hand, *The Bill of Rights* (New York: Macmillan, 1964).

33. *See* works cited in note 31 above.

34. *See* note 1 above.

35. Ronald Dworkin, *Taking Rights Seriously* (Cambridge: Harvard University Press, 1977).

36. *Brown v. Board of Education of Topeka*, 347 U.S. 483 (1954).

37. *See* chapter 1, n. 3 above.

Chapter 8. Rights We Need Today

1. *Cf.* Walter Murphy, *An Ordering of Constitutional Values*, 53 Southern Cal. L. Rev. 703 (1980).

2. On the "original meaning" of "inalienable rights," *see* Jack Rakove, *Original Meanings: Politics and Ideas in the Making of the Constitution* (New York: Alfred A. Knopf, 1996), at 290–91.

3. The leading case is *Furman v. Georgia*, 408 U.S. 238 (1972).

4. *Griswold v. Connecticut*, 381 U.S. 479 (1965).

5. I had the pleasure of authoring the casenote on *Griswold* in 79 Harv. L. Rev. 162 (1965); for a different (and critical) view, *see* David O'Brien, *Privacy, Law, and Public Policy* (New York: Praeger, 1979).

6. *Laird v. Tatum*, 408 U.S. 1 (1972).

7. *Olmstead v. United States*, 277 U.S. 438 (1928) (dissents); *Katz v. United States*, 389 U.S. 347 (1967).

8. *Griswold v. Connecticut*, 381 U.S. 479 (1965).

9. 410 U.S. 113 (1973).

10. *Planned Parenthood v. Danforth*, 428 U.S. 52 (1976).

11. *Compare* Mark Tushnet, *An Essay on Rights*, 62 Texas L. Rev. 1363, 1366 (1984).

12. *See* Daniel Hoffman, *The Theory and Practice of Liberty: A Psychological Contribution* (Ll.B. Thesis, Harvard Law School, 1966).

13. *See Eisenstadt v. Baird*, 405 U.S. 438 (1972); *but see Bowers v. Hardwick*, 478 U.S. 186 (1986).

14. John Stuart Mill, *On Liberty* (D. Spitz, ed.) (New York: W. W. Norton, 1975).

15. *See United States v. Seeger*, 380 U.S. 163 (1965).

16. *See* Isaiah Berlin, *Four Essays on Liberty* (New York: Oxford University Press, 1970).

17. John Hart Ely, *Democracy and Distrust: A Theory of Judicial Review* (Cambridge: Harvard University Press, 1980).

18. *See* Hanna Pitkin, *The Concept of Representation* (Berkeley: University of California Press, 1967), at 14f.

19. For criticism of *Richardson v. Ramirez*, 418 U.S. 24 (1974), which upheld disfranchisement of felons, *see* Frank Michelman, *Conceptions of Democracy in American Constitutional Argument: Voting Rights*, 41 Florida L. Rev. 443, 459 (1989), and works therein cited.

20. *See United States v. Carolene Products Co.*, 304 U.S. 144, 152 n. 4 (1938).

21. *NAACP v. Alabama*, 357 U.S. 449 (1958).

22. *Anderson v. Celebrezze*, 460 U.S. 780 (1983); *but see Storer v. Brown*, 415 U.S. 724 (1974); *Burdick v. Takushi*, 504 U.S. 428 (1992).

23. *E.g., Buckley v. Valeo*, 424 U.S. 1 (1976). *Compare* Stephen Gottlieb, *Compelling Governmental Interests: An Essential but Unanalyzed Term in*

Constitutional Adjudication, 68 Boston U. L. Rev. 917 (1988); casenote, *Opinion of the Justices,* 78 Harvard L. Rev. 1260 (1965).

24. *E.g., First National Bank of Boston v. Bellotti,* 435 U.S. 765 (1978).

25. *Miami Herald v. Tornillo,* 418 U.S. 241 (1974).

26. *Abrams v. United States,* 250 U.S. 616 (1919).

27. *Gideon v. Wainwright,* 372 U.S. 335 (1963); *Harper v. Virginia Board of Elections,* 383 U.S. 663 (1966).

28. *See Smith v. Allright,* 321 U.S. 649 (1944).

29. *See* Morton Halperin and Daniel Hoffman, *Top Secret* (New York: New Republic Books, 1977), at 73.

30. *Lynch v. Donnelly,* 465 U.S. 668 (1984).

31. *Compare* Stephen Gottlieb's argument for symmetry in judicial deference. Stephen Gottlieb, *Introduction: Overriding Public Values,* in Stephen Gottlieb, ed., *Public Values in Constitutional Law* (Ann Arbor: University of Michigan Press, 1993).

32. 83 U.S. (16 Wall.) 36 (1873).

33. A distinction between civil and political rights emerges, with some confusion, from *Corfield v. Coryell,* 6 F. Cas. 546 (C.C.E.D. Pa. 1823), the *Slaughterhouse Cases,* note 32 above, and *Plessy v. Ferguson,* 163 U.S. 537 (1896). Whatever the exact boundary may be, it is impossible to accept Raoul Berger's contention, in *Government by Judiciary: The Transformation of the Fourteenth Amendment* (Cambridge: Harvard University Press, 1977), that the privileges and immunities clause of the Fourteenth Amendment protects only civil and not political rights. While the Article IV privileges and immunities clause may indeed have contemplated political rights as defined and granted primarily by the states, to read the same assumption into the Fourteenth Amendment is clearly inconsistent with its nationalization of citizenship and its express distinction between the special privileges of citizens and the universal rights of persons, each separately protected against state infringement.

34. James Lennertz, *Republicanism and Representation: Districting for Civic Discourse,* presented at 1992 meeting of the American Political Science Association.

35. *Ibid.*

36. *Davis v. Bandemer,* 478 U.S. 109, 132 (1986).

37. Sanford Levinson, *Gerrymandering and the Brooding Omnipresence of Proportional Representation: Why Won't It Go Away?* 33 U.C.L.A. L. Rev. 257 (1985).

38. Stated by Charles Wilson, a former GM official, when asked whether his confirmation as secretary of defense in the Eisenhower administration might not lead to conflict-of-interest problems.

39. *Baker v. Carr*, 369 U.S. 186 (1962).

40. *Reynolds v. Sims*, 377 U.S. 533, 562 (1964).

41. *Davis v. Bandemer*, note 36 above.

42. Daniel Lowenstein, *Bandemer's Gap: Gerrymandering and Equal Protection*, in Bernard Grofman, ed., *Political Gerrymandering and the Courts* (New York: Agathon Press, 1990).

43. Bernard Grofman, *Toward a Coherent Theory of Gerrymandering: Bandemer and Thornburg*, in Bernard Grofman, ed., note 42 above, at 56.

44. 430 U.S. 144 (1977).

45. Voting Rights Act of 1965, sec. 2, *as amended*, 42 U.S.C. sec. 1973 (b) (1982).

46. 478 U.S. 30 (1986).

47. *Shaw v. Reno*, 509 U.S. 630 (1993); *Miller v. Johnson*, 515 U.S. ___, 115 S.Ct. 2475, 131 L. Ed.2d 762 (1995); *Shaw v. Hunt*, ___ U.S. ___ (No. 94-923, June 13, 1996); *Bush v. Vera*, ___ U.S. ___ (No. 94-805, June 13, 1996).

48. For a very different reading, *see* David Ryden, *Representation in Crisis: The Constitution, Interest Groups, and Political Parties* (Albany: State University of New York Press, 1996).

49. Note 36 above.

50. *E.g.*, Bernard Grofman, *Unresolved Issues in Partisan Gerrymandering*, in Bernard Grofman ed., note 42 above.

51. *See Lochner v. New York*, 198 U.S. 45 (1905) (Holmes, J., dissenting).

52. Discussed in chapter 2 above.

53. *Davis v. Bandemer*, note 36 above, at 125 n. 9.

54. Theodore Lowi, *The End of Liberalism* (2d ed.) (New York: W. W. Norton, 1979).

55. Bruce Cain, *Perspectives on Davis v. Bandemer: Views of the Practitioner, Theorist, and Reformer*, in Bernard Grofman, ed., note 42 above.

56. *Civil Rights Cases*, 109 U.S. 3 (1883). For a powerful analysis of the political impact of corporations, *see* Charles Lindblom, *Politics and Markets* (New York: Basic Books, 1977).

57. *Reynolds v. Sims*, 377 U.S. 533 (1964).

58. Charles Reich, *The New Property*, 73 Yale L. J. 733 (1964); Frank Michelman, *Welfare Rights in a Constitutional Democracy*, 1979 Washington U. L. Q. 659 (1979); Margaret Jane Radin, *Reinterpreting Property* (Chicago: University of Chicago Press, 1993).

59. 411 U.S. 1 (1973).

60. *Meyer v. Nebraska*, 262 U.S. 390 (1923).

61. *Slaughterhouse Cases*, note 32 above.

62. Cass Sunstein, *The Partial Constitution* (Cambridge: Harvard University Press, 1993).

63. Note 20 above.

64. *E.g.*, *City of Richmond v. Croson*, 488 U.S. 469 (1989); *Adarand Constructors, Inc. v. Pena*, ___ U.S. ___, 115 S.Ct. 2097, 131 L. Ed.2d 158 (1995).

65. Franz Bienenfeld, *Prolegomena to a Psychoanalysis of Law and Morals*, 53 California L. Rev. 957, 1254 (1965); Margaret Jane Radin, note 58 above.

66. John Rawls, *A Theory of Justice* (Cambridge: Harvard University Press, 1971); *Political Liberalism* (New York: Columbia University Press, 1993).

67. Alexander Hamilton, James Madison, and John Jay, *The Federalist Papers* (C. Rossiter, ed.) (New York: New American Library, 1961), no. 10.

68. *See* Jennifer Nedelsky, *Private Property and the Limits of American Constitutionalism: The Madisonian Framework and Its Legacy* (Chicago: University of Chicago Press, 1990); Stanley Katz, *Thomas Jefferson and the Right to Property in Revolutionary America*, 19 J. Law and Economics 467 (1976).

69. Note 67 above, no. 78.

70. From the keynote speech at the Constitutional Convention. *See* John Reardon, *Edmund Randolph* (New York: Macmillan, 1974), at 100.

71. John Locke, *Two Treatises of Government*, book 2, paras. 87, 124, 182 (New York: Hafner, 1947).

72. Note 68 above.

73. 5 U.S. (1 Cranch) 137 (1803).

74. 10 U.S. (6 Cranch) 87 (1810).

75. 60 U.S. (19 How.) 393 (1857).

76. *Cherokee Nation v. Georgia*, 30 U.S. (5 Pet.) 25 (1831).

77. *Worcester v. Georgia*, 31 U.S. (6 Pet.) 515 (1832).

78. *Slaughterhouse Cases*, note 32 above; *Civil Rights Cases*, note 56 above.

79. *See, e.g.*, Henry Monaghan, *Of "Liberty" and "Property,"* 62 Cornell L. Rev. 405 (1977).

80. Joseph Vining, *Legal Identity: The Coming of Age of Public Law* (New Haven: Yale University Press, 1978), at 156.

81. *Schenck v. Pro-Choice Network of Western New York*, 65 U.S.L.W. 4109 (U.S. Feb. 19, 1997).

82. For a thorough review of the debate, *see* Joyce Appleby, *Liberalism and Republicanism in the Historical Imagination* (Cambridge: Harvard University Press, 1992); *compare* works cited in note 68 above.

83. *See* works cited in note 68 above.

84. Bruce Ackerman, *Private Property and the Constitution* (New Haven: Yale University Press, 1977).

85. Note 58 above.

86. *See* Stuart Scheingold, *The Politics of Rights: Lawyers, Public Policy, and Political Change* (New Haven: Yale University Press, 1974); Samuel Bowles and Herbert Gintis, *Democracy and Capitalism* (New York: Basic Books, 1986).

87. Radin, note 58 above, at 143.

88. *Id.* at 85.

89. *Id.* at 85–86.

90. *Compare* Bruce Ackerman, *Private Property and the Constitution* (New Haven: Yale University Press, 1977).

91. Morris Cohen, *Property and Sovereignty*, 13 Cornell L. Q. 8 (1927). *See also* Bowles and Gintis, note 86 above.

92. Richard Posner, *Economic Analysis of Law* (Boston: Little Brown, 1992).

93. Richard Epstein, *Takings: Private Property and the Power of Eminent Domain* (Cambridge: Harvard University Press, 1985).

94. Radin, note 58 above, at 104.

95. *Id.* at 188.

96. *Id.* at 121.

Bibliography

Cases

Abrams v. United States, 250 U.S. 616 (1919)

Adarand Constructors, Inc. v. Pena, ___ U.S. ___, 115 S.Ct. 2097, 131 L.Ed.2d 158 (1995)

Anderson v. Celebrezze, 460 U.S. 780 (1983)

Aptheker v. United States, 378 U.S. 500 (1964)

Arnett v. Kennedy, 416 U.S. 134 (1974)

Baker v. Carr, 369 U.S. 186 (1962)

Board of Regents v. Roth, 408 U.S. 564 (1972)

Bowers v. Hardwick, 478 U.S. 186 (1986)

Bowsher v. Synar, 478 U.S. 714 (1986)

Brandenburg v. Ohio, 395 U.S. 444 (1971)

Brown v. Board of Education of Topeka, 347 U.S. 483 (1954)

Buckley v. Valeo, 424 U.S. 1 (1976)

Burdick v. Takushi, 504 U.S. 428 (1992)

Bush v. Vera, ___ U.S. ___, 116 S.Ct. 1941, 135 L. Ed. 2d 248 (1996)

Cafeteria Workers v. McElroy, 367 U.S. 886 (1961)

Cherokee Nation v. Georgia, 30 U.S. (5 Pet.) 1 (1831)

Frontiero v. Richardson, 411 U.S. 677 (1973)

Furman v. Georgia, 408 U.S. 238 (1972)

Garcia v. San Antonio Metropolitan Transit Authority, 469 U.S. 528 (1985)

Georgia v. Stanton, 73 U.S. (6 Wall.) 50 (1867)

Gideon v. Wainwright, 372 U.S. 335 (1963)

Goldwater v. Carter, 444 U.S. 996 (1979)

Greene v. McElroy, 360 U.S. 474 (1959)

Griswold v. Connecticut, 381 U.S. 479 (1965)

Haig v. Agee, 453 U.S. 280 (1981)

Hamilton v. Kentucky Distilleries and Warehouse Co., 251 U.S. 146 (1919)

Harisiades v. Shaughnessy, 342 U.S. 580 (1952)

Harper v. Virginia Board of Elections, 383 U.S. 663 (1966)

Hirabayashi v. United States, 320 U.S. 81 (1943)

Hirota v. MacArthur, 338 U.S. 197 (1948)

Home Building and Loan Association v. Blaisdell, 290 U.S. 398 (1934)

Humphrey's Executor v. United States, 295 U.S. 602 (1935)

Immigration and Naturalization Service v. Chadha, 462 U.S. 919 (1983)

Japan Whaling Association v. American Cetacean Society, 478 U.S. 221 (1986)

Katz v. United States, 389 U.S. 347 (1967)

Kennedy v. Mendoza-Martinez, 372 U.S. 144 (1963)

Kent v. Dulles, 357 U.S. 116 (1958)

Kleindienst v. Mandel, 408 U.S. 753 (1972)

Knauff v. Shaughnessy, 338 U.S. 537 (1950)

Knote v. United States, 95 U.S. 149 (1877)

Korematsu v. United States, 323 U.S. 214 (1944)

Kovacs v. Cooper, 336 U.S. 77 (1949)

La Abra Silver Mining Co. v. United States, 175 U.S. 423 (1899)

Laird v. Tatum, 408 U.S. 1 (1972)

Pan American World Airlines v. CAB, 392 F.2d 483 (D.C. Cir. 1968)

Panama Refining Co. v. Ryan, 293 U.S. 388 (1935)

Peters v. Hobby, 349 U.S. 331 (1955)

Planned Parenthood v. Danforth, 428 U.S. 52 (1976)

Plessy v. Ferguson, 163 U.S. 537 (1896)

Plyler v. Doe, 457 U.S. 202 (1982)

Powell v. McCormack, 395 U.S. 486 (1969)

Prize Cases, 67 U.S. (2 Black) 635 (1863)

Raymond v. Thomas, 91 U.S. 712 (1876)

Reed v. Reed, 404 U.S. 71 (1971)

Regan v. Wald, 468 U.S. 222 (1984)

Regents of the University of California v. Bakke, 438 U.S. 265 (1978)

Reynolds v. Sims, 377 U.S. 533 (1964)

Richardson v. Ramirez, 418 U.S. 24 (1974)

Riggs v. Palmer, 115 N.Y. 506, 22 N.E. 188 (1889)

Rochin v. California, 342 U.S. 165 (1952)

Roe v. Wade, 410 U.S. 113 (1973)

Romer v. Evans, ___ U.S. ___, 116 S.Ct. 1620, 134 L. Ed. 2d 855 (1996)

San Antonio Independent School District v. Rodriguez, 441 U.S. 1 (1973)

Santa Clara County v. Southern Pacific Railroad Co., 118 U.S. 394 (1886)

Schechter Poultry Corp. v. United States, 295 U.S. 495 (1935)

Schenck v. Pro-Choice Network of Western New York, 65 U.S.L.W. 4109 (U.S. Feb. 19, 1997)

Seminole Tribe of Florida v. Florida, ___ U.S. ___, 116 S.Ct. 1114, 134 L. Ed. 2d 252 (1996)

Service v. Dulles, 354 U.S. 363 (1957)

Shaw v. Hunt, ___ U.S. ___, 116 S.Ct. 1894, 135 L. Ed. 2d 207 (1996)

Shaw v. Reno, 509 U.S. 630 (1993)

Slaughterhouse Cases, 83 U.S. (16 Wall.) 36 (1873)

Smith v. Allright, 321 U.S. 649 (1944)

Books

Abelson, Raziel, *Persons: A Study in Philosophical Psychology* (New York: St. Martin's Press, 1977)

Abramson, Paul, *Political Attitudes in America* (San Francisco: Freeman, 1986)

Ackerman, Bruce, *We, the People: Foundations* (Cambridge: Belknap Press, 1991)

——— , *Social Justice in the Liberal State* (New Haven: Yale University Press, 1980)

——— , *Private Property and the Constitution* (New Haven: Yale University Press, 1977)

Adler, David, and Larry George, eds., *The Constitution and the Conduct of American Foreign Policy* (Lawrence: University Press of Kansas, 1996)

Anderson, Benedict, *Imagined Communities: Reflections on the Origin and Spread of Nationalism* (New York: Verso, 1991)

Appleby, Joyce, *Liberalism and Republicanism in the Historical Imagination* (Cambridge: Harvard University Press, 1992)

——— , *Capitalism and a New Social Order* (New York: New York University Press, 1984)

Bailyn, Bernard, *Ideological Origins of the American Revolution* (Cambridge: Belknap Press, 1967)

Balbus, Isaac, *The Dialectics of Legal Repression: Black Rebels before the American Criminal Courts* (New Brunswick: Transaction Books, 1973)

Barber, Benjamin, *Strong Democracy* (Berkeley: University of California Press, 1984)

Barber, Sotirios, *The Constitution of Judicial Power* (Baltimore: Johns Hopkins University Press, 1993)

——— , *On What the Constitution Means* (Baltimore: Johns Hopkins University Press, 1984)

Beard, Charles, *An Economic Interpretation of the Constitution of the United States* (New York: Free Press, 1986)

Beitz, Charles, *Political Equality* (Princeton: Princeton University Press, 1989)

Berger, Raoul, *Government by Judiciary: The Transformation of the Four-teenth Amendment* (Cambridge: Harvard University Press, 1977)

Berlin, Isaiah, *Four Essays on Liberty* (New York: Oxford University Press, 1970)

Berns, Walter, *The First Amendment and the Future of American Democracy* (New York: Basic Books, 1976)

Bernstein, Richard, *Amending America* (New York: Times Books, 1993)

Bickel, Alexander, *The Least Dangerous Branch: The Supreme Court at the Bar of Politics* (Indianapolis: Bobbs-Merrill, 1962)

Bix, Brian, *Law, Language, and Legal Determinacy* (New York: Clarendon Press, 1993)

Boorstin, Daniel, *The Genius of American Politics* (Chicago: University of Chicago Press, 1953)

Bork, Robert, *The Tempting of America: The Political Seduction of the Law* (New York: Free Press, 1990)

Bowles, Samuel, and Herbert Gintis, *Democracy and Capitalism* (New York: Basic Books, 1986)

Braybrooke, David, *Meeting Needs* (Princeton: Princeton University Press, 1987)

Breuilly, John, *Nationalism and the State* (2d ed.) (Chicago: University of Chicago Press, 1994)

Brigham, John, *The Cult of the Court* (Philadelphia: Temple University Press, 1987)

Burgess, Susan, *Contest for Constitutional Authority: The Abortion and War Powers Debates* (Lawrence: University of Kansas Press, 1992)

Burnham, Walter Dean, *Critical Elections and the Mainsprings of American Politics* (New York: W. W. Norton, 1970)

Calhoun, John, *A Disquisition on Government, and Selections from the Discourses* (Indianapolis: Bobbs-Merrill, 1953)

Carmen, Ira, *Cloning and the Constitution: An Inquiry into Governmental Policymaking and Genetic Experimentation* (Madison: University of Wisconsin Press, 1985)

Carruthers, Michael, Steven Collins, and Steven Lukes, eds., *The Category of the Person* (New York: Cambridge University Press, 1985)

Corwin, Edward, *The President: Office and Powers, 1787-1957* (4th rev. ed.) (New York: New York University Press, 1957)

———, *The "Higher Law" Background of American Constitutional Law* (Ithaca: Great Seal Books, 1955)

Dennison, George, *The Dorr War: Republicanism on Trial, 1831-1861* (Lexington: University Press of Kentucky, 1976)

Dworkin, Ronald, *Law's Empire* (Cambridge: Belknap Press, 1986)

———, *A Matter of Principle* (Cambridge: Harvard University Press, 1985)

———, *Taking Rights Seriously* (Cambridge: Harvard University Press, 1977)

Ely, John Hart, *Democracy and Distrust: A Theory of Judicial Review* (Cambridge: Harvard University Press, 1980)

Epstein, David, *The Political Theory of the Federalist* (Chicago: University of Chicago Press, 1984)

Epstein, Richard, *Takings: Private Property and the Power of Eminent Domain* (Cambridge: Harvard University Press, 1985)

Erikson, Robert, Norman Lutbeg, and Kent Tedin, *American Public Opinion: Its Origins, Content, and Impact* (4th ed.) (New York: Macmillan, 1991)

Falk, Ze'ev, *Law and Religion* (Jerusalem: Mesharim Publishers, 1981)

Fehrenbacher, Don, *The Dred Scott Case: Its Significance in American Law and Politics* (New York: Oxford University Press, 1978)

Fei Hsiao-Tung, *Peasant Life in China* (Cambridge: Oxford University Press, 1946)

Fish, Stanley, *There's No Such Thing as Free Speech . . . and It's a Good Thing, Too* (New York: Oxford University Press, 1994)

Foley, Michael, *The Silence of Constitutions* (New York: Routledge, 1989)

Foner, Philip, ed., *The Life and Writings of Frederick Douglass*, vol. 5 (New York: International Publishers, 1975)

Freeman, David, ed., *Political Concepts* (Dubuque: Kendall/Hunt, 1994)

Friedman, Leon, and Bert Neuborne, *Unquestioning Obedience to the President: The ACLU Case against the Legality of the War in Vietnam* (New York: W. W. Norton, 1972)

Galston, William, *Liberal Purposes: Goods, Virtues, and Diversity in the Liberal State* (Cambridge: Cambridge University Press, 1991)

Gillman, Howard, *The Constitution Besieged: The Rise and Demise of Lochner Era Police Powers Jurisprudence* (Durham: Duke University Press, 1993)

Gottlieb, Stephen, ed., *Public Values in Constitutional Law* (Ann Arbor: University of Michigan Press, 1993)

Graber, Mark, *Transforming Free Speech: The Ambiguous Legacy of Civil Libertarianism* (Berkeley: University of California Press, 1991)

Grady, Robert, *Restoring Real Representation* (Urbana: University of Illinois Press, 1993)

Greenfield, Liah, *Nationalism: Five Roads to Modernity* (Cambridge: Harvard University Press, 1992)

Griffin, Stephen, *American Constitutionalism: From Theory to Politics* (Princeton: Princeton University Press, 1996)

Grofman, Bernard, ed., *Political Gerrymandering and the Courts* (New York: Agathon Press, 1990)

Grofman, Bernard, Lisa Handley, and Richard Niemi, *Minority Representation and the Quest for Voting Equality* (Cambridge: Cambridge University Press, 1992)

Guinier, Lani, *The Tyranny of the Majority: Fundamental Fairness in Representative Democracy* (New York: Free Press, 1994)

Gutmann, Amy, *Democratic Education* (Princeton: Princeton University Press, 1987)

Habermas, Jürgen, *Between Facts and Norms* (Cambridge: MIT Press, 1996)

Halperin, Morton, and Daniel Hoffman, *Top Secret* (New York: New Republic Books, 1977)

———, eds., *Freedom vs. National Security* (New York: Chelsea House, 1977)

Hamilton, Alexander, James Madison, and John Jay, *The Federalist Papers* (C. Rossiter, ed.) (New York: New American Library, 1961)

Hand, Learned, *The Bill of Rights* (New York: Macmillan, 1964)

Hanke, Louis, *Aristotle and the American Indians* (Chicago: Henry Regnery, 1959)

Harris, William, *The Interpretable Constitution* (Baltimore: Johns Hopkins University Press, 1993)

Hartz, Louis, *The Liberal Tradition in America: An Interpretation of American Political Thought since the Revolution* (New York: Harcourt Brace, 1955)

Henderson, Dan, *Conciliation and Japanese Law: Tokugawa and Modern* (Seattle: University of Washington Press, 1965)

Herzog, Don, *Happy Slaves: A Critique of Consent Theory* (Chicago: University of Chicago Press, 1989)

————— , *Without Foundations: Justification in Political Theory* (Ithaca: Cornell University Press, 1985)

Hobsbawm, Eric, *Nations and Nationalism since 1780: Programme, Myth, Reality* (New York: Cambridge University Press, 1992)

Hoffman, Daniel, *Governmental Secrecy and the Founding Fathers: A Study in Constitutional Controls* (Westport, Ct.: Greenwood Press, 1981)

Holmes, Oliver Wendell, Jr., *Collected Legal Papers* (New York: P. Smith, 1952)

Horowitz, Donald, *The Courts and Social Policy* (Washington: Brookings Institution, 1977)

Horwitz, Morton, *The Transformation of American Law, 1870-1960* (New York: Oxford University Press, 1992)

————— , *The Transformation of American Law, 1780-1860* (Cambridge: Harvard University Press, 1977)

Hunt, Alan, *Explorations in Law and Society* (New York: Routledge, 1993)

Kahn, Paul, *Legitimacy and History: Self-Government in American Constitutional Theory* (New Haven: Yale University Press, 1992)

Kairys, David, ed., *The Politics of Law: A Progressive Critique* (New York: Pantheon, 1982)

Kaufman, Allen, *Capitalism, Slavery and Republican Values: American Political Economists, 1819-1848* (Austin: University of Texas Press, 1982)

Key, V. O., Jr., *Politics, Parties, and Pressure Groups* (5th ed.) (New York: Crowell, 1964)

Kocourek, Albert, and John Wigmore, eds., *Formative Influence of Legal Development*, Evolution of Law Series, vol. 3 (Boston: Little Brown, 1918)

Koh, Harold, *The National Security Constitution: Sharing Power After the Iran-Contra Affair* (New Haven: Yale University Press, 1990)

Kramer, Matthew, *Legal Theory, Political Theory, and Deconstruction: Against Rhadamanthus* (Bloomington: Indiana University Press, 1991)

Kyvig, David, *Explicit and Authentic Acts: Amending the U.S. Constitution, 1776–1995* (Lawrence: University Press of Kansas, 1996)

Lefcourt, Robert, ed., *Law against the People: Essays to Demystify Law, Order and the Courts* (New York: Random House, 1971)

Levinson, Sanford, *Constitutional Faith* (Princeton: Princeton University Press, 1988)

———— , ed., *Responding to Imperfection: The Theory and Practice of Constitutional Amendment* (Princeton: Princeton University Press, 1995)

Levy, Leonard, *Essays on the Making of the Constitution* (New York: Oxford University Press, 1987)

Leyh, Gregory, ed., *Legal Hermeneutics: History, Theory, and Practice* (Berkeley: University of California Press, 1992)

Lindblom, Charles, *Politics and Markets* (New York: Basic Books, 1977)

Lipset, Seymour, *Political Man: The Social Bases of Politics* (Baltimore: Johns Hopkins University Press, 1981)

Lipset, Seymour, and William Schneider, *The Confidence Gap* (Baltimore: Johns Hopkins University Press, 1987)

Locke, John, *Two Treatises of Government* (New York: Hafner, 1947)

Lomasky, Loren, *Persons, Rights, and the Moral Community* (New York: Oxford University Press, 1987)

Lowi, Theodore, *The End of Liberalism* (2d ed.) (New York: W. W. Norton, 1979)

Macedo, Stephen, *Liberal Virtues: Citizenship, Virtue, and Community in Liberal Constitutionalism* (New York: Clarendon Press, 1991)

MacIntyre, Alasdair, *After Virtue* (Notre Dame: University of Notre Dame Press, 1981)

Madison, James, *Letters and Other Writings of James Madison*, vol. 4 (Philadelphia: J. P. Lipincott, 1865)

Mansbridge, Jane, *Beyond Adversary Democracy* (New York: Basic Books, 1980)

Marshall, Thomas, *Public Opinion and the Supreme Court* (Boston: Unwin Hyman, 1989)

McCann, Michael, and Gerald Houseman, eds., *Judging the Constitution: Critical Essays on Judicial Lawmaking* (Glenview, Il.: Scott, Foresman, 1989)

McClosky, Herbert, and Alida Brill, *Dimensions of Tolerance* (New York: Russell Sage Foundation, 1983)

McDonald, Forrest, *Novus Ordo Seclorum: The Intellectual Origins of the Constitution* (Lawrence: University Press of Kansas, 1985)

McDowell, Gary, *The Constitution and Contemporary Constitutional Theory* (Cumberland, Va.: Center for Judicial Studies, 1986)

Melden, Abraham, *Rights and Persons* (New York: Oxford University Press, 1977)

Mill, John Stuart, *On Liberty* (D. Spitz, ed.) (New York: W. W. Norton, 1975)

Moore, Wayne, *Constitutional Rights and Powers of the People* (Princeton: Princeton University Press, 1996)

Mostov, Julie, *Power, Process, and Popular Sovereignty* (Philadelphia: Temple University Press, 1992)

Munzer, Stephen, *A Theory of Property* (Cambridge: Cambridge University Press, 1990)

Nedelsky, Jennifer, *Private Property and the Limits of American Constitutionalism: The Madisonian Framework and Its Legacy* (Chicago: University of Chicago Press, 1990)

Neely, Mark, Jr., *The Fate of Liberty: Abraham Lincoln and Civil Liberties* (New York: Oxford University Press, 1991)

Neuman, W. Russell, *The Paradox of Mass Politics: Knowledge and Opinion in the American Electorate* (Cambridge: Harvard University Press, 1986)

Nozick, Robert, *Anarchy, State and Utopia* (New York: Basic Books, 1974)

O'Brien, David, *Privacy, Law, and Public Policy* (New York: Praeger, 1979)

Ollman, Bertell, and Jonathan Birnbaum, eds., *The United States Constitution* (New York: New York University Press, 1990)

Parfit, Derek, *Reasons and Persons* (New York: Oxford University Press, 1984)

Patterson, Orlando, *Slavery and Social Death: A Comparative Study* (Cambridge: Harvard University Press, 1982)

Pennock, J. R., and John Chapman, eds., *Representation, Nomos X* (New York: Atherton Press, 1968)

Perry, Michael, *Morality, Politics, and Law: A Bicentennial Essay* (New York: Oxford University Press, 1988)

Philips, Michael, *Between Universalism and Skepticism* (New York: Oxford University Press, 1994)

Pitkin, Hanna, *Wittgenstein and Justice: On the Significance of Ludwig Wittgenstein for Social and Political Thought* (Berkeley: University of California Press, 1972)

———, *The Concept of Representation* (Berkeley: University of California Press, 1967)

Pocock, J. G. A., *The Machiavellian Moment: Florentine Political Thought and the Atlantic Republican Tradition* (Princeton: Princeton University Press, 1975)

Podell, Janet, and Steven Anzovin, eds., *Speeches of the American Presidents* (New York: H. W. Wilson, 1988)

Posner, Richard, *Economic Analysis of Law* (Boston: Little Brown, 1992)

Postone, Moishe, *Time, Labor, and Social Domination: A Reinterpretation of Marx's Critical Theory* (New York: Cambridge University Press, 1993)

Radin, Margaret Jane, *Reinterpreting Property* (Chicago: University of Chicago Press, 1993)

Rakove, Jack, *Original Meanings: Politics and Ideas in the Making of the Constitution* (New York: Alfred A. Knopf, 1996)

Rawls, John, *Political Liberalism* (New York: Columbia University Press, 1993)

———, *A Theory of Justice* (Cambridge: Harvard University Press, 1971)

Reardon, John, *Edmund Randolph* (New York: Macmillan, 1974)

Rodgers, Daniel, *Contested Truths* (New York: Basic Books, 1987)

Roelofs, H. Mark, *The Poverty of American Politics: A Theoretical Interpretation* (Philadelphia: Temple University Press, 1992)

Roosevelt, Theodore, *An Autobiography* (New York: Scribner, 1958)

Rorty, Amelie, ed., *The Identities of Persons* (Berkeley: University of California Press, 1976)

Rosenberg, Gerald, *The Hollow Hope* (Chicago: University of Chicago Press, 1991)

Rossum, Ralph, and G. Alan Tarr, eds., *American Constitutional Law: Cases and Interpretation* (3d ed.) (New York: St. Martin's Press, 1991)

Rousseau, Jean-Jacques, *The Social Contract and Discourses* (G. D. H. Cole, ed.) (New York: Dutton, 1950)

Ryden, David, *Representation in Crisis: The Constitution, Interest Groups, and Political Parties* (Albany: State University of New York Press, 1996)

Sandel, Michael, *Democracy's Discontent: America in Search of a Public Philosophy* (Cambridge: Harvard University Press, 1996)

———, *Liberalism and the Limits of Justice* (New York: Cambridge University Press, 1982)

Sarat, Austin, and Thomas Kearns, eds., *Identities, Politics, and Rights* (Ann Arbor: University of Michigan Press, 1995)

———, *Legal Rights* (Ann Arbor: University of Michigan Press, 1995)

Schauer, Frederick, *Playing by the Rules: A Philosophical Examination of Rule-Based Decision-Making in Law and in Life* (Oxford: Clarendon Press, 1991)

Scheingold, Stuart, *The Politics of Rights: Lawyers, Public Policy, and Political Change* (New Haven: Yale University Press, 1974)

Schlesinger, Arthur, Jr., *The Imperial Presidency* (Boston: Houghton Mifflin, 1973)

Schlossberger, Eugene, *Moral Responsibility and Persons* (Philadelphia: Temple University Press, 1992)

Segal, Jeffrey, and Harold Spaeth, *The Supreme Court and the Attitudinal Model* (New York: Cambridge University Press, 1993)

Seidman, Louis, and Mark Tushnet, *Remnants of Belief: Contemporary Constitutional Issues* (New York: Oxford University Press, 1996)

Shapiro, Ian, *The Evolution of Rights in Liberal Theory* (New York: Cambridge University Press, 1986)

Shaw, Margery, and A. E. Doudera, eds., *Defining Human Life: Medical, Legal, and Ethical Implications* (Ann Arbor: AUPHA Press, 1983)

Smith, Adam, *The Wealth of Nations* (New York: Viking Penguin, 1986)

Story, Joseph, *Commentaries on the Constitution of the United States* (New York: Da Capo, 1970)

Strum, Philippa, *The Supreme Court and "Political Questions": A Study in Judicial Evasion* (University, Ala.: University of Alabama Press, 1974)

Sundquist, James, *Constitutional Reform and Effective Government* (Washington: Brookings Institution, 1986)

Sunstein, Cass, *The Partial Constitution* (Cambridge: Harvard University Press, 1993)

Tamir, Yael, *Liberal Nationalism* (Princeton: Princeton University Press, 1993)

Thompson, E. P., *Whigs and Hunters: The Origin of the Black Act* (New York: Pantheon Books, 1975)

Tushnet, Mark, *The American Law of Slavery* (Princeton: Princeton University Press, 1981)

Unger, Roberto, *False Necessity: Anti-Necessitarian Social Theory in the Service of Radical Democracy* (New York: Cambridge University Press, 1987)

——— , *Social Theory: Its Situation and Its Task* (New York: Cambridge University Press, 1987)

——— , *Knowledge and Politics* (New York: Macmillan, 1975)

Vile, M. J. C., *Constitutionalism and the Separation of Powers* (Oxford: Clarendon Press, 1967)

Vining, Joseph, *Legal Identity: The Coming of Age of Public Law* (New Haven: Yale University Press, 1978)

Wellman, Carl, *Real Rights* (New York: Oxford University Press, 1995)

Wittgenstein, Ludwig, *Philosophical Investigations* (New York: Macmillan, 1958)

Wolff, Robert, ed., *The Rule of Law* (New York: Simon and Schuster, 1971)

Wood, Gordon, *The Radicalism of the American Revolution* (New York: Alfred A. Knopf, 1992)

Articles and Papers

Aleinikoff, T. Alexander, *Constitutional Law in the Age of Balancing*, 96 Yale L. J. 943 (1987)

Bienenfeld, Franz, *Prolegomena to a Psychoanalysis of Law and Morals*, 53 California L. Rev. 957, 1254 (1965)

Brest, Paul, *The Fundamental Rights Controversy*, 90 Yale L. J. 1063 (1981)

Cohen, Morris, *Property and Sovereignty*, 13 Cornell L. Q. 8 (1927)

Cover, Robert, *Violence and the Word*, 95 Yale L. J. 1601 (1986)

Derrida, Jacques, *Declarations of Independence*, 8 New Political Science 7 (1986)

Dworkin, Ronald, *What Is Equality?* 10 Philosophy and Public Affairs 185, 283 (1981)

Fiss, Owen, *Groups and the Equal Protection Clause*, 5 Philosophy and Public Affairs 107 (1976)

Gottlieb, Stephen, *Compelling Governmental Interests: An Essential but Unanalyzed Term in Constitutional Adjudication*, 68 Boston U. L. Rev. 916 (1988)

Griswold, Erwin, *Secrets Not Worth Keeping*, Washington Post, Feb. 15, 1989, p. 25A

Harris, William, *Binding Word and Polity*, 76 Amer. Pol. Sci. Rev. 34 (1982)

Haskell, Thomas, *The Curious Persistence of Rights Talk in the "Age of Interpretation,"* 74 J. Amer. Hist. 984 (1987)

Henkin, Louis, *Is There a "Political Question" Doctrine?* 85 Yale L. J. 597 (1976)

Herzog, Don, *Some Questions for Republicans*, 14 Political Theory 473 (1986)

Hoffman, Daniel, *What Makes a Right Fundamental?* 49 Review of Politics 515 (1987)

———— , *Personhood and Rights*, 19 Polity 74 (1986)

———— , *The Theory and Practice of Liberty: A Psychological Contribution* (Ll.B. thesis, Harvard Law School, 1966)

Katz, Stanley, *Thomas Jefferson and the Right to Property in Revolutionary America*, 19 J. Law and Economics 467 (1976)

Kelly, R. F., *Historical and Political Interpretations of Jurisprudence and the Social Action Perspective in Sociology*, 15 J. Hist. Behav. Sciences 47 (1979)

Lennertz, James, *Republicanism and Representation: Districting for Civic Discourse* (Paper presented at 1992 meeting of the American Political Science Association)

Levinson, Sanford, *Gerrymandering and the Brooding Omnipresence of Proportional Representation: Why Won't It Go Away?* 33 U.C.L.A. L. Rev. 257 (1985)

Lutz, Donald, *Toward a Theory of Constitutional Amendment*, 88 Amer. Pol. Sci. Rev. 355 (1994)

Michelman, Frank, *Conceptions of Democracy in American Constitutional Argument: Voting Rights*, 41 Florida L. Rev. 443 (1989)

———— , *Law's Republic*, 97 Yale L. J. 1493 (1988)

———— , *Welfare Rights in a Constitutional Democracy*, 1979 Washington U. L. Q. 659 (1979)

Monaghan, Henry, *Of "Liberty" and "Property,"* 62 Cornell L. Rev. 405 (1977)

Murphy, Walter, *An Ordering of Constitutional Values*, 53 Southern Cal. L. Rev. 703 (1980)

Peter, Kenneth, *Foundation of the Empire of Factions* (Paper presented at 1989 meeting of the American Political Science Association)

Reich, Charles, *The New Property*, 73 Yale L. J. 733 (1964)

Scharpf, Fritz, *Judicial Review and the Political Question: A Functional Analysis*, 75 Yale L. J. 517 (1966)

Stone, Christopher, *Should Trees Have Standing?—Toward Legal Rights for Natural Objects*, 45 Southern Cal. L. Rev. 450 (1972)

Sunstein, Cass, *Beyond the Republican Revival*, 97 Yale L. J. 1539 (1988)

Tribe, Lawrence, *The Puzzling Persistence of Process-Based Theories of Constitutional Law*, 89 Yale L. J. 1063 (1980)

Tushnet, Mark, *An Essay on Rights*, 62 Texas L. Rev. 1363 (1984)

Wolin, Sheldon, *The People's Two Bodies*, 1 Democracy 9 (1981)

Miscellaneous

Note, *A "Frightful Political Dragon" Indeed: Why Constitutional Challenges Cannot Subdue the Gerrymander*, 13 Harvard J. Law and Pub. Policy 949 (1990)

Casenote, *Griswold v. Connecticut*, 79 Harvard L. Rev. 162 (1965)

Casenote, *Opinion of the Justices*, 78 Harvard L. Rev. 1260 (1965)

Voting Rights Act of 1965, sec. 2, *as amended*, 42 U.S.C. sec. 1973 (b) (1982)

Hearings on S. 158 before the Subcommittee on Separation of Powers of the Senate Judiciary Committee, 97th Cong., 1st Sess., Serial #J-97-16

Caucus for a New Political Science Newsletter, Fall, 1994

Index

5070

DATE DUE